IMAGES
of America

DOWNTOWN ANN ARBOR

On the Cover: This Red Cross parade used the wagons of local delivery companies to simulate World War I ambulances. Together with other floats, they paraded on Main Street at William Street in May 1918.

IMAGES
of America

DOWNTOWN ANN ARBOR

Patti Smith
Foreword by Mayor John Hieftje

ARCADIA
PUBLISHING

ISBN 978-1-4671-1283-3

Published by Arcadia Publishing
Charleston, South Carolina

Printed in the United States of America

Library of Congress Control Number: 2014938042

For all general information, please contact Arcadia Publishing:
Telephone 843-853-2070
Fax 843-853-0044
E-mail sales@arcadiapublishing.com
For customer service and orders:
Toll-Free 1-888-313-2665

Visit us on the Internet at www.arcadiapublishing.com

My parents, Judy Smith and Tim Smith, encouraged me to be a writer from the very beginning. This book is for them.

Contents

Foreword

Many people tell me that they came to Ann Arbor for school and never left. Ann Arbor is that kind of town; you might think you are only here for a college, but soon you find yourself in love with the city's parks, people, restaurants, nightlife, and downtown. With each passing year, there are fewer downtowns that allow someone to visit an original 1864 building in one block, eat in a restaurant with an original tin-pressed ceiling in another, and view the still visible lettering advertising a business that is long gone.

The businesses have changed: from dry goods and harness shops to brewpubs, galleries, and salons. The names have changed: from St. James, Bach, and Muehlig to Grizzly Peak, Jessica's Apothecary, and People's Food Co-Op. The blocks are no longer the Bank Block, the Hoban Block, or the Masonic Block. Gone are the hitching posts, gaslights, and muddy streets. Yet, one thing remains: downtown Ann Arbor is a special place. It hosts the Ann Arbor Art Fairs, a Mayor's Green Fair promoting sustainable practices, an annual Festifools parade featuring large papier-mâché puppets, a Dancing in the Streets celebration, car shows, block parties, festivals, outdoor lunchtime concerts in the summertime—and those are only the special events. People from all over the state and country come to our downtown, and like those students who only came here for college, some of them end up staying.

It is easy to become involved in a town like this. People serve on city council, on committees and task forces, and in neighborhood associations. People want to keep this place special. In my 14 years as mayor, I have had the privilege to serve this community, these people, and our downtown.

—Mayor John Hieftje

ACKNOWLEDGMENTS

I cannot thank enough the people who helped me with this book. Our local "brain trusts," including Grace Shackman (especially her "Then & Now" articles), Susan Cee Wineberg, and Dale Leslie, were extremely friendly and helpful to me. The "Ann Arbor Townies" Facebook page was also full of fun hints and nice people. Our own unofficial historian, Wystan Stevens, was a huge help, and I feel like he should get a cowriting credit for all of the work he did on a very raw manuscript! A huge thank-you goes to my friend Kevin Sharp for helping me take some last-minute shots.

The Bentley Historical Library and especially Karen Jania were simply amazing as they helped me in the archives. The Ann Arbor District Library archives and Amy Cantu and its staff were similarly welcoming. The Washtenaw County Historical Society encouraged me from the beginning. The existence of Arbor Wiki and the *Ann Arbor Observer* also helped immensely. All images are from the Bentley Historical Library unless otherwise acknowledged.

Thank you to Mayor John Hieftje for writing the foreword and for serving our city for so many years. I want to acknowledge Tiffany Browning Tscherne for bringing me to Ann Arbor during our college years and lighting the spark that became my love for this town.

Thank you to my better half, Ken Anderson, for spending so many hours helping me edit this and for all of your love and support. You are a gem, and I do not know how I would have done this project without you.

Thank you to all of the residents of Ann Arbor—past and present—for being you.

INTRODUCTION

There is no place like downtown Ann Arbor on a bright summer day, a crisp fall afternoon, a warm spring morning, or even a blustery winter night. It is a special place—any time of year. On any given street, you will hear music from a business, passing car, or street musician. People are happy to be here and are engaging and pleasant. It is a place where one can run into a friend while crossing the street or make a new friend while hanging out in a coffeehouse. It is not a stretch to believe that this welcoming spirit is not recent and that it existed during the times the photographs in this book were taken.

On a cold February day in 1824, John Allen and Elisha Rumsey registered a claim with the federal land office in Detroit for a settlement named "Annarbour." It is believed to be named for their wives, but whether this was true or not, it certainly offered the notion of a settled and civilized place. Three months later, they registered the town's original plat. In June, the two men placed an ad in the *Detroit Gazette* and offered lots for sale, appealing for mechanics and artisans to locate in their new village.

Before the town could be settled, Allen and Rumsey had to do so themselves. Their initial stop was at a creek that fed into the river. That creek would later become known as Allen's Creek. One account states that the traveling party hunkered down here, turned over the box of their sleigh, draped blankets and carpets over it, and called it home. Their next important task was to build a log cabin, which was how their first few days were spent. The structure was later described as being a "pen" without a permanent roof. This pen became the home of Rumsey and his wife, who arrived later. Allen slept in a tent just north of this site. The three settlers waited for spring, which arrived in the form of torrential rains that caused the region to become a "mud-hole." Eventually, the rains stopped, the land dried, and the first residents, Mr. and Mrs. Asa Smith and their infant daughter, arrived in town in late May.

At first, Elisha and Mary Ann Rumsey's home was opened to new settlers and visitors. Eventually, it became known as a coffeehouse at which all were welcome. It remained the social spot for newcomers even after Allen's home at the corner of Huron and Main Streets was built that fall; meanwhile, more and more settlers began to arrive in the little village. Asa Smith built a home near the courthouse square, and other settlers put down logs at Washington and Main Streets and William and Main Streets. The town began to take shape.

The first schoolhouse was built at the northwest corner of Ann and Main Streets. John Hereford opened a general store. A sawmill began to operate in 1825, a tannery was started in 1827, and a shoemaker arrived in 1830. Groceries and agricultural tools were sold at the corner of Huron and Main Streets. Blacksmith shops followed. Taverns flourished in the new village, and the Rumseys' home/coffeehouse continued entertaining newcomers. Soon, downtown Ann Arbor became a place of dry good stores, hotels, and music stores.

Today's downtown looks a lot different than it did even just a few years ago, but you can still see it as it was in many places. I am lucky enough to live within a half mile of downtown, and when walking into town, I try to imagine what it was like for Allen and Rumsey as they looked at this wooded area and said, "Here." If I try hard enough, I can almost see the men hauling logs up from the river and through the mud. I wonder what the wooden sidewalks were like and how people dealt with the constant muck. I do not know if Allen and Rumsey had any idea of what a special town they were founding. Rumsey passed away not long after the town was founded; John Allen lived on, becoming a postmaster, newspaper publisher, village president, and school organizer. At the risk of sounding metaphysical, I will say that I hope somehow, some way, they know.

On a final note, I hope that readers will be generous with my definition of "downtown"—I know that there are myriad ideas of what defines downtown, Kerrytown, and so on. I have tried to limit the first two chapters to locations that fall within the area bounded by Catherine Street on the north, Thompson Street on the east, William Street on the south, and First Street on the west. I had to pick which chapter to put in businesses that were located on corners and again ask for generosity with my placement. I included the third chapter on the "near" areas because while not part of the traditional definition of downtown, they still are close enough as to have the vibe of a bustling downtown. Also, I hope that someone will be inspired to do a follow-up book focusing on Lower Town or Kerrytown, as both of those areas have additional stories to tell.

Downtown Ann Arbor is a special place. It does not have tanneries or gristmills anymore, and there are not any coopers or blacksmiths. There are, like then, city employees, teachers, bartenders, and businessmen, and there are some special restaurants, shops, and offices. It is a diverse town full of people who have relocated from all 50 states and beyond alongside those who were born right here. Downtown is still like the Rumseys' coffeehouse—a place that gives newcomers and travelers a place to rest and feel welcome. This town takes people as they are and finds a place for them. May that good spirit never perish from this fine city.

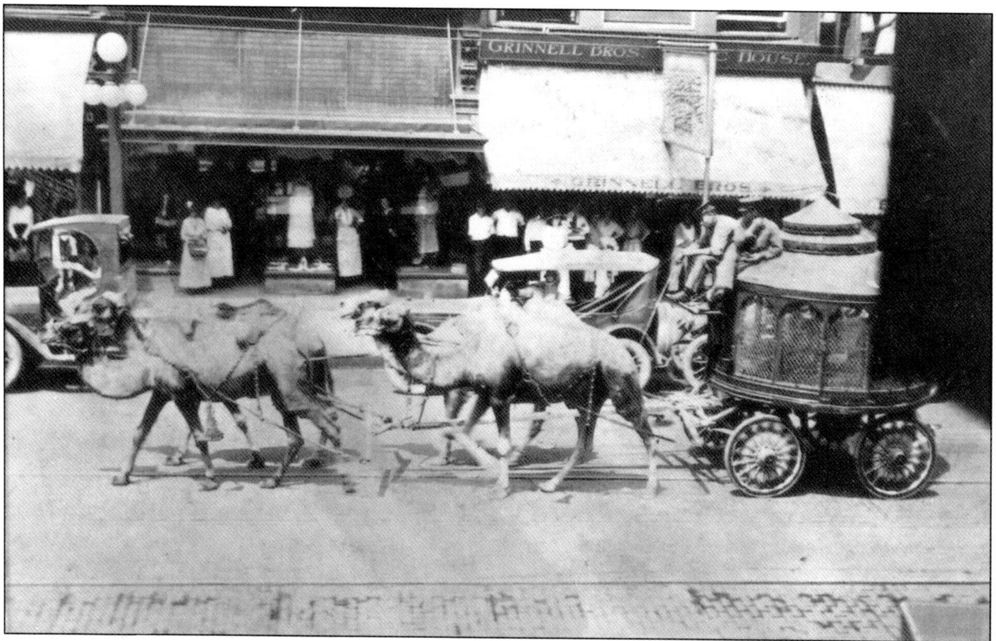

Before the Internet, television, and radio, the circus served as a distraction from daily life for people around the country—and it was certainly true in Ann Arbor. In 1916, this circus parade came down Main Street. Note the Grinnell Brothers business in the background. Located at 323 South Main Street, both the music store and the brothers became well known for offering outstanding products.

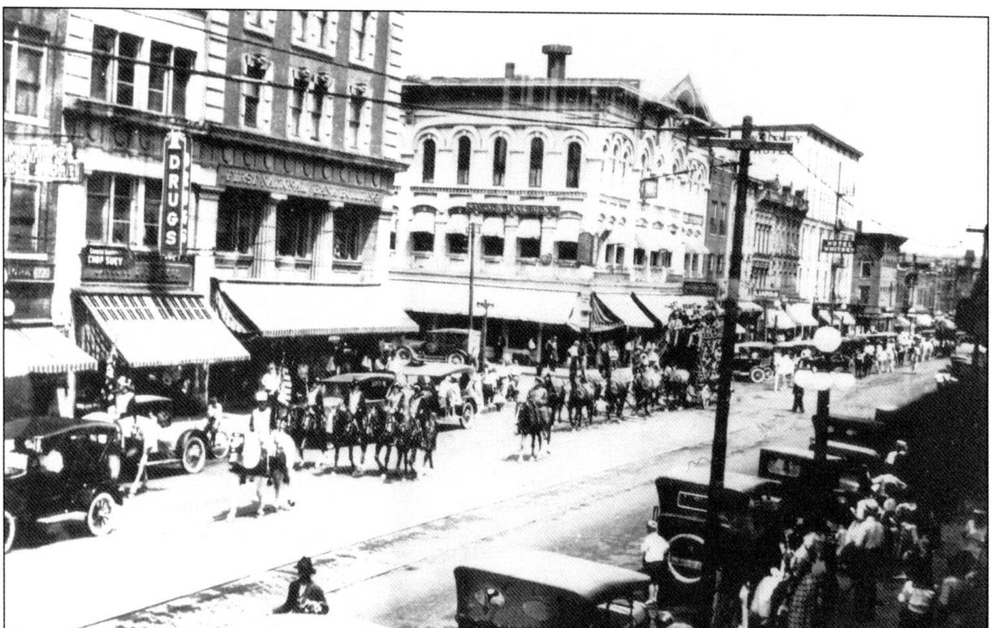

Here is another view of the parade as it comes down Main Street. Note the chop suey restaurant in the row of businesses on the left side of the street. It is generally agreed upon that the Chinese laborers, who laid the track for the Pacific Railroad in the 1860s and after, created chop suey.

One

North-South Streets

When John Allen and Elisha Rumsey bought the land that became Ann Arbor, they needed to divide it, hence Division Street. Headed west from Division Street, the streets were simply numbered Fifth, Fourth, Third (alternately called Main Street), Second, and First.

In the 1840s, William Maynard began to plat what is now called the "Old West Side." Heading west from First Street, Maynard created a mirror image of Allen's original system, using Second, Third, Fourth, Fifth, Sixth, and Seventh as street designations. This created confusion, so at some point Maynard asked the city to designate the original Fourth and Fifth Streets as avenues, and they are called such today.

Second Avenue has a different name today: Ashley Street. In 1889, it was renamed in honor of James "Big Jim" Ashley, whose Toledo and Ann Arbor Railroad depot was located on that street. Big Jim Ashley was also a congressman from Ohio and the governor of the Montana Territory; however, he liked Ann Arbor so much that he moved here.

There is much to do today on these blocks, especially in the summertime. One of the earliest outdoor activities is the annual Festifools parade that takes place on the first Sunday in April. The parade features large papier-mâché puppets made by city residents and University of Michigan students. In June, Main Street welcomes the annual Mayor's Green Fair, which features clean-energy exhibits and other activities that promote the local environment. The Taste of Ann Arbor festival takes place in early June and is a wonderful way to sample Ann Arbor's established and newer restaurants. During the summer, numerous car shows and block parties close the streets and provide residents and visitors with opportunities to listen to live music and dance the night away. And speaking of dancing, the annual Dancing in the Streets festival takes place the day before Labor Day. This book's journey will begin on Main Street and then move to the other north-south streets.

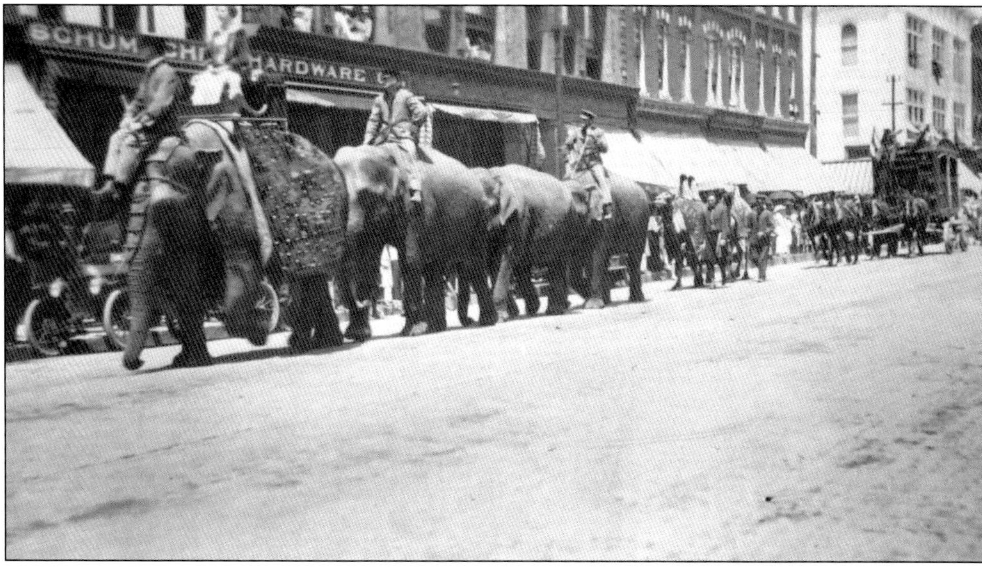

These are two views of a 1913 circus as it parades downtown. The importance and excitement surrounding the "greatest show on earth" cannot be understated. The late 1870s to the 1910s were the golden age of the circus. Its decline in popularity coincided with the increase of entertainment found in nickelodeons and silent movie houses. The days leading up to the circus were eventful as a squad of circus workers came into town before a performance to set up stakes. The rest of the workers, including performers and animals, followed on the train cars. The railroad revolutionized circuses, as the mode of transportation took them off of the dusty back roads and into bigger towns and cities. The performers would come into town, do their show, and then get right back on the train to head to the next destination.

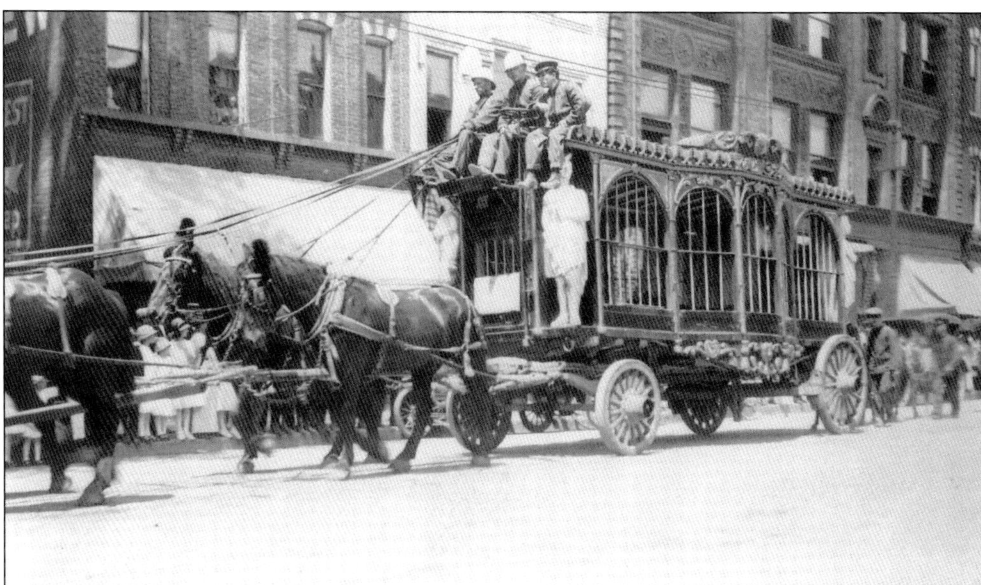

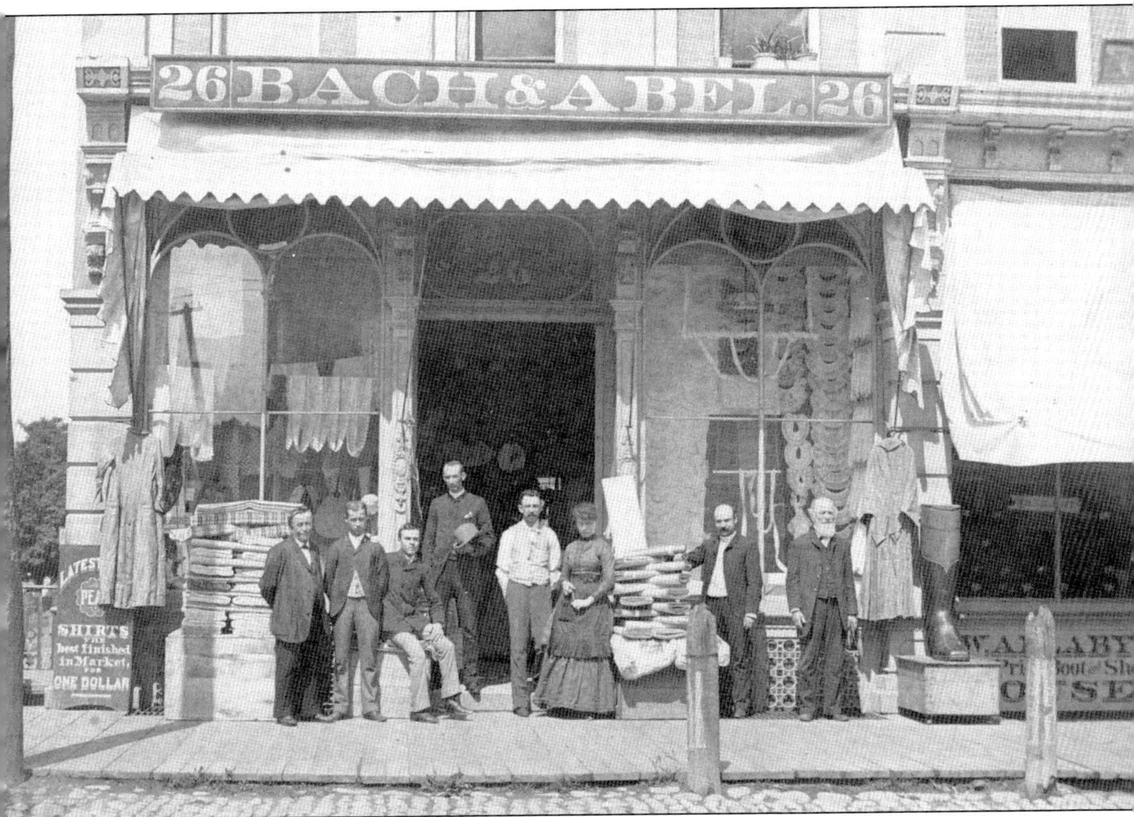

Bach & Abel at Main Street and Liberty Street sold shirts for just $1! As a sort of alternative to the traditional advertisement, Bach & Abel had a column in the *Ann Arbor Courier*. In 1886, it informed the "careful people" reading that "ladies of the city" let them know that the muslin underwear line at the store was the "finest line ever brought to Ann Arbor." In addition to selling lines of underwear, the early dry goods store sold other household goods, such as blankets, linen, and fabric. Months before his death, Philip Bach sold his store to Bruno St. James, co-owner of Goodyear and St. James, the store located next door. Upon taking over the business, St. James installed an "innovative spring-operated cash carrier" that sent money and sales slips to the cashier at the back of the store. After St. James's death in 1911, his longtime employee Bertha Muehlig bought the business and renamed it after herself. The store thrived under the auspices of Bertha Muehlig. When she passed away in 1955, Muehlig left the store to two of her employees, and they ran the business until 1976, when it was sold and renamed DeFord's. The quaint cash carriers remained in use until the store closed.

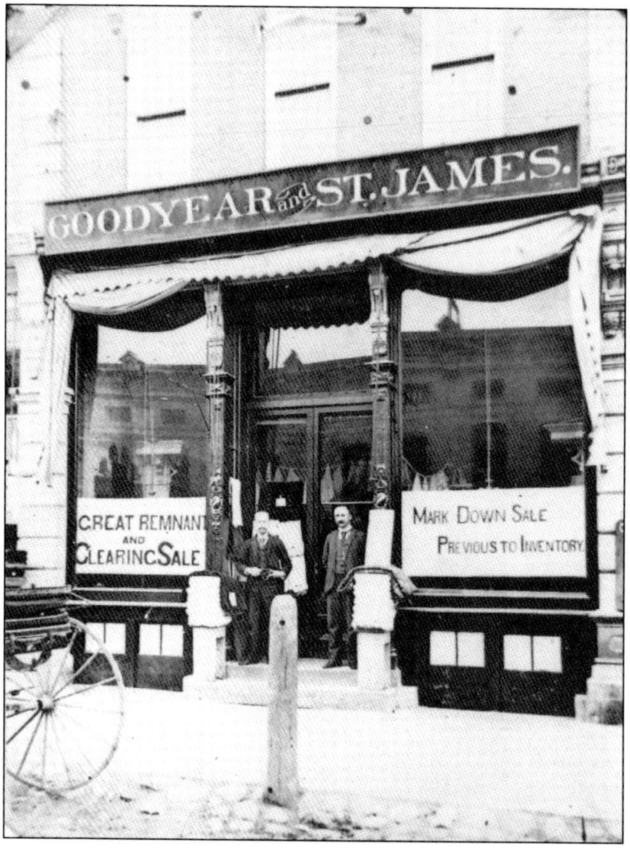

Bruno St. James partnered with William Goodyear when the latter arrived in Ann Arbor in 1888. They were in business together until 1895. When they began their partnership, they had little capital, and many predicted failure. Not only did they not fail, but Goodyear enjoyed great success after buying out his partner's interest.

At 126 South Main Street, Bruno St. James sold dry goods and notions. His frequent advertisements in the *Argus-Democrat* promised customers that their money would be "cheerfully returned" if not satisfied.

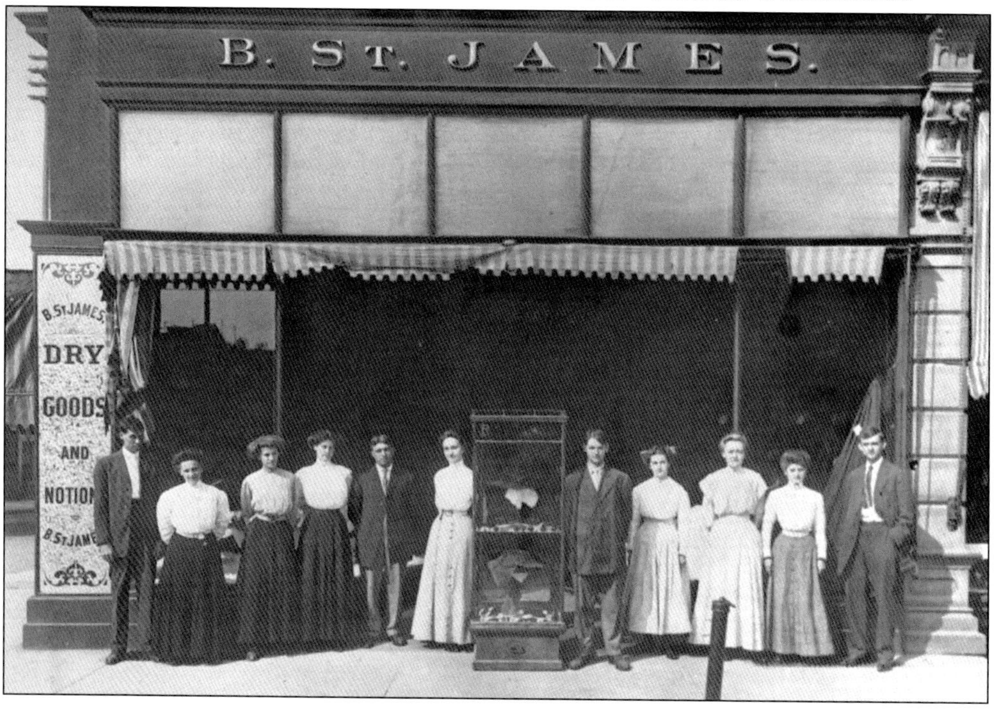

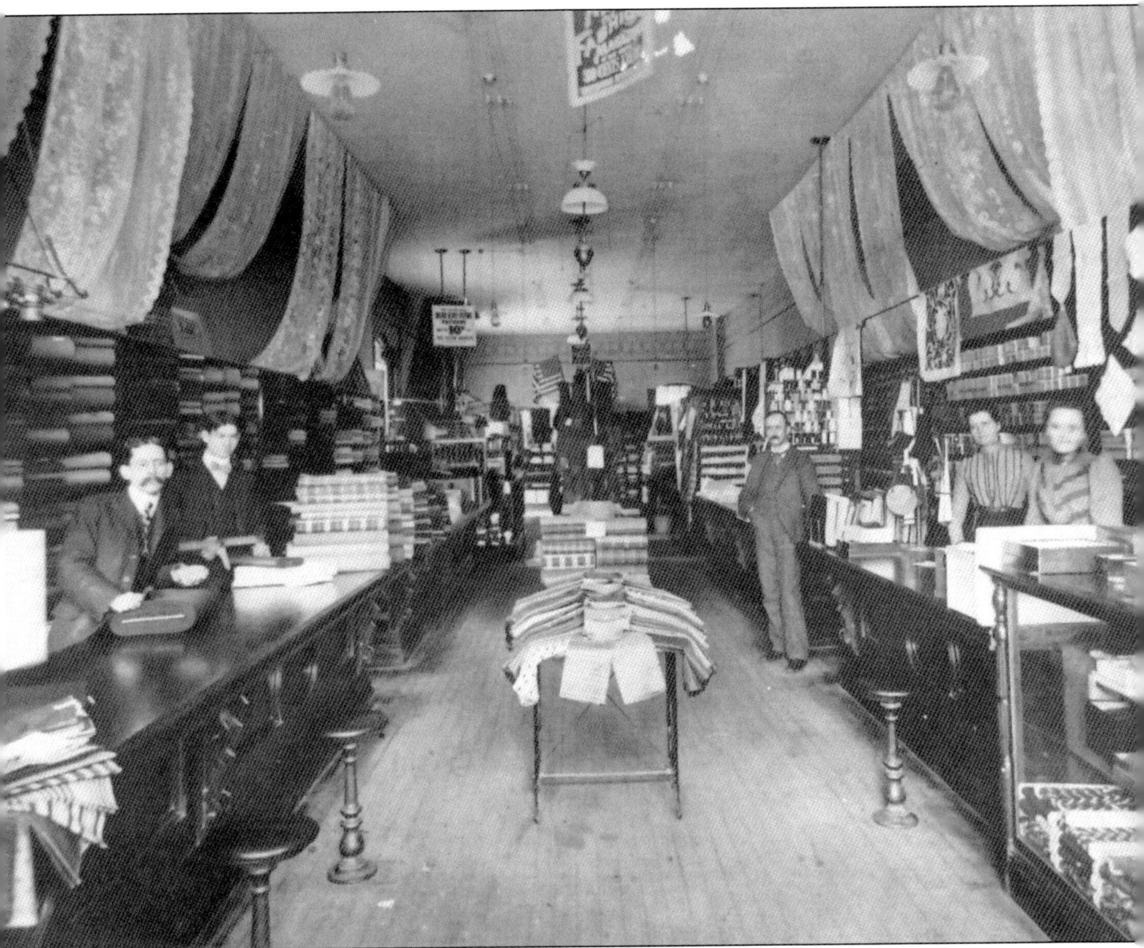

Featured here is a c. 1909 photograph of the interior of Bruno St. James's store. Dry good stores dominated Main Street at the time. These businesses sold everything from manufactured cloth to coffee to oil and specialized in selling items for the person who sewed at home. St. James was just one of the several dry goods store in the downtown area in the late 1800s that operated into the early 20th century. St. James passed away in 1911 and was interred in St. Thomas Catholic Cemetery. On the day of St. James's funeral, St. Thomas Catholic School closed for the day.

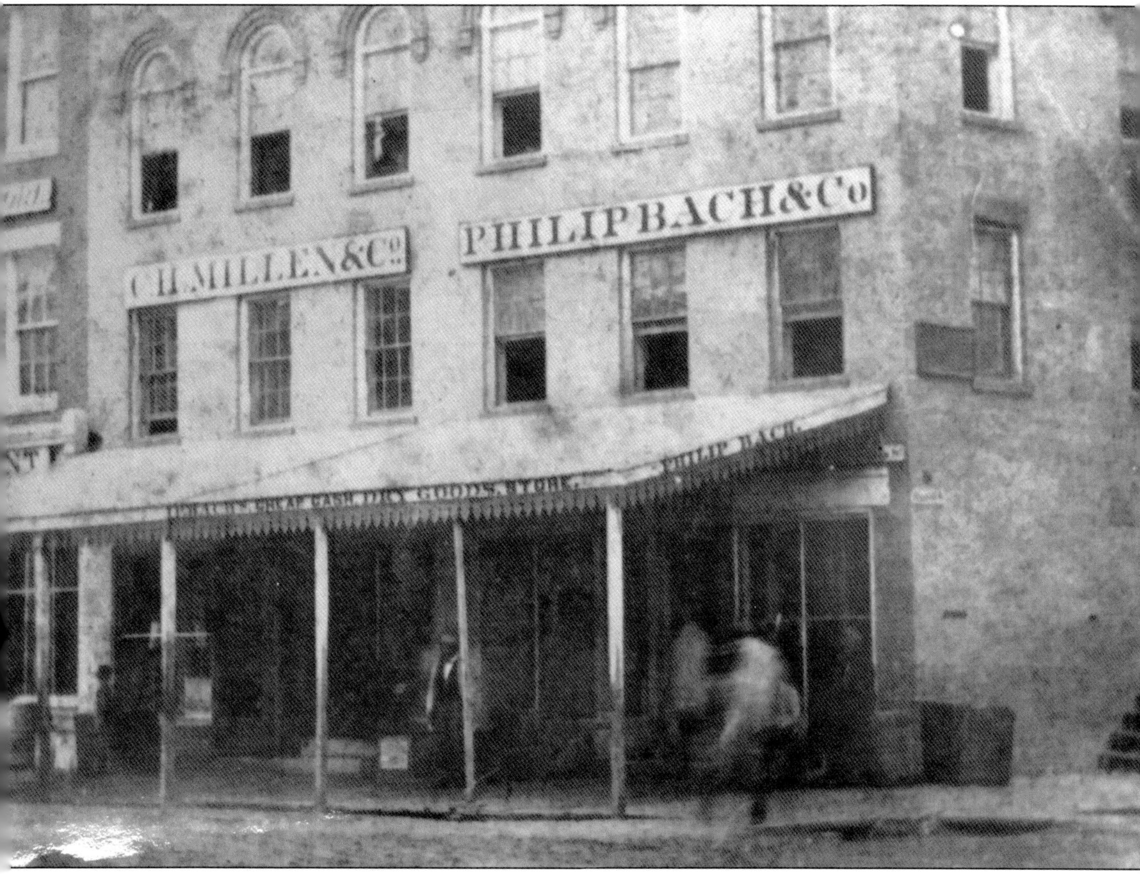

Philip Bach's store anchored the Main Street corner building that also housed C.H. Millen & Co. An emigrant from Karlsruhe, Germany, Bach also served as the mayor of Ann Arbor from 1858 to 1859 and on the school board. Bach Elementary School is named in his honor. Bach married Anna Botsford, who also served on the local school board and has the distinction of the being the first female president of that board. The two lived in a 14-room home on Main Street. Chauncey H. Millen was one of Ann Arbor's most respected citizens. Born in Connecticut, Millen eventually made his way to Ann Arbor where he ran a successful dry goods business and insurance agency. Additionally, he served as the US Internal Revenue collector under Pres. Ulysses S. Grant. Millen passed away in 1891.

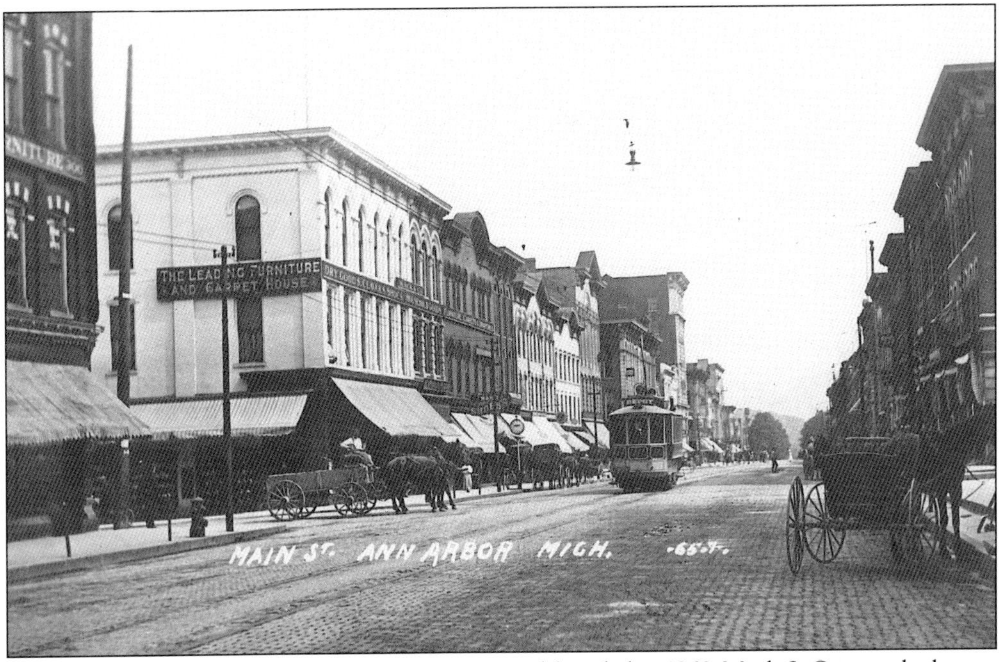

Located at the corner of Main and Liberty Streets and founded in 1860, Mack & Co. was the largest department store in the city for a time. Mack's boasted ornate window displays at Christmastime and at one point was the premier destination of the Main Street shopping district. Unfortunately, it did not survive the Great Depression and closed in the late 1930s.

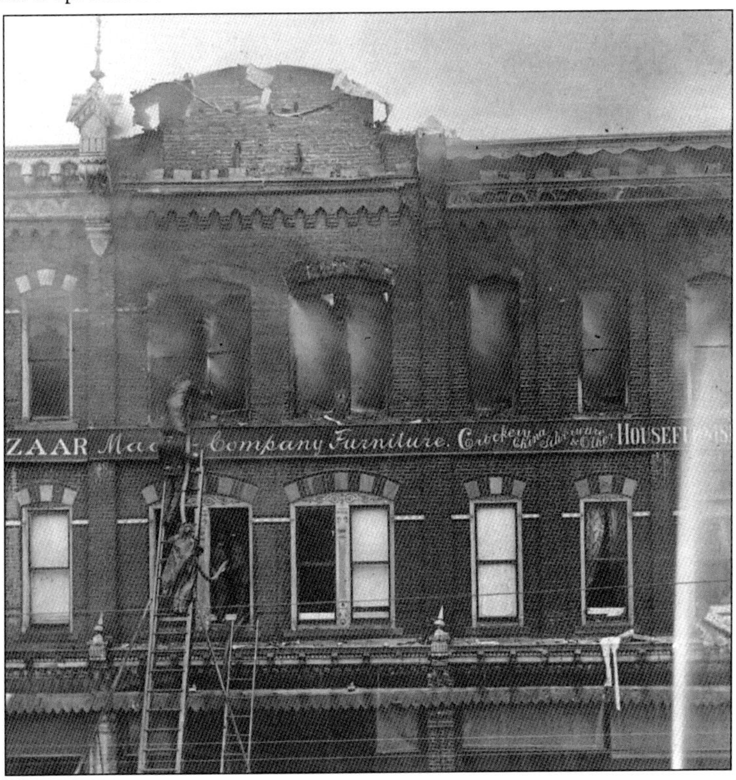

Fire broke out at the Mack & Co. store on May 15, 1899. The *Ann Arbor Argus-Democrat* reported that the cause was unknown but possibly was a result of "combustion" or the sun's refraction on cotton and oils. If the wind had been blowing in a different direction, the fire could have spread up Main Street.

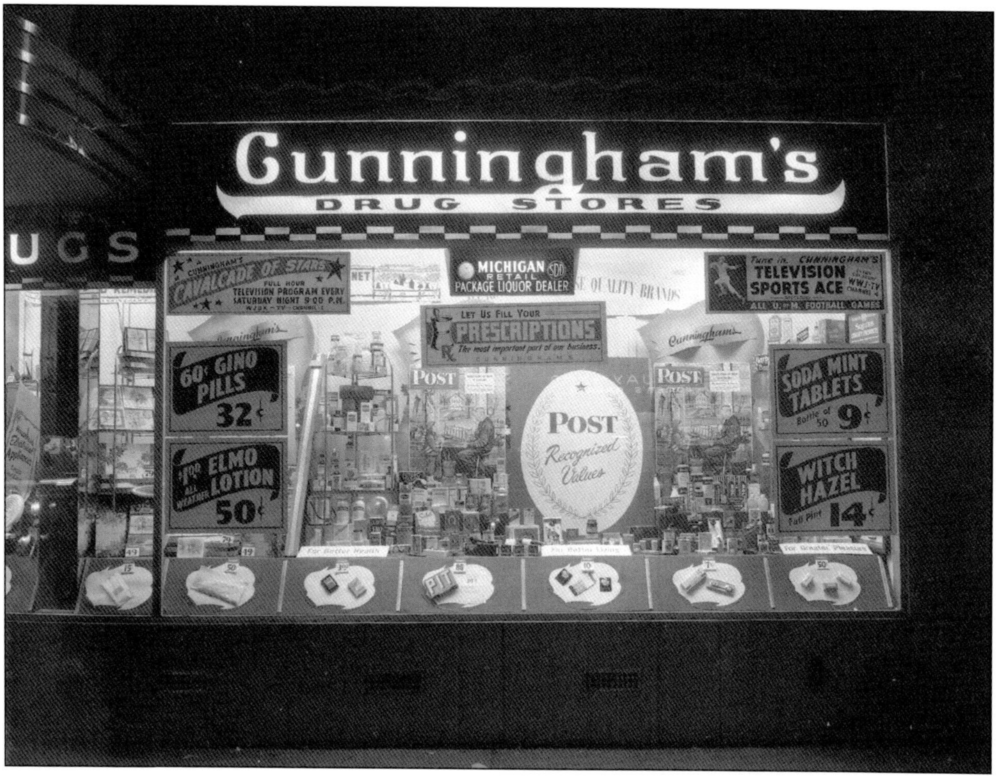

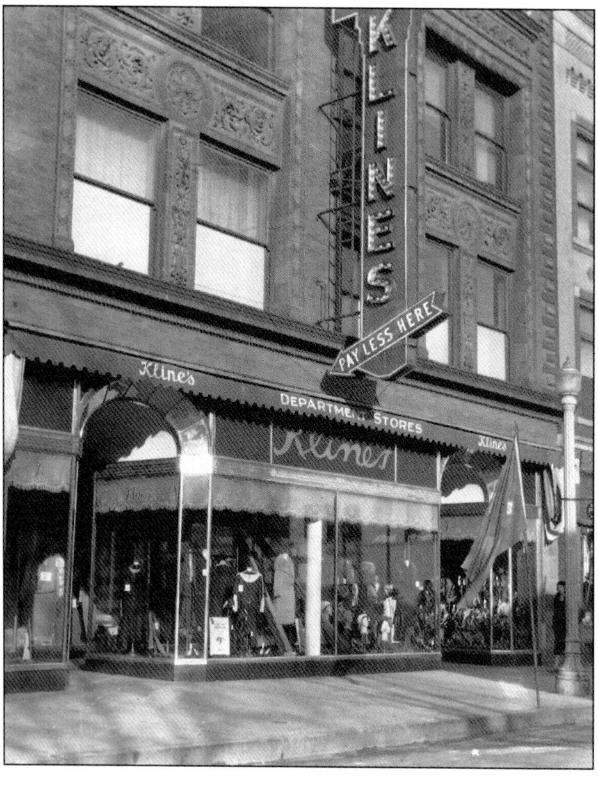

In 1940, the Cunningham Drugstore chain took over part of the Mack & Co. location. The drugstore featured green panels that were eventually removed as businesses and owners changed hands. In 2012, the restaurant Lena moved in and included panels the color of Cunningham's green, which now shine proudly over Main Street once again.

The Pratt Block was located on Main Street south of Liberty Street. It was named for its owner, Stephan Pratt, an industrialist from Detroit. Kline's Department Store took over an entire building in 1930. At the time, other local businesses like Mack & Co. and Goodyear's were still in business; however, Kline's offered mass-produced items that were less expensive.

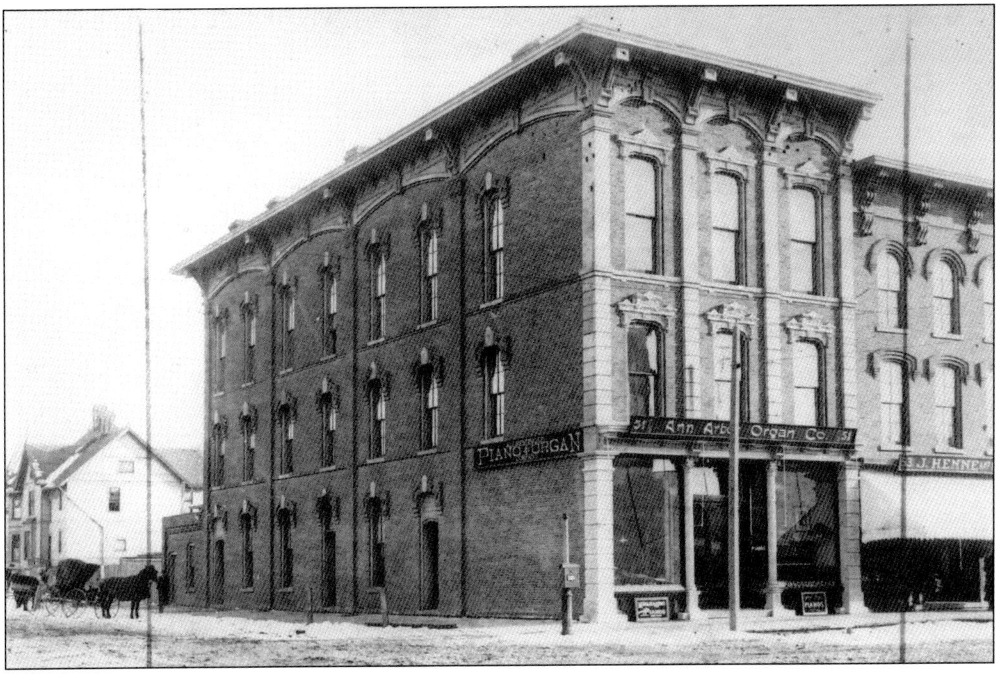

The Ann Arbor Organ Company sold locally made reed organs at this store on the southeast corner of Main and Liberty Streets. David Frederick Allmendinger established the organ company, originally called the Ann Arbor Organ Works. According to an 1893 piece in the *Ann Arbor Argus*, Allmendinger looked at every aspect of organ construction. At one point in his career, he also tuned each organ himself. Eventually, he relinquished that task to a "trusted employee"; still, no organ left the building without his approval. The image below features some of those employees so trusted by Allmendinger.

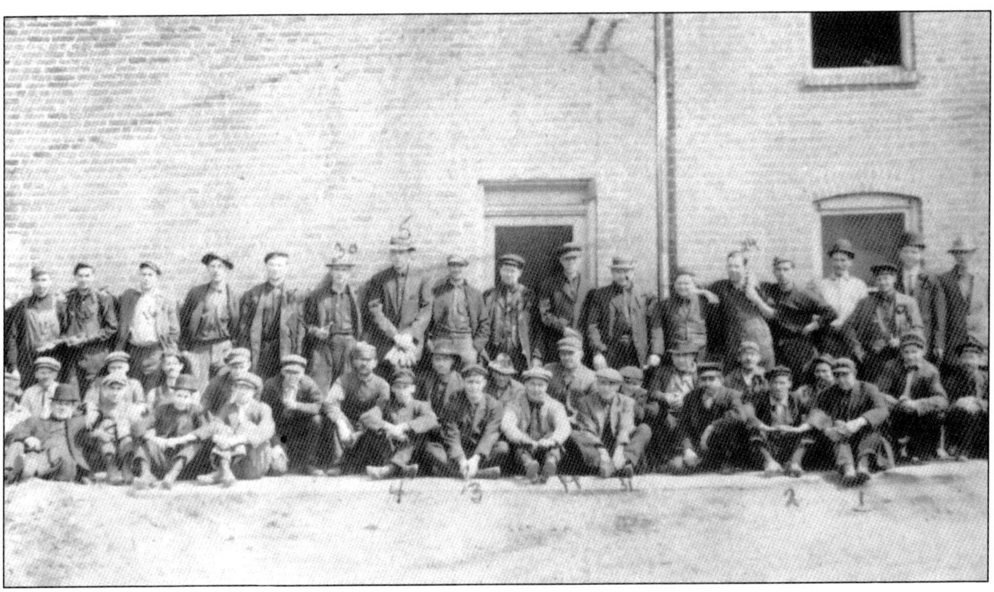

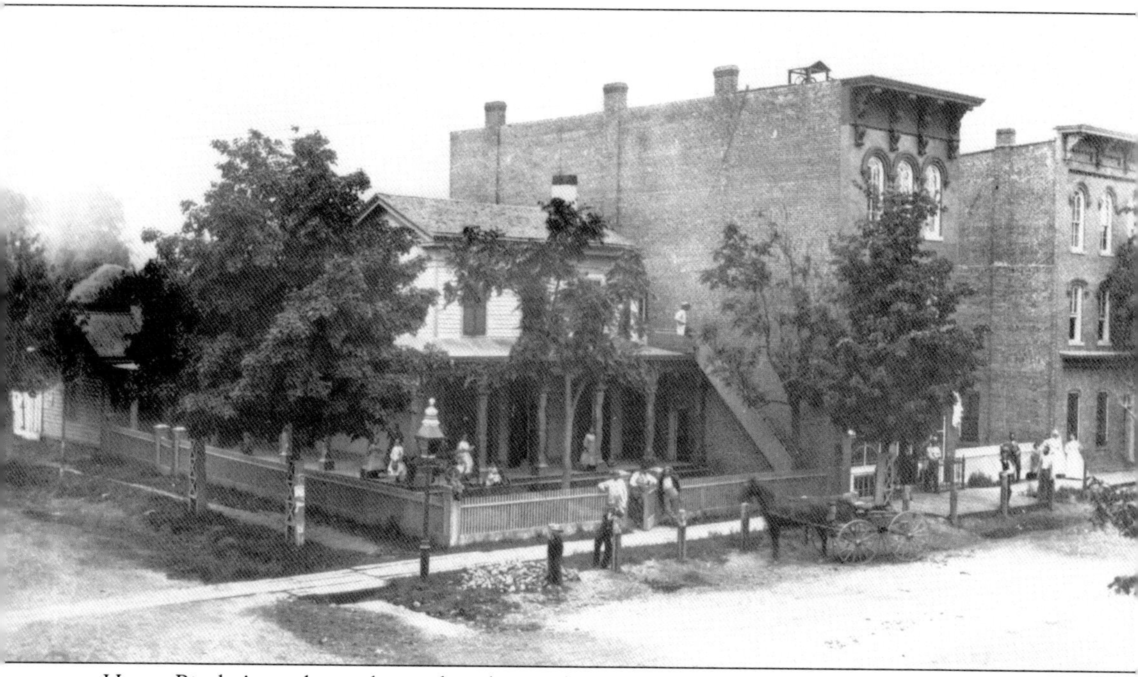

Henry Binder's residence, located at the southeast corner of Main and Liberty Streets, is shown here; the house number was 51 South Main Street. Binder also owned a saloon at 50 South Main Street. The saloon saw trouble in 1856, when several uninvited students entered the establishment during a private function and helped themselves to some liquor. Upon being discovered, most of the students managed to escape, but Binder and other party guests held up one. Shortly thereafter, the students who had escaped came back to get their buddy, and they brought a mob of friends with them. The matter escalated to the point that the students beat the building with logs and killed Binder's dog. The next day, Binder swore out warrants for six of the students, who quickly reminded him about an old charge against him involving the selling of alcohol to minors. After receiving this reminder, Binder dropped the charges. Binder died on November 13, 1894, when a lantern exploded on him as he was climbing the stairs of his barn. Neighbors rushed to his rescue but were too late to save him.

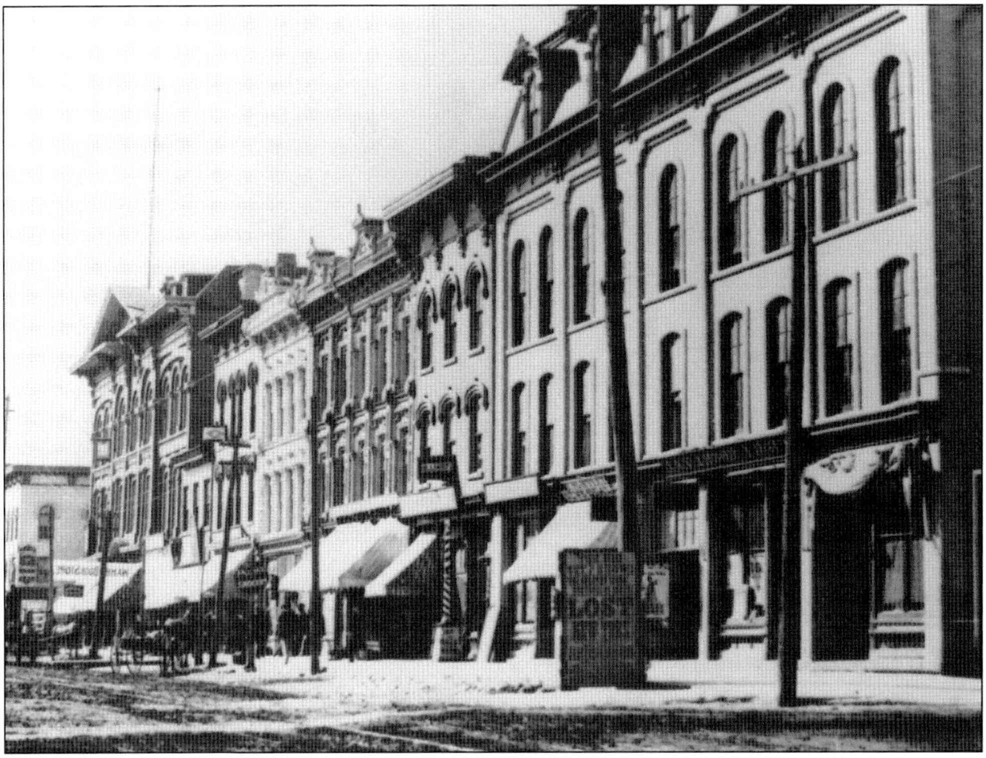

From the book *Art Work of Washtenaw County*, this 1893 view of Main Street looking south from Ann Street shows (from front to back) the Ann Arbor Argus Building, a billiards room, a grocery store, baths, and Wahr's Book Store. George Wahr's bookstore was a staple on Main Street until it closed in the 1950s. Wahr also had a publishing business and eventually opened a second bookstore on State Street.

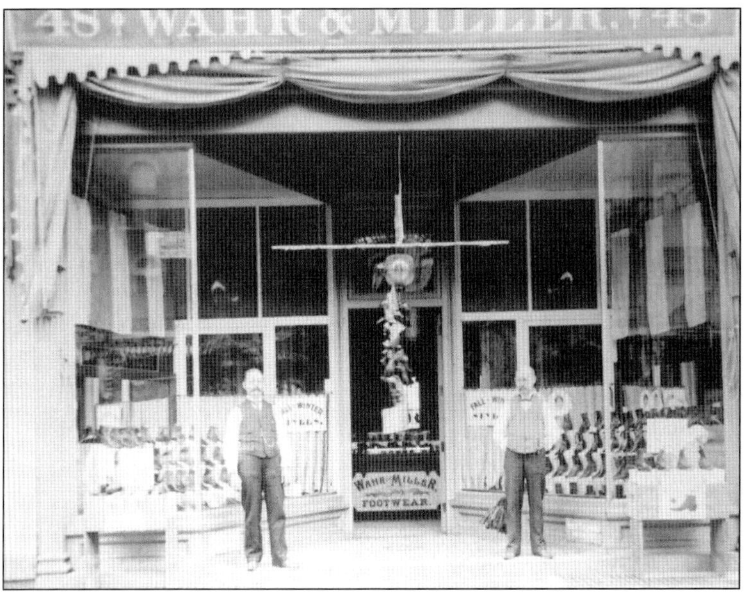

John Wahr and George H. Miller sold boots and shoes at what was then 48 South Main Street. Calling themselves "the shoe men," the two sold a variety of footwear, including calf-lined shoes (for only $3 according to an 1898 *Argus-Democrat* ad) and Mishawaka all-knit boots. Wahr was a cousin of George Wahr, the bookstore owner and publisher.

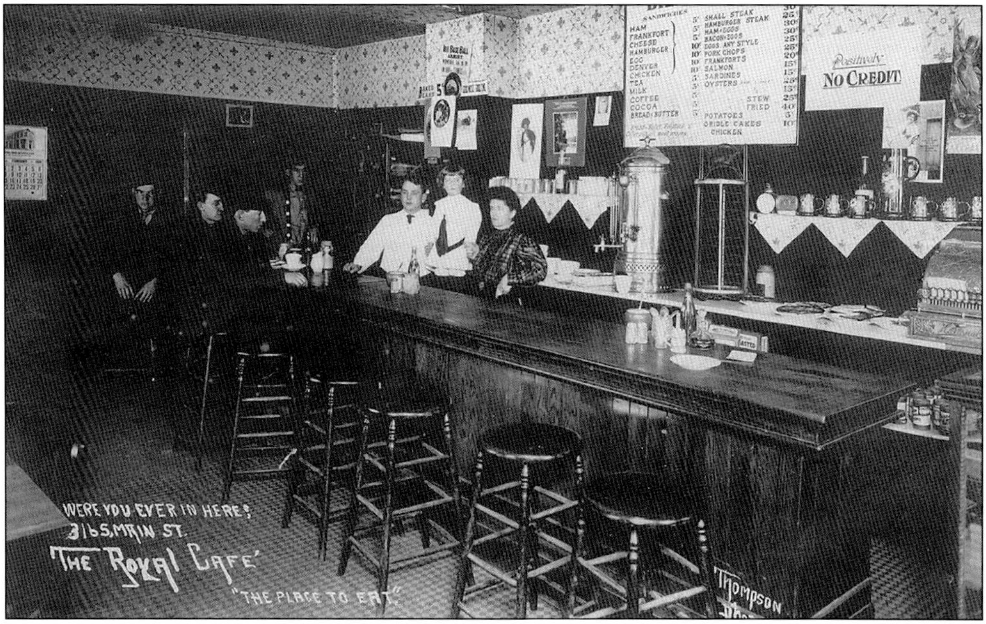

The Royal Café at 316 South Main Street was "the place to eat," but only if one paid in cash—note the "no credit" sign on the wall. Guy Bissell opened the restaurant in 1909. Described as a "casual restaurant," it had a simple menu and counter service. It later moved across the street and then to Church Street with the idea of catering to the university population. Two years after that move, the university purchased the building.

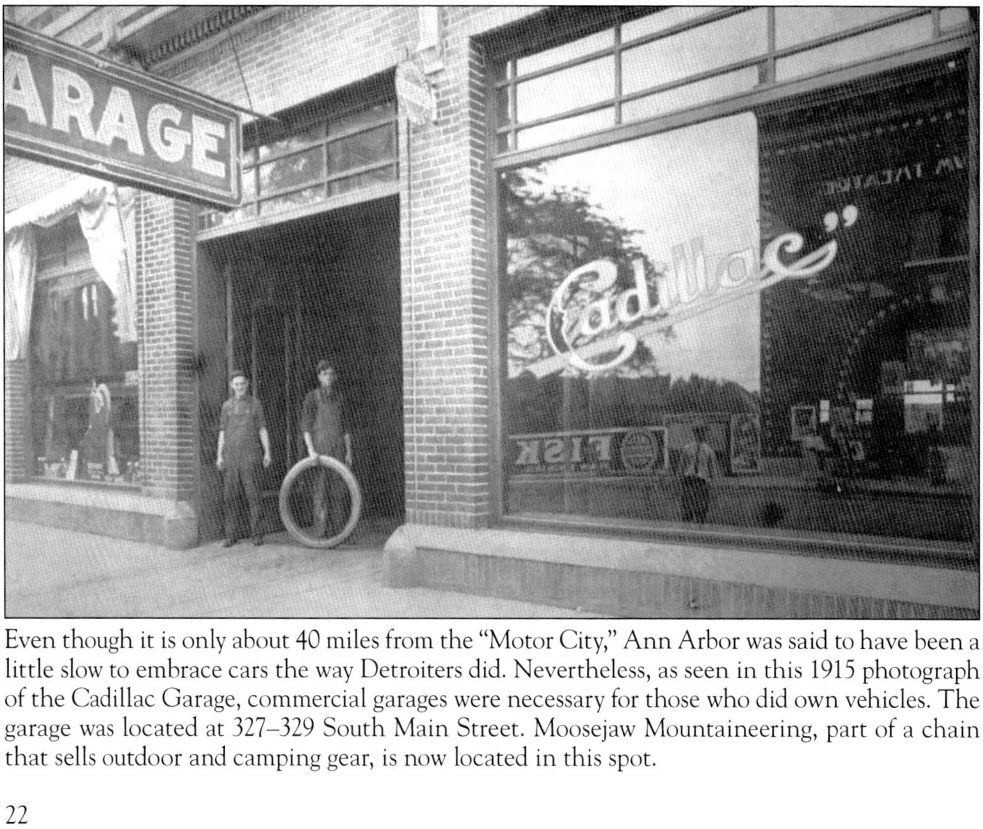

Even though it is only about 40 miles from the "Motor City," Ann Arbor was said to have been a little slow to embrace cars the way Detroiters did. Nevertheless, as seen in this 1915 photograph of the Cadillac Garage, commercial garages were necessary for those who did own vehicles. The garage was located at 327–329 South Main Street. Moosejaw Mountaineering, part of a chain that sells outdoor and camping gear, is now located in this spot.

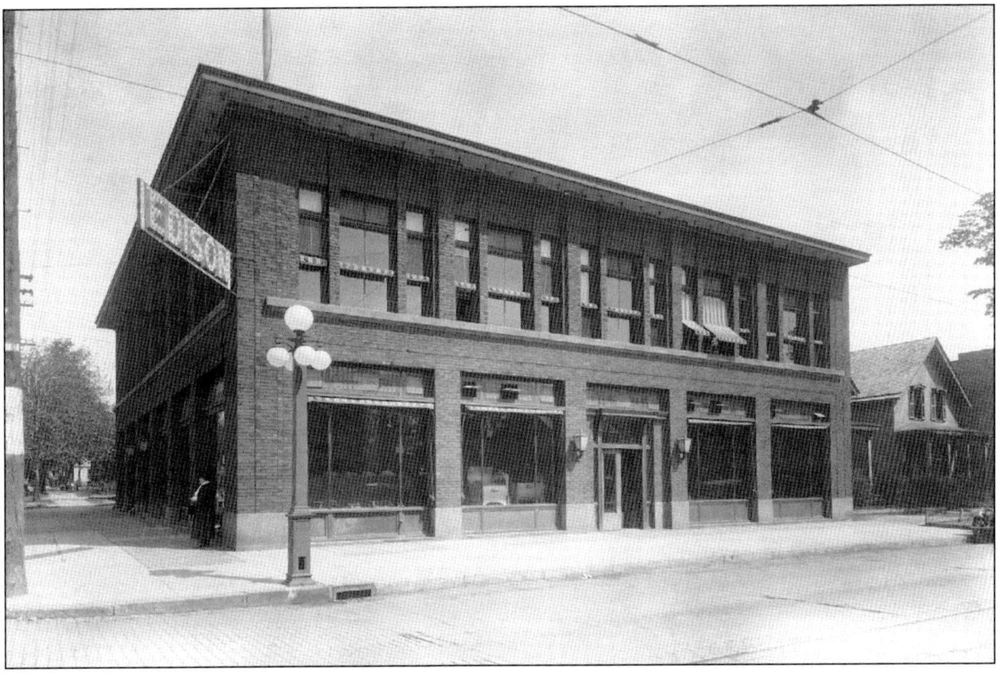

Fireplaces and lard lamps lit the earliest homes in Ann Arbor. In time, oil and coal provided light after the sun went down. In the late 1800s, electric power came to Ann Arbor when a plant powered by coal-fired steam was built just west of the Ann Arbor Railroad. Later, dams began generating hydropower along the river. After the turn of the century, the Edison Company began purchasing water rights, mills, and small power plants, eventually turning itself into the largest supplier of electricity in the county. Edison built Barton Dam in 1912, but the power it supplied was insufficient for the needs of the growing town; thus, coal-powered plants were expanded. Detroit Edison not only supplied Ann Arbor's power but also sold home appliances and gave away free lightbulbs in its Main Street showrooms until 1983.

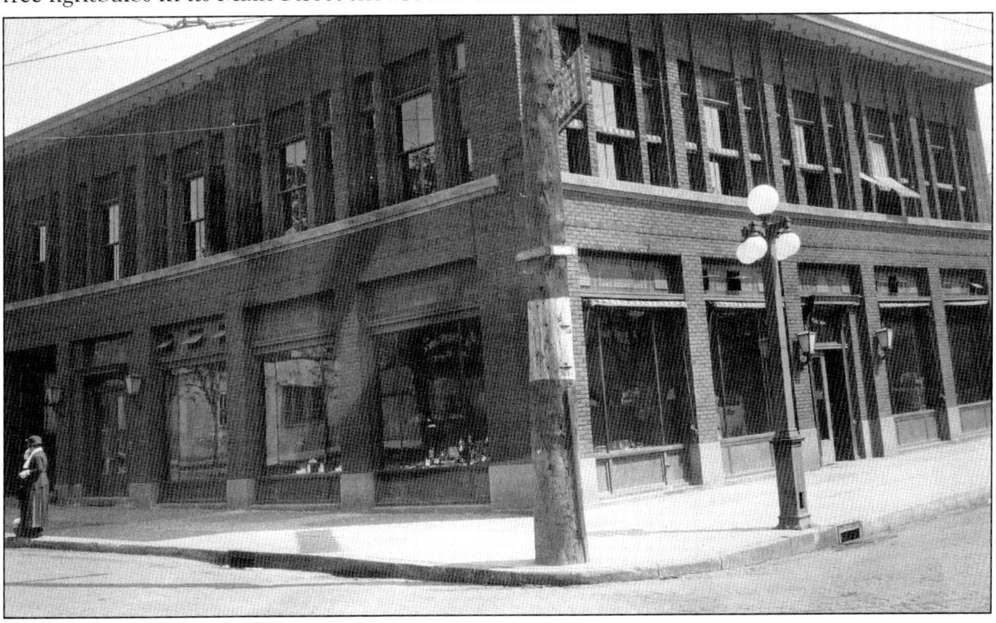

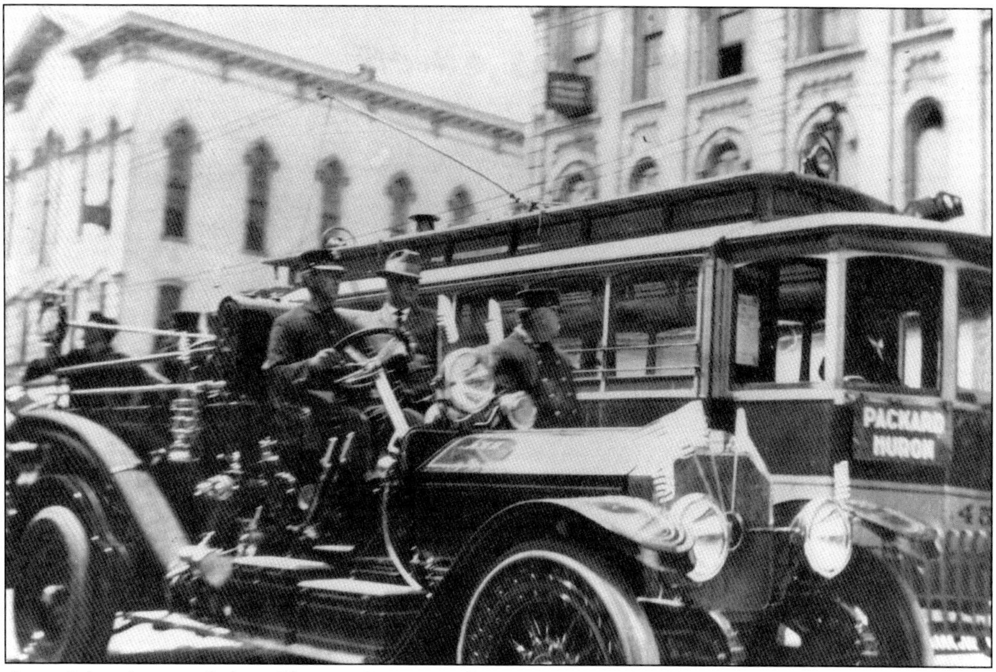

Ann Arbor has prided itself on its "town-and-gown" spirit of collaboration between businesses, townspeople, and the university. This was also true during World War I, as seen in a photograph of an Armistice Day parade where townsfolk, faculty, and students marched together to celebrate the end of the Great War.

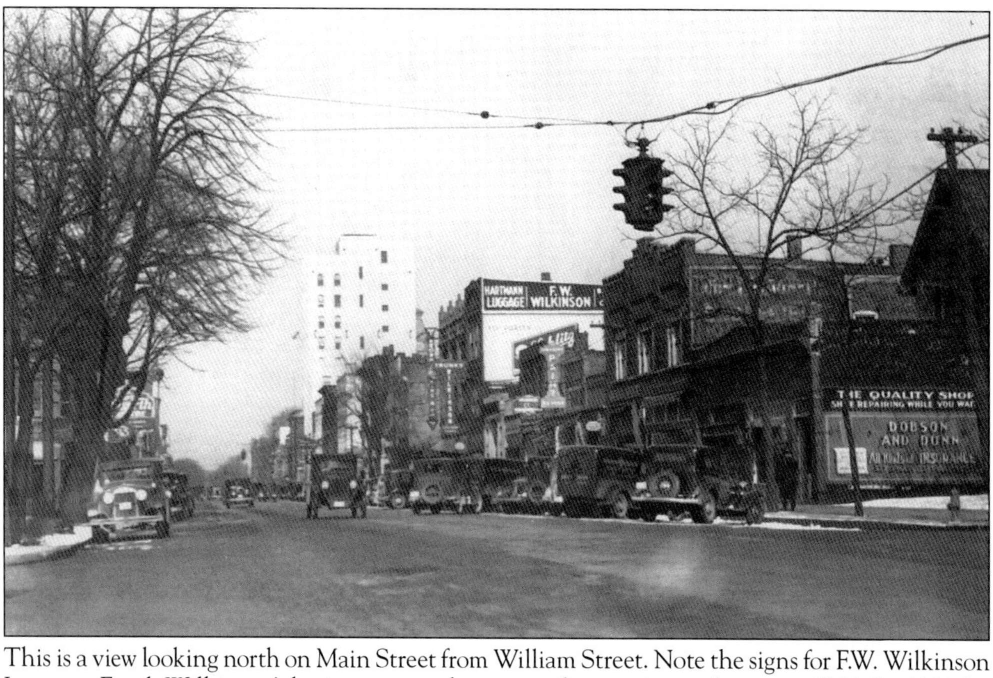

This is a view looking north on Main Street from William Street. Note the signs for F.W. Wilkinson Luggage. Frank Wilkinson's business was a downtown fixture since it began in 1904. By 1924, he was selling trunks to students, and from there the store evolved into a luggage store. Wilkinson retired in 1951. The store briefly moved to Scio Township in 2006 but closed in 2008.

Wagner & Co. was located at 21 South Main Street. According to the 1890–1891 "Polk Directory," this business provided tailoring, clothing, and "gents' furnishing." In 1888, proprietors William and Charles Wagner advertised in the *Ann Arbor Courier*, stating their need to sell 12 dozen "white Merino undershirts" in sizes 44 and 46. The price was reduced from 50¢ to 25¢ for the occasion.

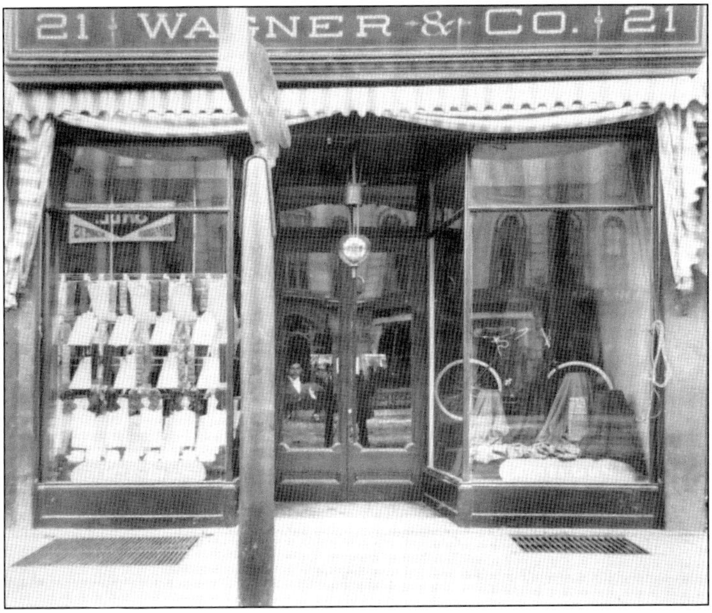

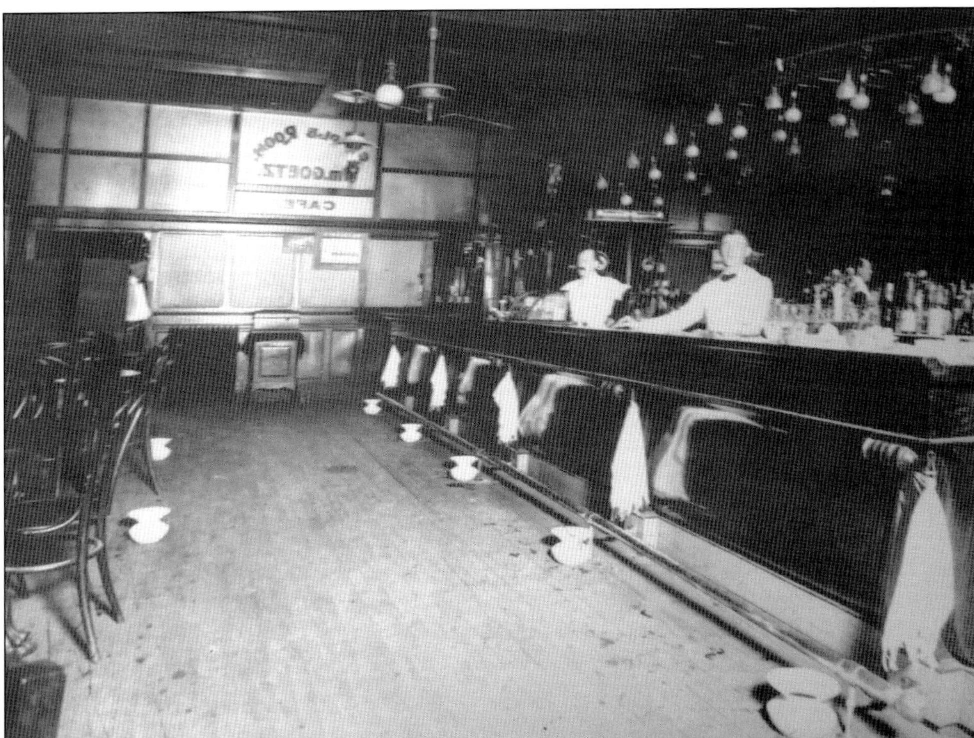

John Goetz and his son operated a business at 221 South Main Street that was billed as both a grocery store and a saloon. The "Polk Directory" indicated that John Sr. and John Jr. both worked at the business, with the elder man living at the same location. An earlier directory listed another family member, William, in their employ.

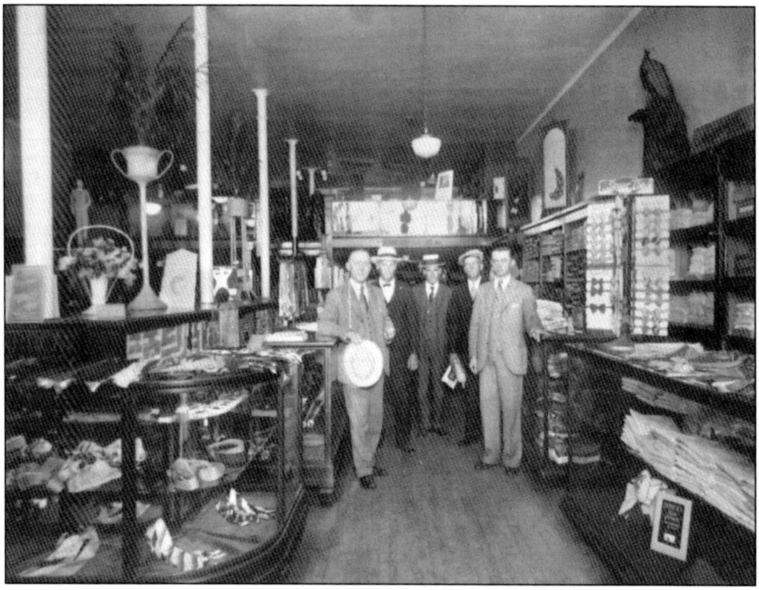

The interior of Wadhams, Ryan & Reule menswear store, located at 200–202 Main Street, is shown here in 1898. Its 1897 ad in the *Argus* proclaimed that the store had just acquired the "best clothing in the world." Also, stiff hats were for sale for 96¢. Note the nice selection of bow ties.

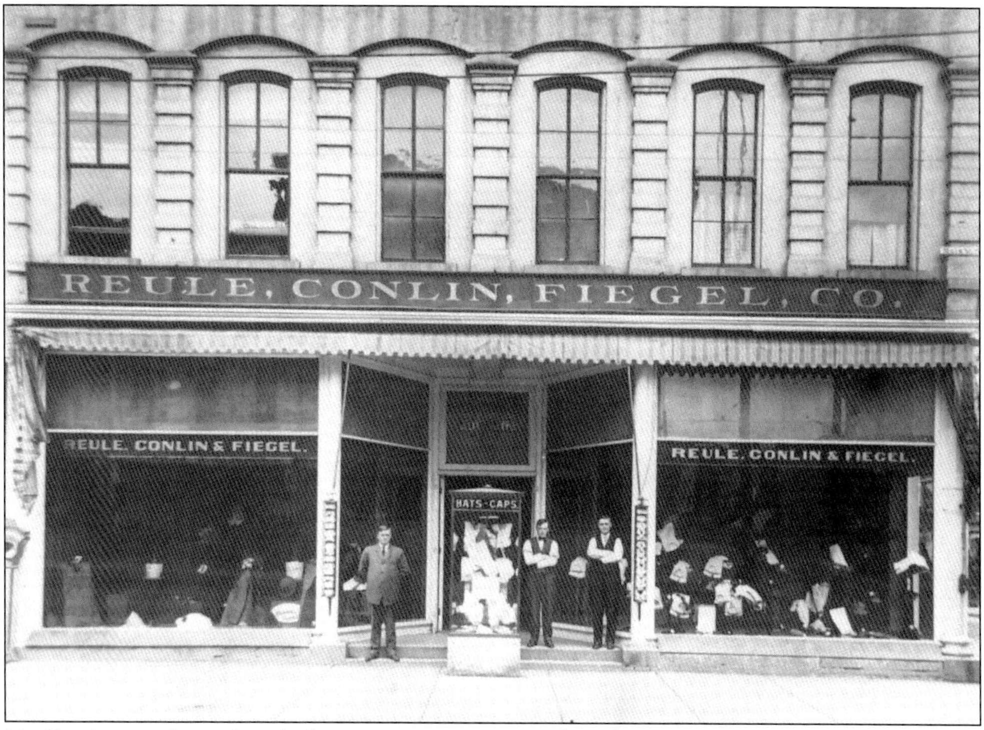

Mr. Reule owned another clothing store in 1916 named Reule, Conlin & Fiegel Co., also located at 200–202 Main Street. Mr. Reule's partner, Albert Fiegel, began his career in the clothing business when he was 18 years old. Fiegel originally planned to become a minister, but after his father's untimely and tragic death, he went to work for what was then named Wadhams, Ryan & Reule. He did well enough to buy in as a partner and change the name of the store. Fiegel passed away in the 1940s, but his store operated into the 1990s.

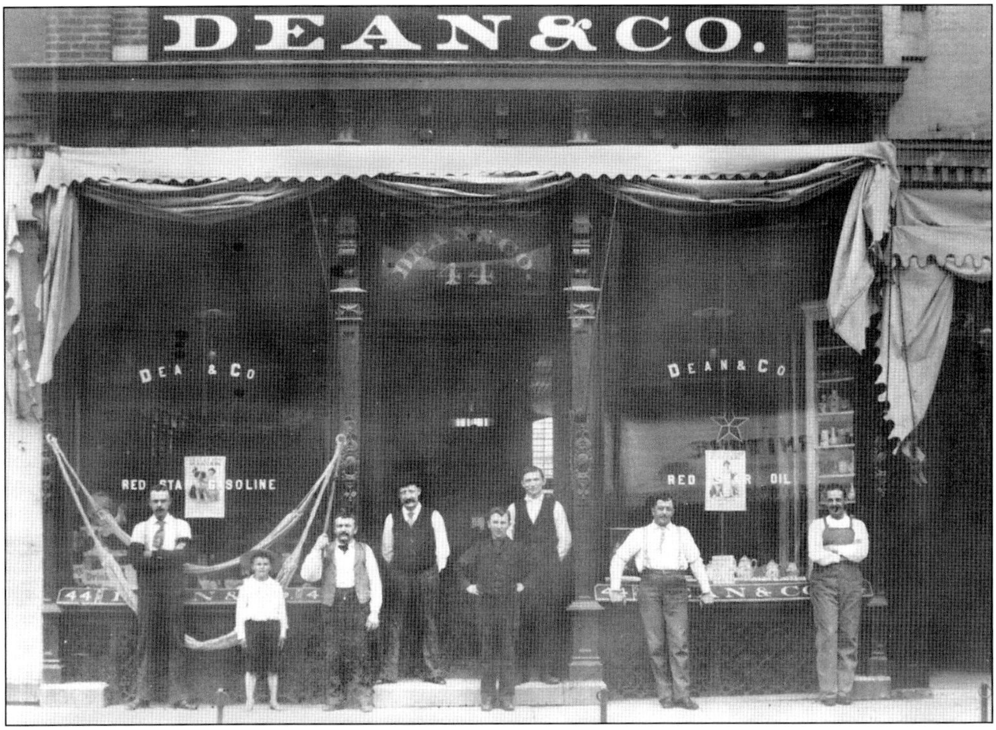

This photograph shows the exterior of Dean & Co. In 1964, Elizabeth Dean, daughter of Sedgwick Dean, willed $2 million to the city to establish a fund for trees. Every year, the Elizabeth Dean Tree Fund allocates its annual interest to maintain and plant trees in Ann Arbor.

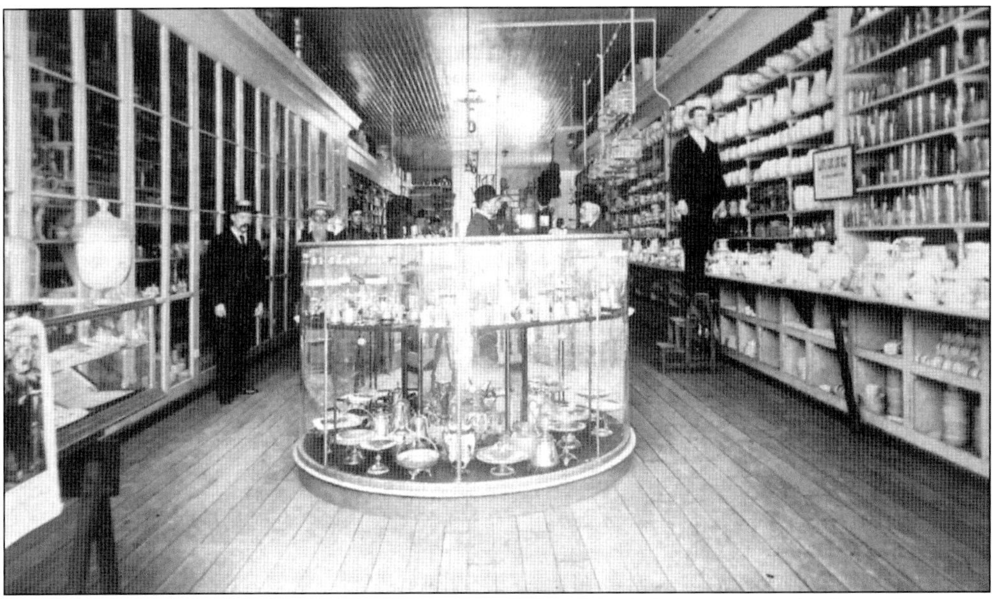

Dean & Co. was located at 214 South Main Street between Washington and Liberty Streets. It was another store that offered a wide variety of goods, such as candy, peanuts, fine dishware, and eventually gasoline. An 1892 ad in the *Argus* offered mocha coffee for just 35¢ per pound. Coffee is still available at this location, now in the Espresso Royale coffee shop.

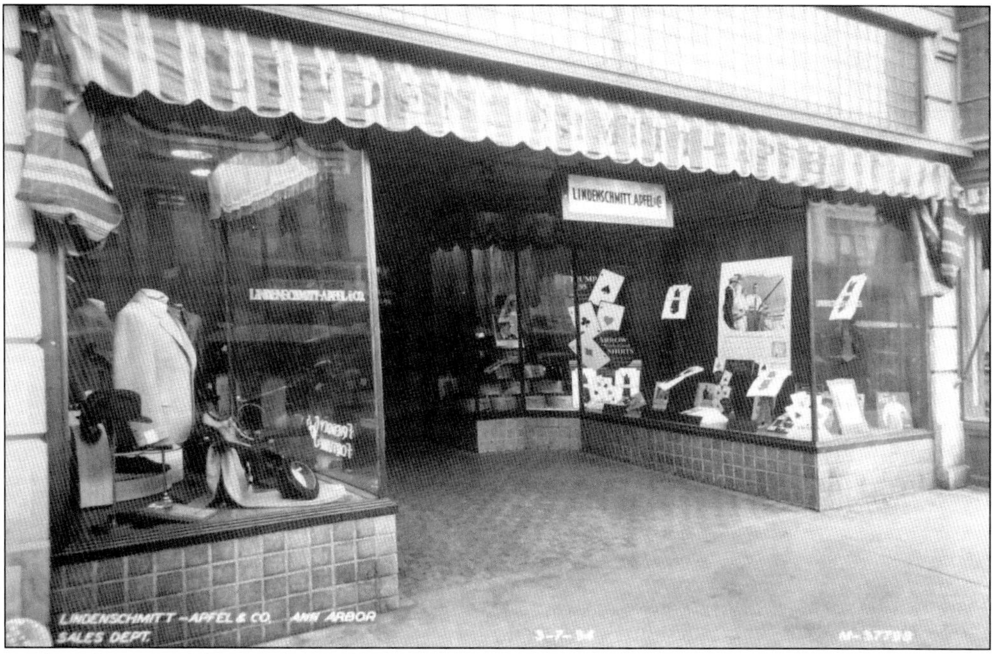

Lindenschmitt-Apfel & Co., located at 209 South Main Street, advertised itself as selling inexpensive clothes, "The very best merchandise for the least money." The store, which primarily sold men's and boys' clothing, started before 1900 and continued through the Great Depression. Lindenschmitt-Apfel & Co. was one of the stores in Ann Arbor to issue "Depression scrip" in 5¢ denominations.

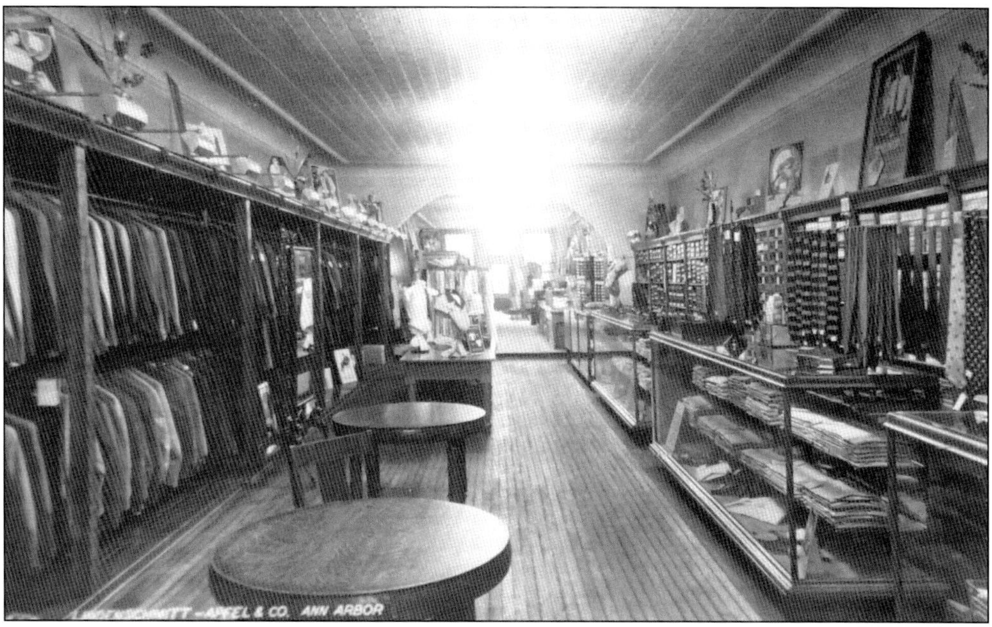

Examples are shown here of the fine clothing sold by Lindenschmitt-Apfel & Co. An employee named J. Herman Goetz purchased the store and later went into partnership with George Haarer. The two renamed the store after themselves. Haarer & Goetz menswear existed until the 1960s. Goetz passed away in 1964.

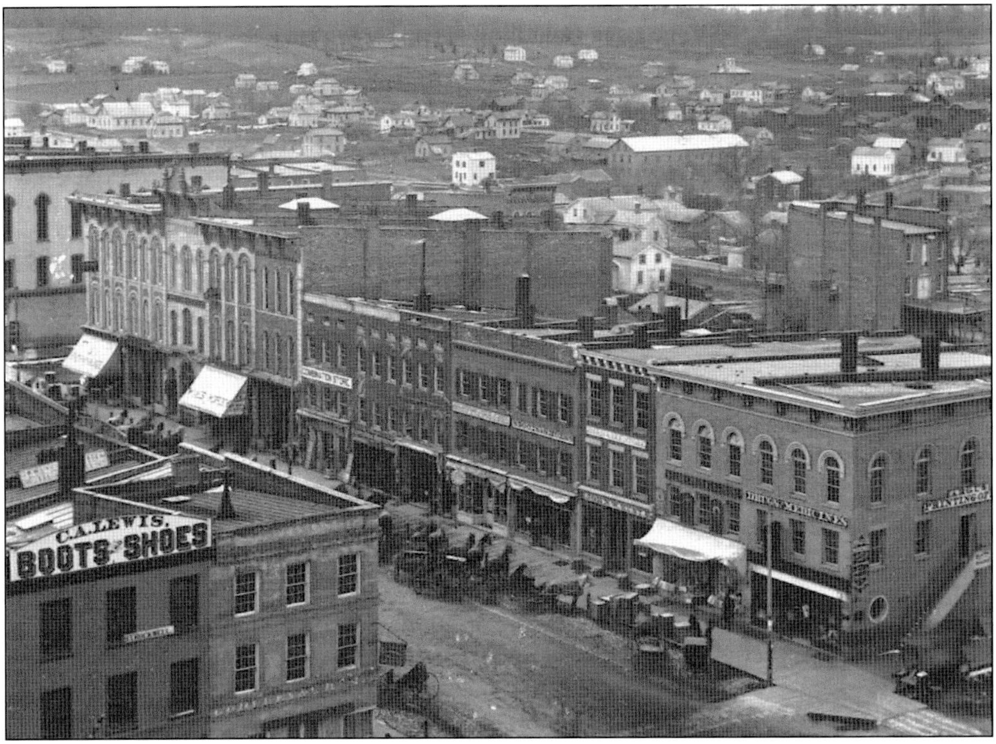

An aerial photograph of Main Street is shown here. Note the printing offices of the *Argus* at the corner of Main and Huron Streets. The *Ann Arbor Argus* grew out of the *Michigan Argus*. In 1898, it merged with the *Ann Arbor Democrat* and *Ypsilanti Weekly Times*, creating the *Ann Arbor Argus-Democrat*.

Ann Arbor had many newspapers in the past, as seen in this image looking north. The 1906 "Polk Directory" lists no fewer than five publications. In the foreground is the *Times News*, which ran from 1919 to 1927. A produce market is also visible in the background.

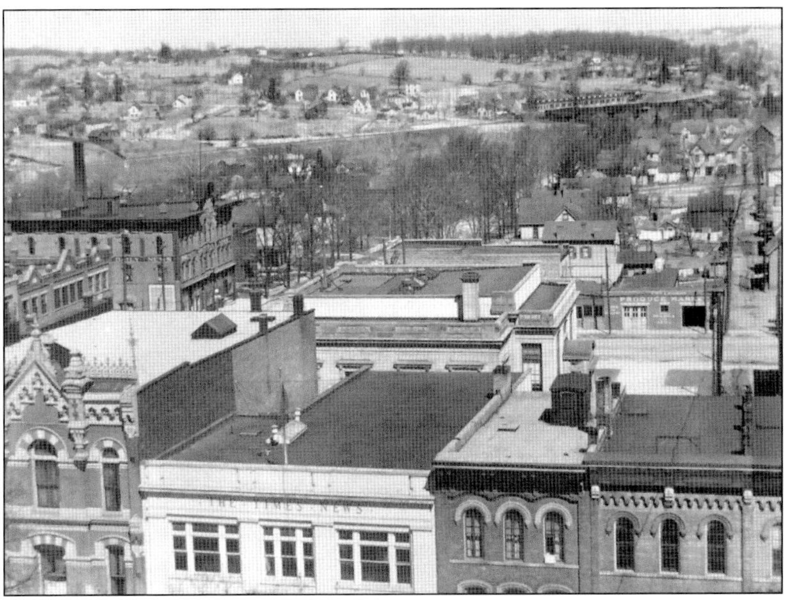

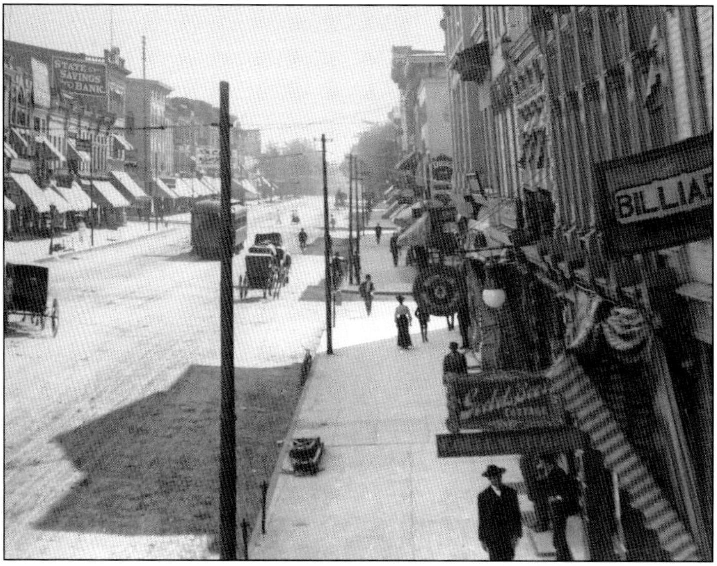

This 1910 photograph shows Main Street looking south. Note the sign in the foreground announcing that Goebel's beer can be found at that location. Goebel Brewing Company was in business in Detroit from 1873 to 1964. The Stroh Brewing Company acquired it late in its existence. Goebel's was a longtime sponsor of the Detroit Tigers and was very popular in the region.

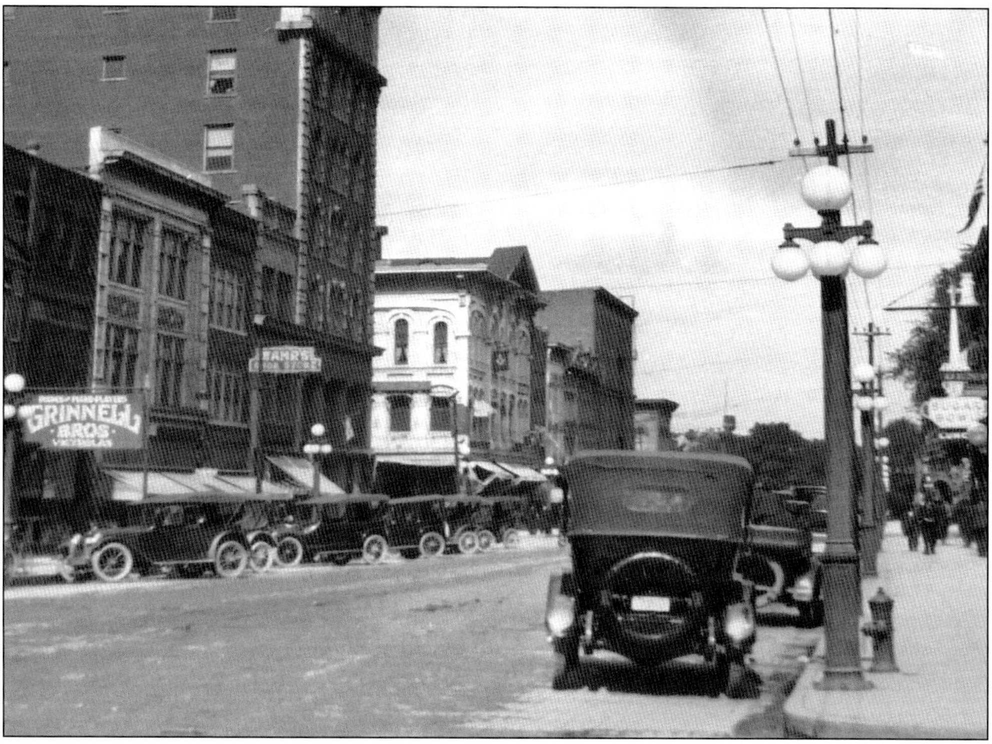

This view of Main Street shows businesses, including the Sugar Bowl, Grinnell Brothers, and Wahr's Book Store, which are discussed elsewhere in this book. Note the picturesque streetlamps in the foreground. Today, Ann Arbor uses LED streetlights in an effort to reduce energy usage and costs.

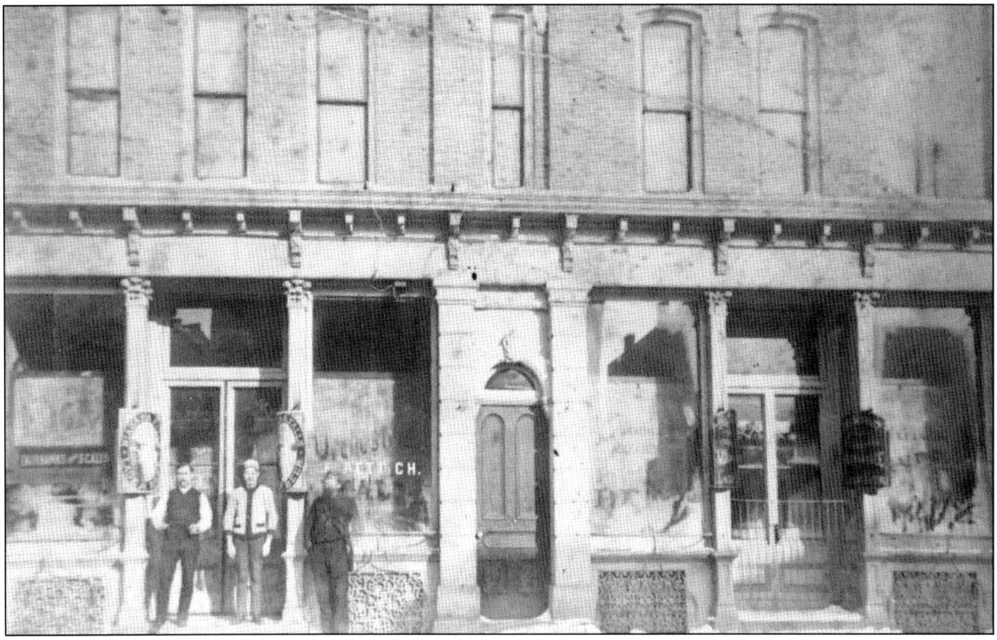

This undated image of Fred Rettich's orchestra hall on Main Street features ads for Niagara Falls and Milwaukee lager beer. The large German population of Ann Arbor formed many German clubs, some of which met at this location on Main Street. On February 10, 1893, the *Argus* reported the death of Fred Rettich at the age of 36.

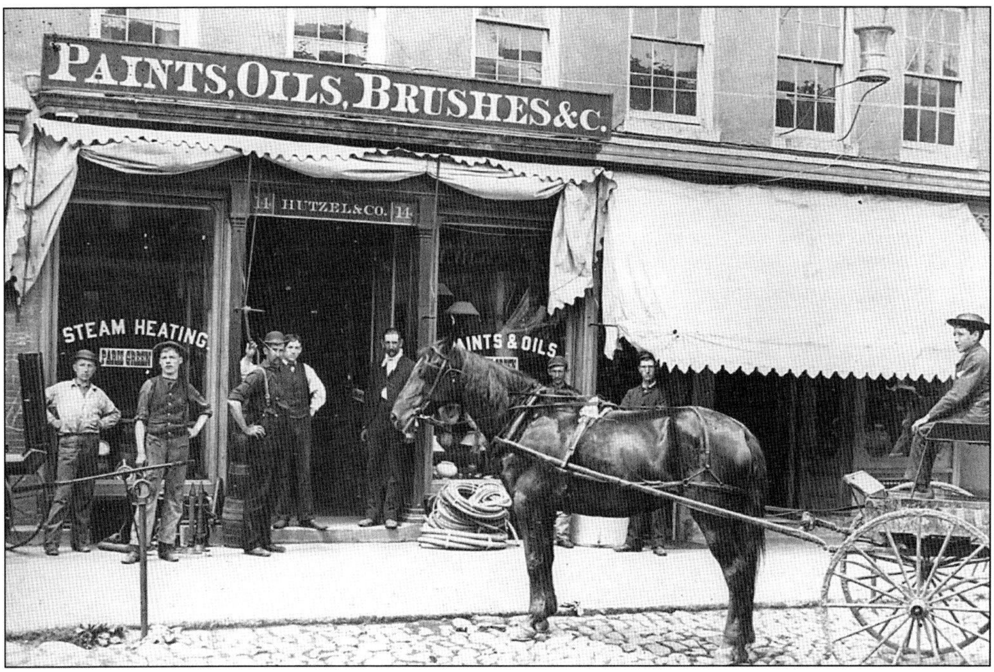

August F. Hutzel began his business, Hutzel & Co., in 1857 as a three-man operation. The store featured a variety of items for sale, including groceries, paints, oils, and glass, and it quickly became a gathering place for businessmen and farmers. Hutzel's original storefront was on Main Street, but he later moved its headquarters to 119 East Washington Street.

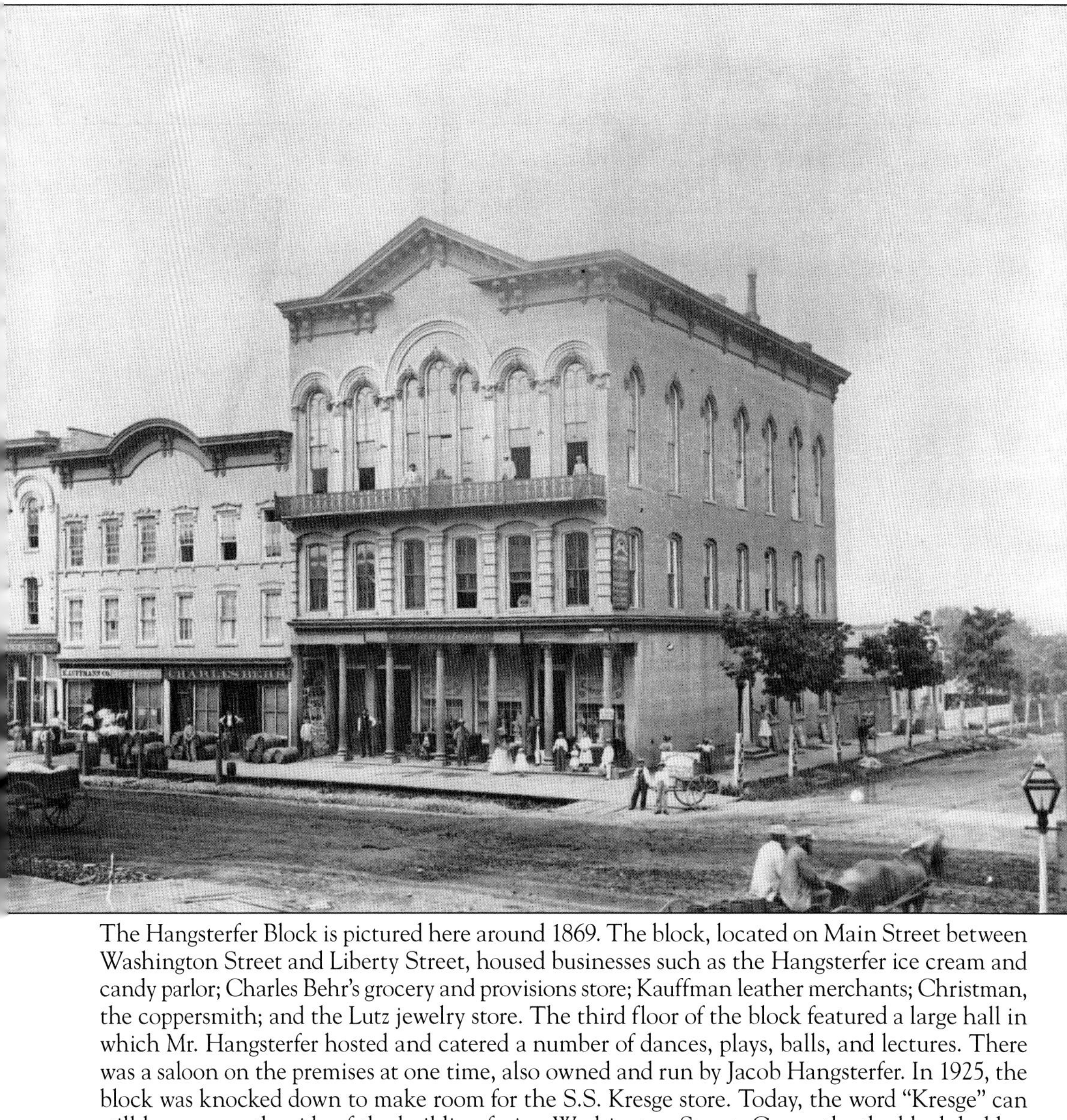

The Hangsterfer Block is pictured here around 1869. The block, located on Main Street between Washington Street and Liberty Street, housed businesses such as the Hangsterfer ice cream and candy parlor; Charles Behr's grocery and provisions store; Kauffman leather merchants; Christman, the coppersmith; and the Lutz jewelry store. The third floor of the block featured a large hall in which Mr. Hangsterfer hosted and catered a number of dances, plays, balls, and lectures. There was a saloon on the premises at one time, also owned and run by Jacob Hangsterfer. In 1925, the block was knocked down to make room for the S.S. Kresge store. Today, the word "Kresge" can still be seen on the side of the building facing Washington Street. Currently, the block holds a number of businesses and restaurants, such as B.D.'s Mongolian Barbecue, Café Felix, a Verizon Wireless store, and the Peaceable Kingdom.

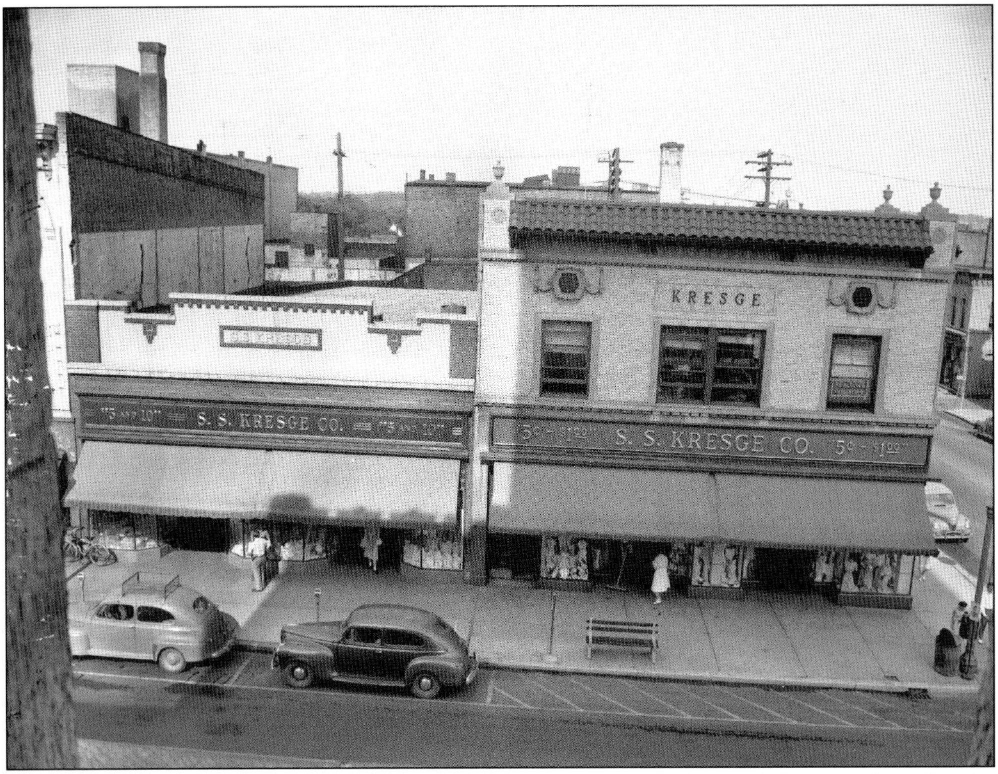

When Kresge's store took over the Hangsterfer space, it not only changed the name but also the type of business. Kresge was a chain of five-and-dime stores that offered mass-produced goods at lower prices than its predecessor. At one time, the S.S. Kresge Company owned four five-and-dime stores in Ann Arbor.

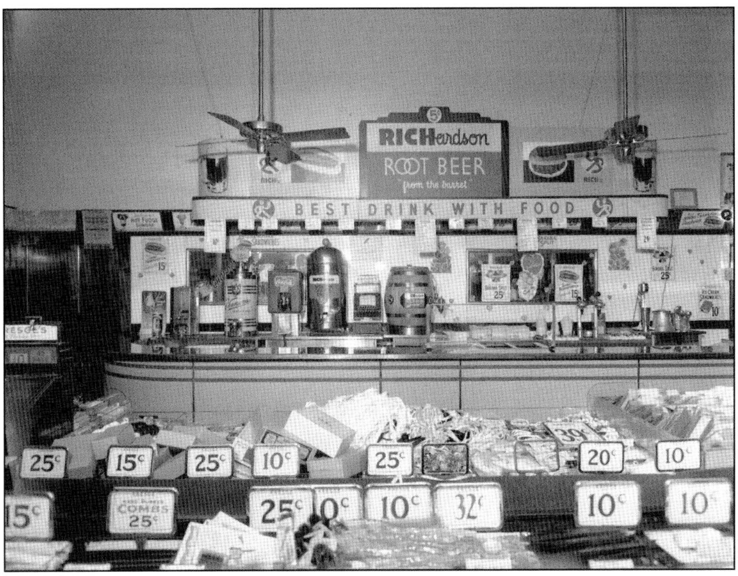

Kresge's soda fountain is shown here. The first Kresge store, owned by Sebastian S. Kresge, opened in Detroit in 1899. By 1912, he owned a chain of 85 five-and-dime stores. In the 1930s and 1940s, the business expanded to become variety stores that offered a wider choice of goods. By 1966, the year Sebastian S. Kresge passed away, there were over 900 stores in the chain.

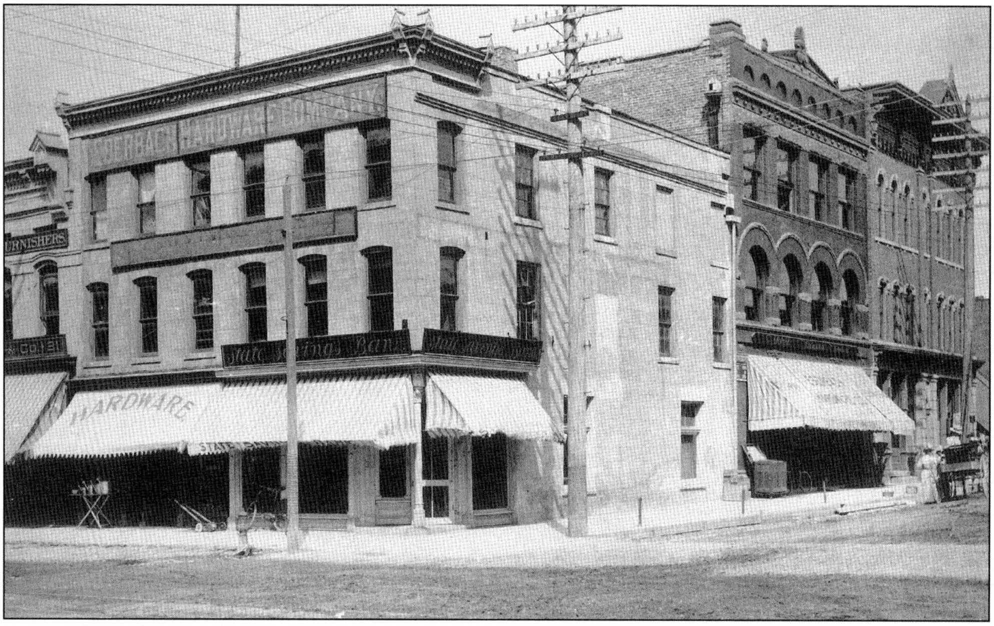

Located on the northeast corner of Main and Washington Streets, Eberbach Hardware was acquired by Christian Eberbach in 1875 and run by Ernest and Edward Eberbach. The December 15, 1893, issue of the *Ann Arbor Argus* described Eberbach's "special business" of heating buildings with hot air and called Eberbach's tin department the "best equipped" in the state, served by artisan Ernest Dieterle.

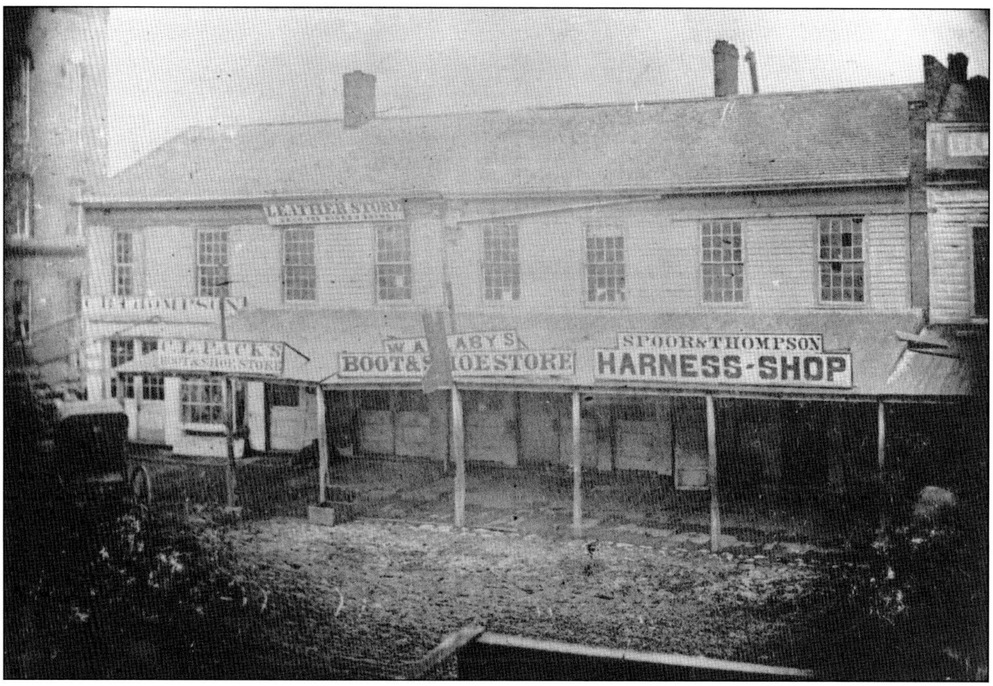

The American Block, built in 1836 and located on Main Street at Washington Street, is shown here in the 1860s. These primitive structures were replaced by Philip Bach's building in 1867. Later, this was the site of the B.E. Muehlig Company and Goodyear's.

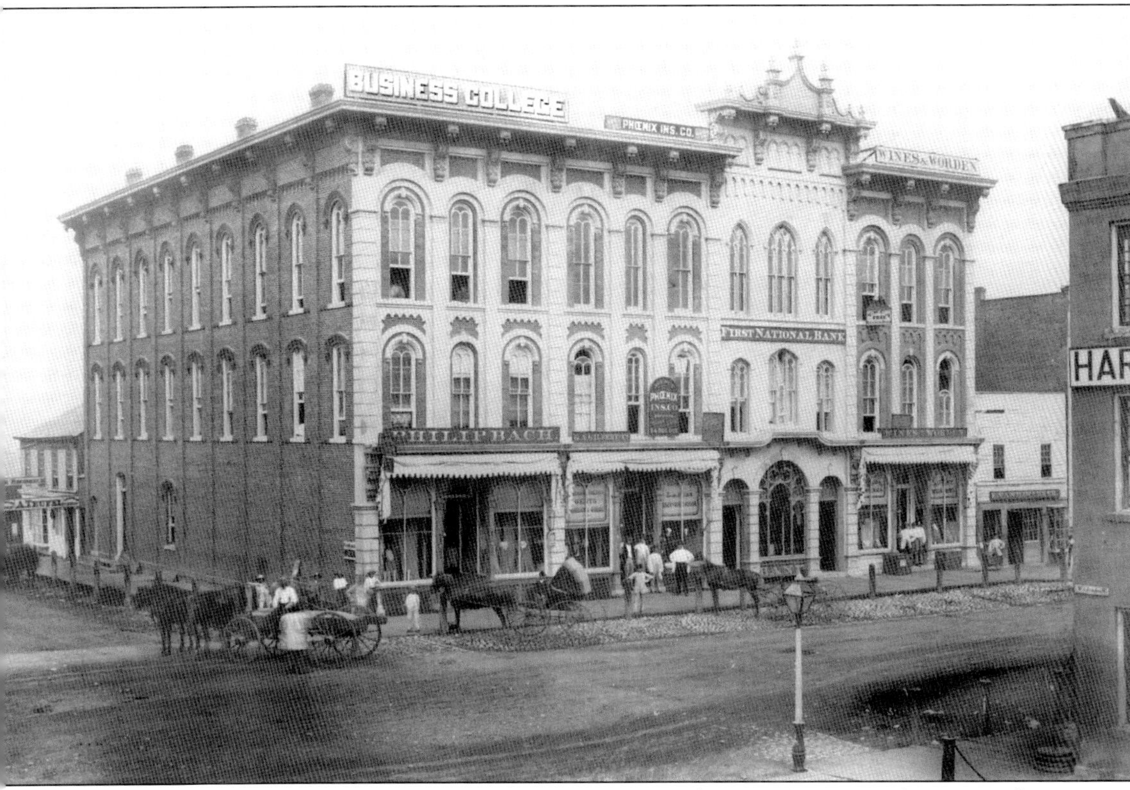

The block of buildings at 120–124 South Main Street at Washington Street was known as the Bank Block. It held the First National Bank and the Phoenix Insurance Company. In those days, fire was a very real danger and constant threat to both businesses and homes. In the late 1800s, over 19 local insurance companies existed to address this threat. Also note the Ann Arbor Business College and Telegraph Institute located over Bach's dry goods store. The college was opened in the wake of the local economic surge following the Civil War. It offered courses in "Bookkeeping, Railroading, Steamboating, Banking, Jobbing and Importing, Commercial Law, Business Penmanship, and Telegraphing." Courses for women were priced $5 less than courses for men. Judge Thomas Cooley, for whom the Cooley Law School is named, administered the law department.

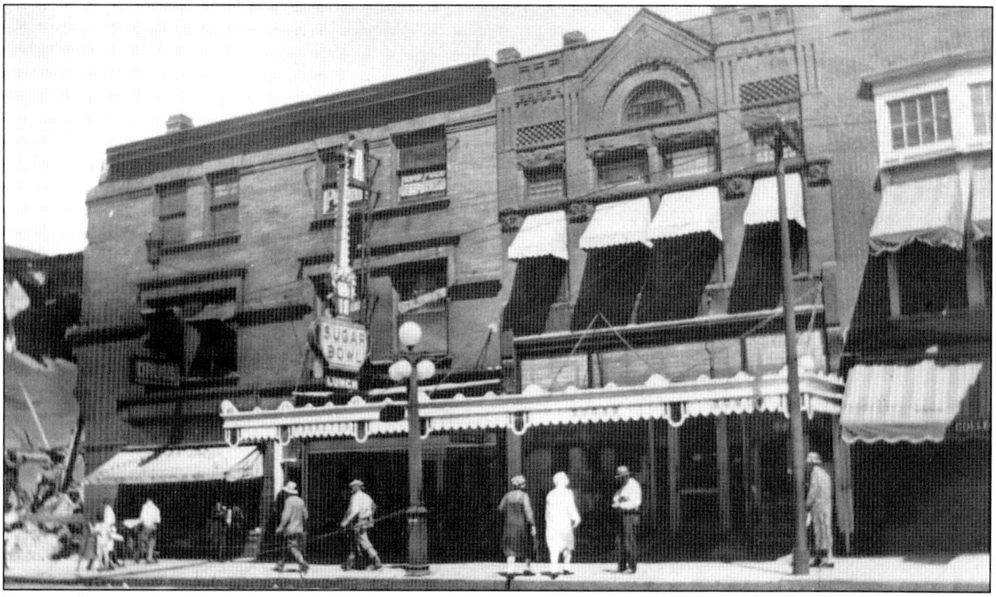

Located at 109 South Main Street, the Preketes family's Sugar Bowl restaurant served hungry patrons from 1911 until 1967. Originally from Greece, Paul Preketes came to the United States in 1903 and to Ann Arbor a year later. Paul and his brother Charles first opened a candy store at the 109–111 South Main Street location in 1911. Brothers Frank and Tony later joined the business as teenagers. During the 1930s, a University of Michigan student by the name of Gerald Ford worked part-time at the restaurant.

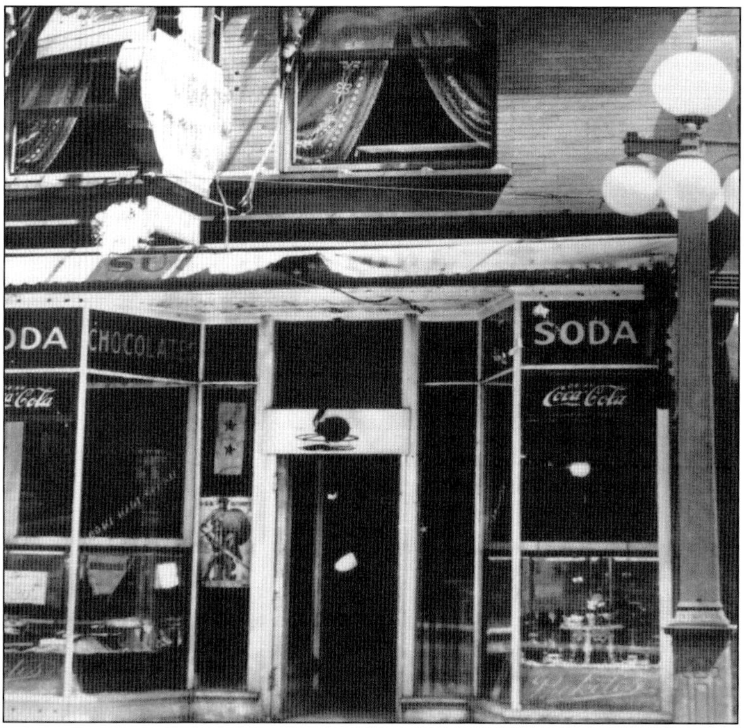

Here is another view of the Sugar Bowl. It was one of the first restaurants on Main Street to have an electric sign. After its time specializing in candy and ice cream, the shop became a restaurant and cocktail lounge. Charles Preketes passed away in 1965, and Paul Preketes passed away in 1975 at the age of 85. Currently, part of a PNC bank branch occupies the space at 109 South Main Street.

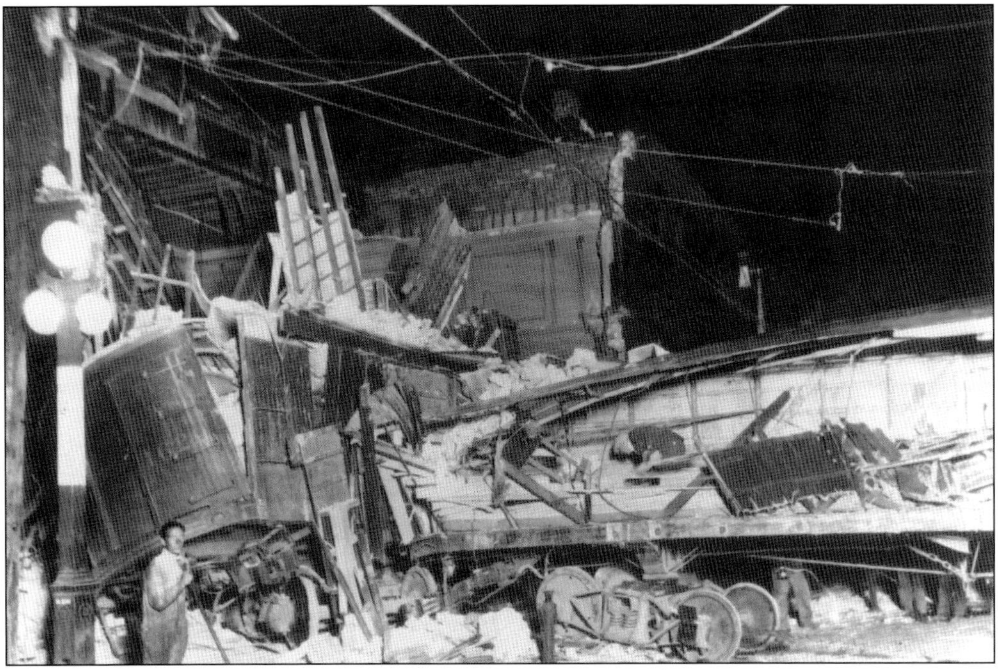

Pictured here is the interurban wreck at the corner of Huron and Main Streets on August 5, 1927. The Farmers & Mechanics Bank was destroyed when four train cars left the track at a turn on Main Street. The conductor, Fern Garn, survived when he jumped out of the train car he was in. The incident began near the county fairgrounds, which were located where Veterans Park on Jackson Street is now. Somehow, four fully loaded interurban freight cars broke loose and began to roll into town. The cars rolled down Jackson Street, to Huron Street, and under the Ann Arbor Railroad bridge. They slowed on the Huron Street hill as they approached First Street and Ashley Street. When the cars hit a 90-degree turn onto Main Street, they departed the tracks and crashed into the lobby of the Farmers & Mechanics Bank. Upon impact, bricks flew, walls shook, and diners at nearby restaurants were thrown from their seats. As people ran into the street, they were greeted with a shower of dust and brick from the tremendous collision. Thankfully, no one was injured. Later, a director of the bank said, "This is the largest deposit in the history of the Farmers & Mechanics Bank . . . I hope we shall never have another like it."

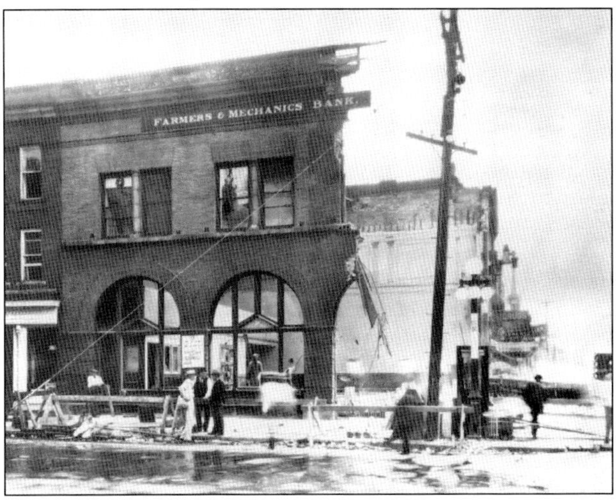

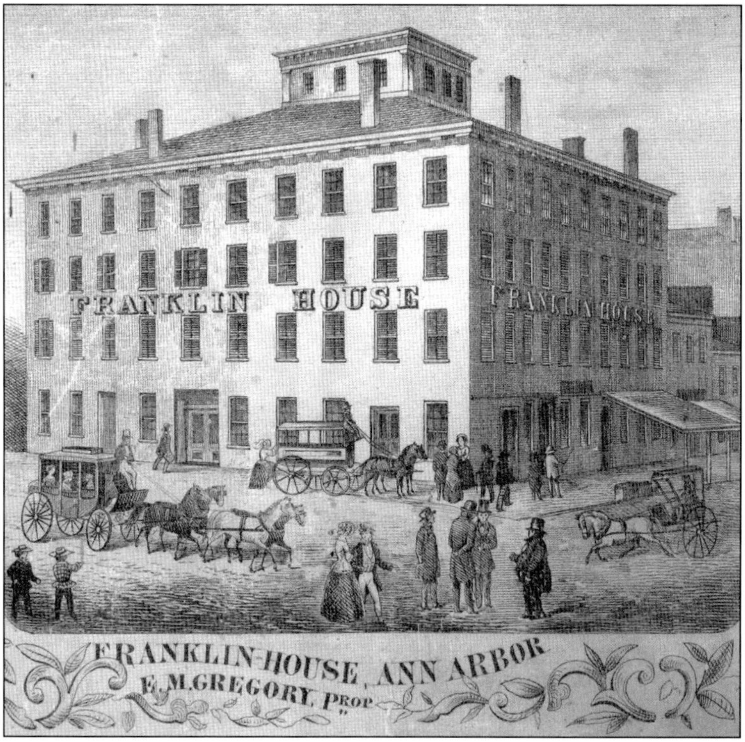

This 1856 drawing shows the Franklin House at the northwest corner of Main and Huron Streets. The corner blockhouse had earlier hosted a general store, an inn, and a tavern that at some point was painted bright red. Perhaps not surprisingly, it was then given the name "Bloody Corners."

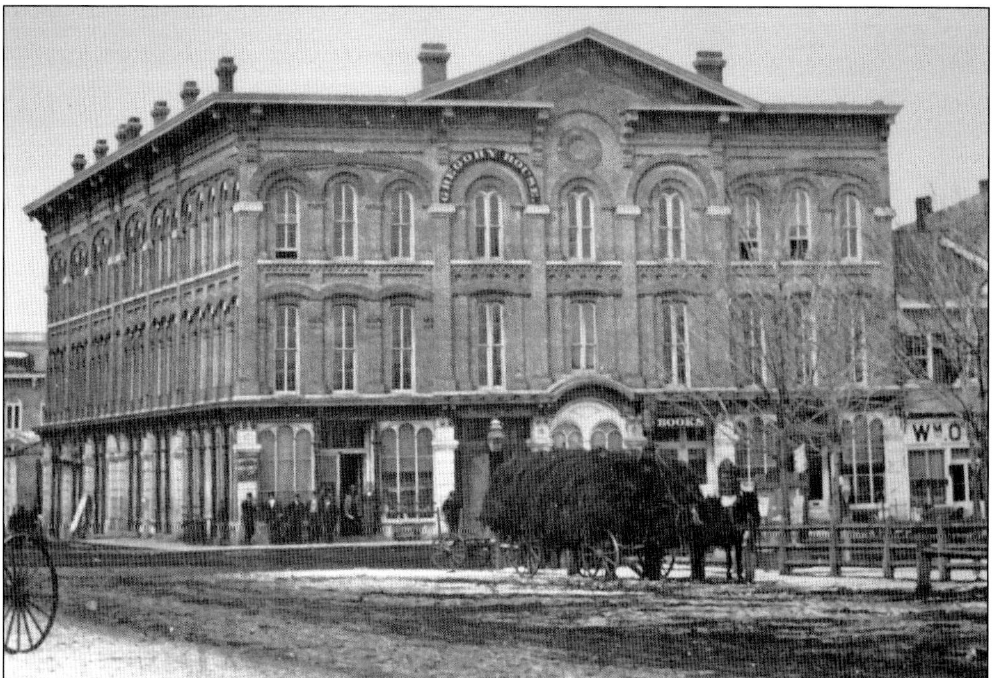

Built in 1862, the Gregory House was located at the northwest corner of Main and Huron Streets. It took the place of the Franklin House, which was the city's first large hotel. In 1885, the building was renovated as the Masonic hall, and later it became known as the Savings Bank Building.

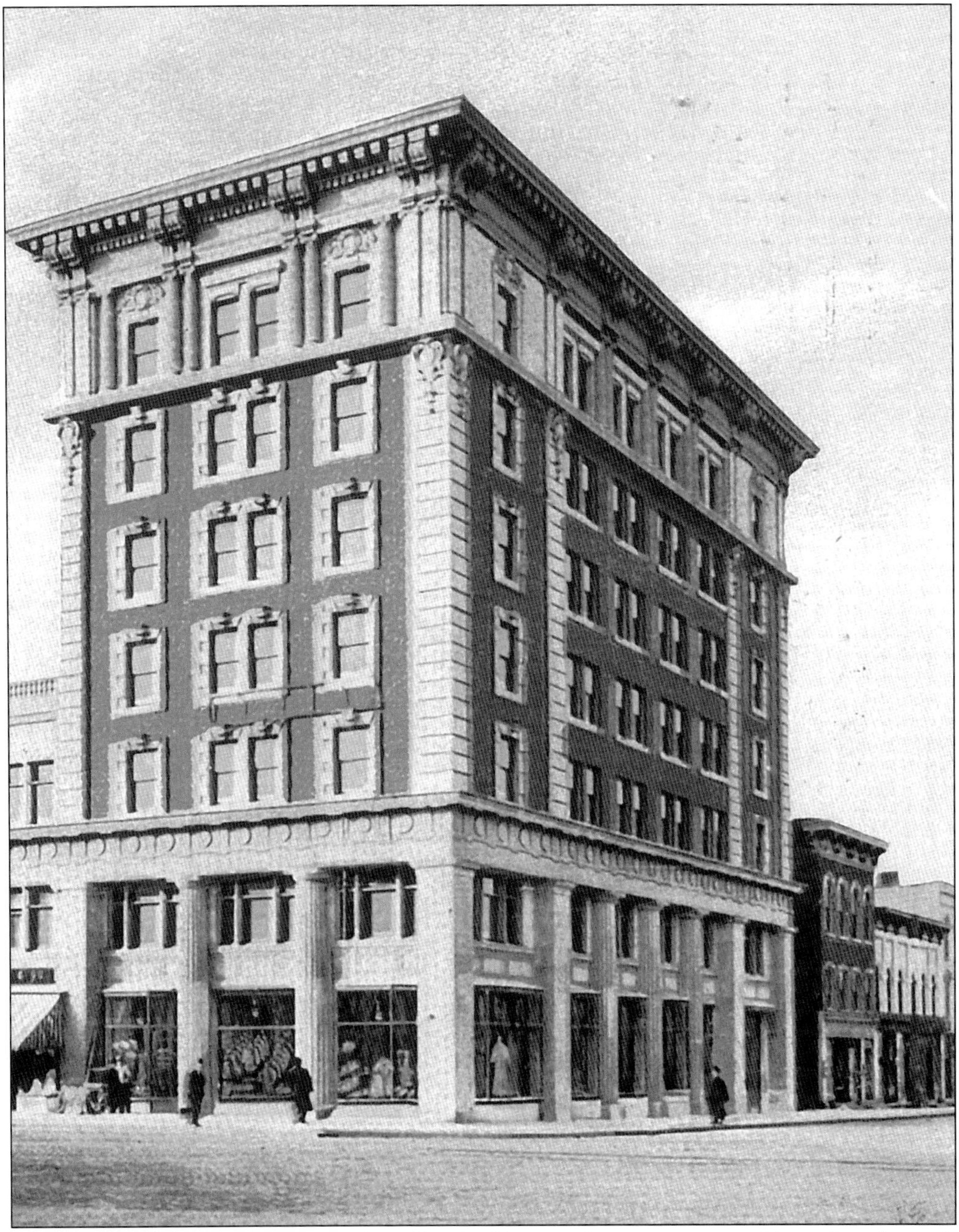

The Glazier Building, at one time the tallest building in the city, is pictured here. It still stands proudly on Main Street at the corner of Huron Street. The building was constructed by Frank P. Glazier, who was state treasurer, a banker, owner of newspapers, and manufacturer of Chelsea stoves. Glazier never got to occupy the building, as he was forced to resign his post as state treasurer after filing for personal bankruptcy and being convicted of embezzlement. It was said that his goal was to be the governor of Michigan, but his conviction, prison sentence, and subsequent loss of a financial empire ended that dream.

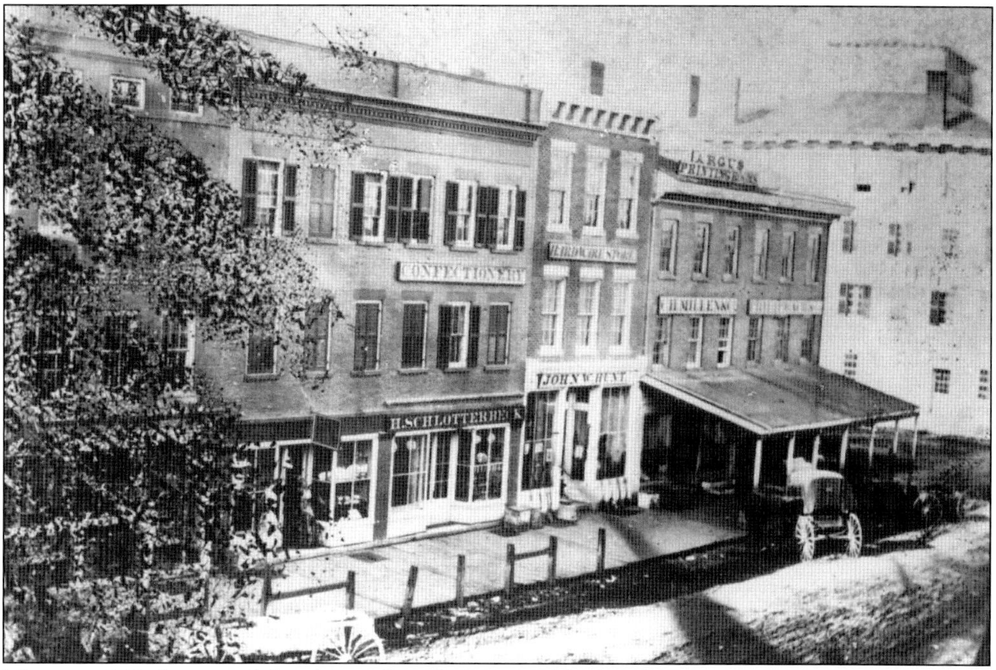

This pre-1860 photograph has been identified as possibly the oldest of Ann Arbor. It is an image of the west side of Main Street, just south of Huron Street. The Glazier Building would now be at the corner on the far left. Next door is Herman Schlotterbeck's confectionery and bakery, and farther right is John Hunt's store, which specialized in hardware, nails, and iron. Vinology restaurant and the Crazy Wisdom bookstore occupy these spaces now.

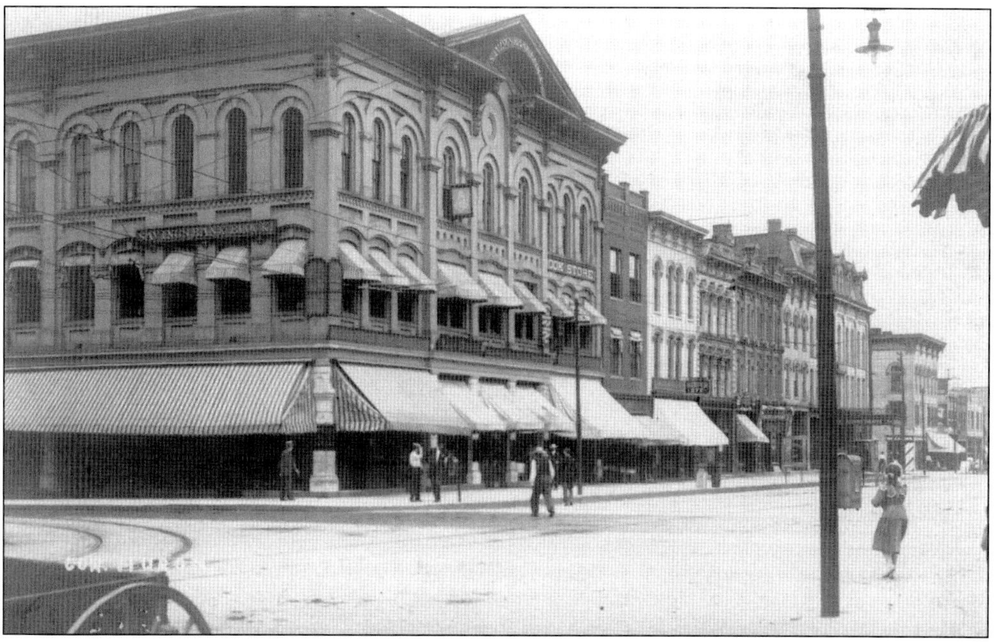

This is a later view of Main and Huron Streets. The Savings Bank Building is visible in the northwest corner. This same corner once housed the Gregory House, the Franklin House, and the Masonic Block. From the looks of the photograph, it was a windy day in Ann Arbor.

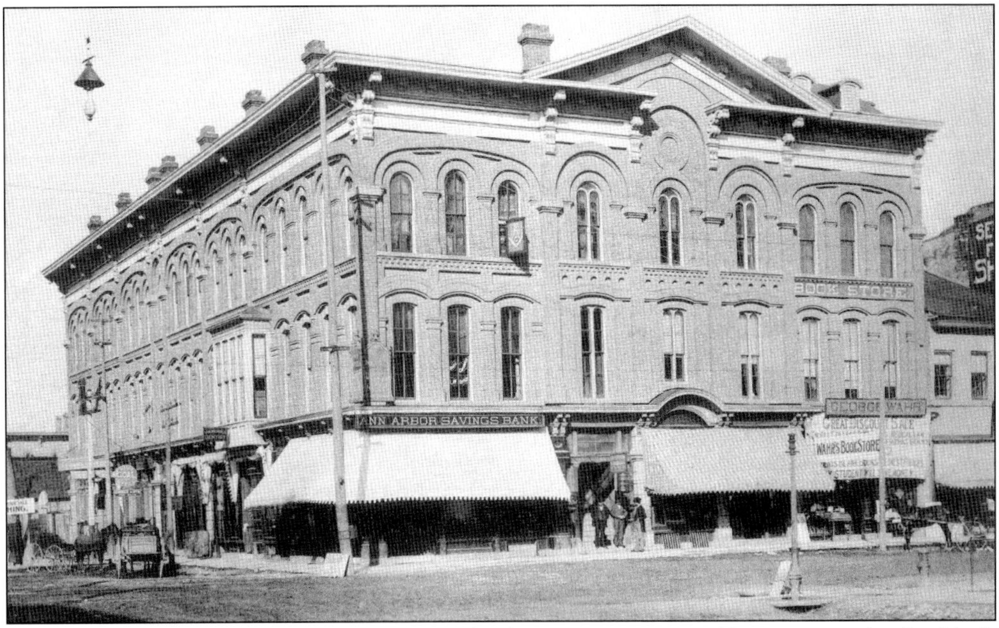

The Masonic Block was on Main Street north of East Huron Street. Not surprisingly, this block took its name when the upper floors were remodeled as Masonic rooms in 1885. Masons have a long history in the city; their first meeting was reportedly in 1824 at Allen's Tavern (the log blockhouse built by founder John Allen). In 1885, the group leased the third floor of the St. James Building at the northwest corner of Main and Huron Streets. Eventually, five more Masonic organizations joined them, and the block was then referred to as the "Masonic Block."

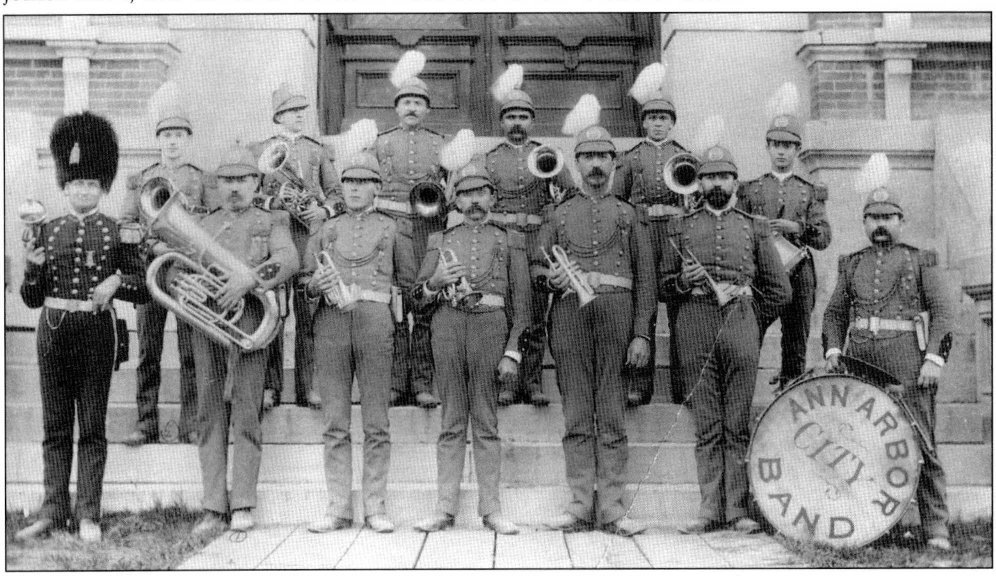

Otto's Ann Arbor City Band marched on Main Street many times and is said to have given the city "its sound track for half a century." Henry Otto Sr. started the band in 1875, and his son Louis assumed command 20 years later. The band performed in parades and dances and also sent soldiers marching off to both the Spanish-American War and World War I. They joined the musicians' union after Louis took over and hold the distinction of being the first band to play "The Victors," the fight song of the University of Michigan.

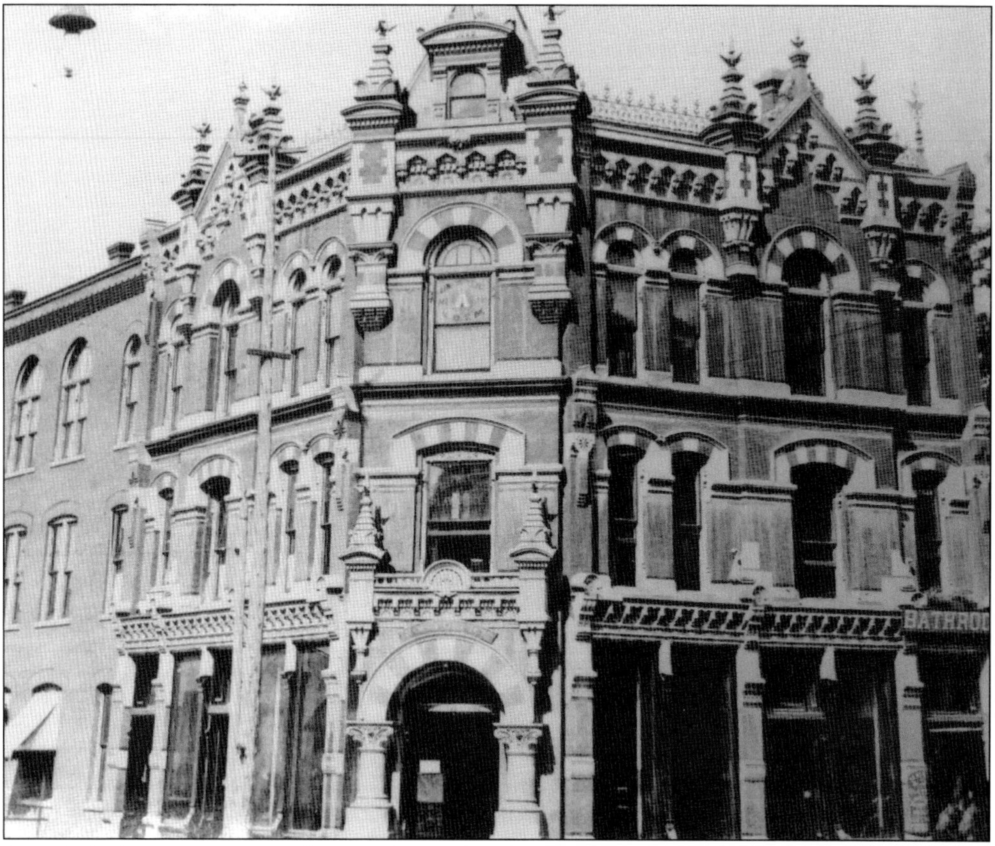

Ann Arbor's majestic post office was located at the northeast corner of Main and Ann Streets (now home of Washtenaw County Clerk/Register of Deeds) and was on the site that is believed to be the original location of John Allen's vegetable garden. Built in 1882, it also became a social hub, as mail had to be picked up in person. Four years later, home delivery began, and the post office was no longer a social meeting place. It was eventually replaced by the new post office at another location, seen below. This site is now the home of the Washtenaw County Administration Building. The old structure was demolished in 1940, and all that remains are photographs such as these, taken in the 1890s.

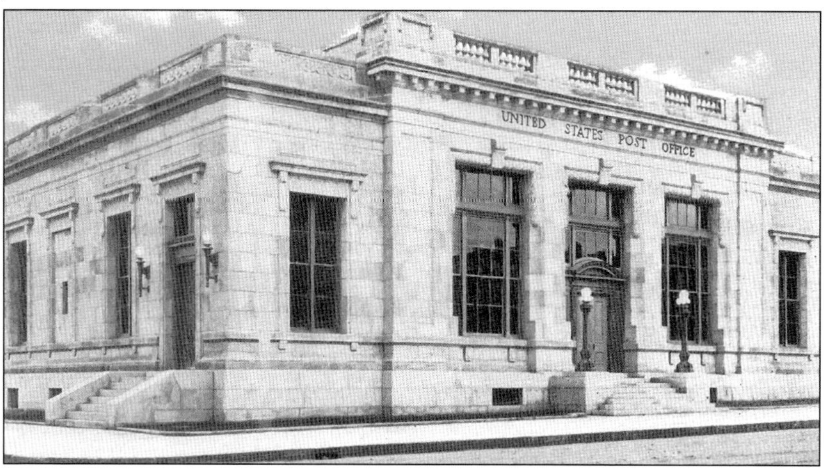

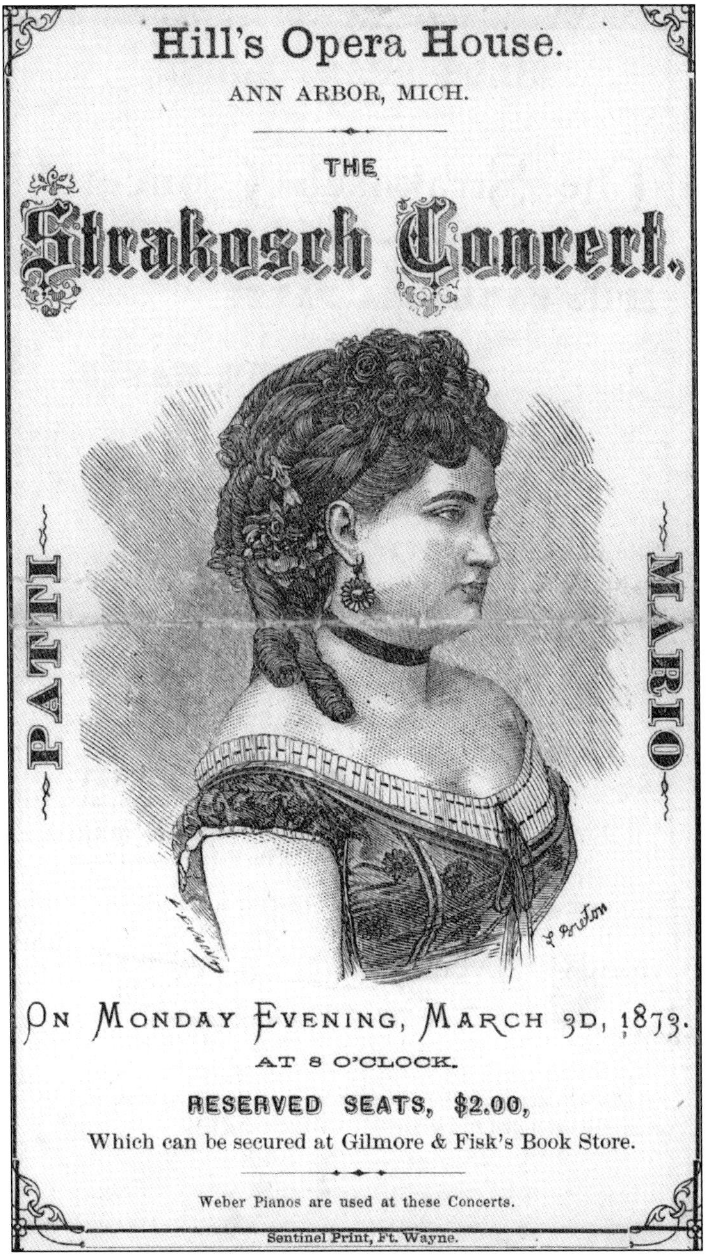

Hill's Opera House was on the southwest corner of Main and Ann Streets. Its location across the street from the courthouse square was extremely helpful for business. The Civil War drama *The Spy of Shiloh* was the opening-night play, and it continued for five nights of sold-out performances. There had been some concern that Ann Arbor was not a large enough town for the theater, but those worries were eased by the play's success. Prior to the opera house, the building on that corner housed a food and clothing store, along with a hotel. When that site burned down, owner George D. Hill replaced what had been lost and added a theater upstairs. Eventually, the theater experienced financial difficulties and was sold to a man from New York, who turned out to be the first of several absentee landlords. When the opera house became too expensive to repair, it was closed and condemned as a firetrap.

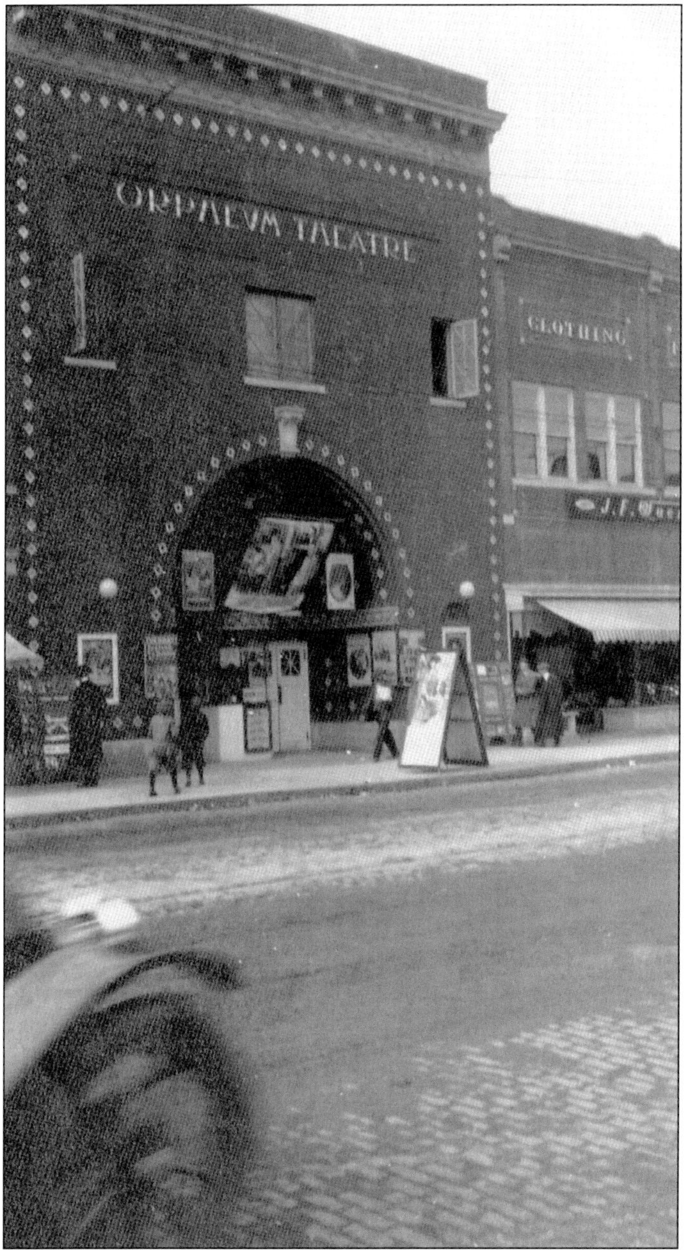

Fred J. Wuerth constructed the Orpheum, the first theater in town to show movies. Located at 326 South Main Street, the Orpheum opened in 1913. Prior to this, Ann Arbor residents could see one-reel films at nickelodeons like the Star Theater. The Star was located nearby at 118 East Washington Street and featured vaudeville acts in addition to the nickelodeons. It is perhaps best remembered as the theater at which over a thousand university students rioted in 1908. The manager of the theater asked a football player to throw the upcoming game so he and an accomplice could bet against the game and share their bounty. The player refused, and students got wind of the incident and then marched to the Star to demand that the manager "talk." When he refused to do so, the students threw bricks at the building, broke in, and destroyed the interior. The riot resulted in the complete destruction of the Star Theater. (Courtesy of Susan Cee Weinburg.)

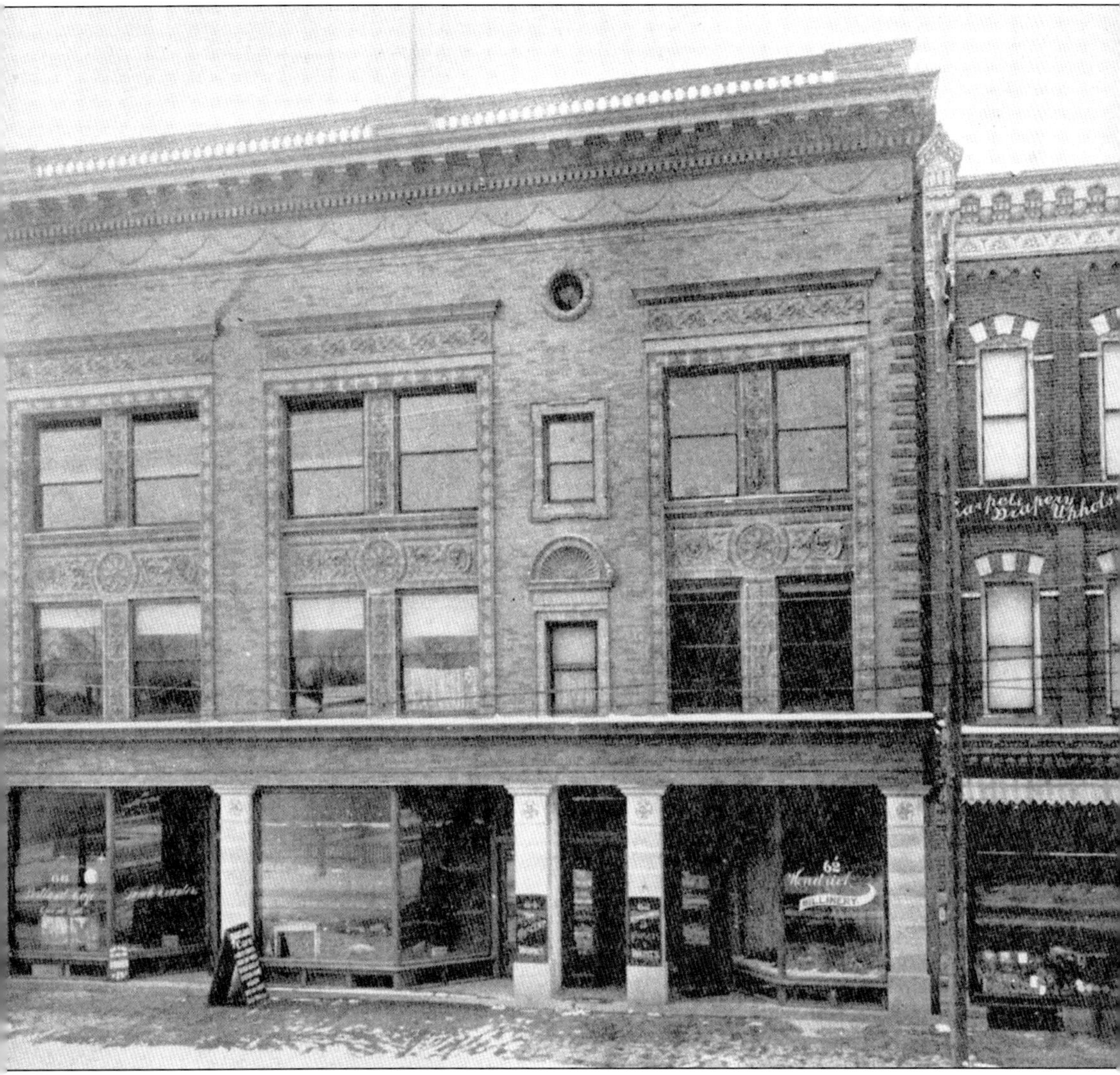

Ann Arbor has long been a town that enjoys its entertainment. The Theatorium nickelodeon opened in 1906 on Liberty Street and was quickly followed by the Casino on Main Street (now home of the Real Seafood Company). Other nickelodeons followed, including the People's Popular Family Theater, which was later called the Vaudette. There were also vaudeville houses, such as the Bijou on Liberty Street and the Star on Washington Street. This photograph shows the site of Fred J. Wuerth's theater that opened in 1918. The Wuerth's marquee welcomed guests to walk through a skylit arcade on their way into the theater. In 1929, it was the first theater in town to convert to "talkie films." Smaller than the Orpheum, the Wuerth specialized in children's matinees. In addition to owning the theaters, Wuerth also owned a self-named menswear store. One can see images of some of these long-departed theaters in the screening room of the Michigan Theater. (Courtesy of Susan Cee Weinburg.)

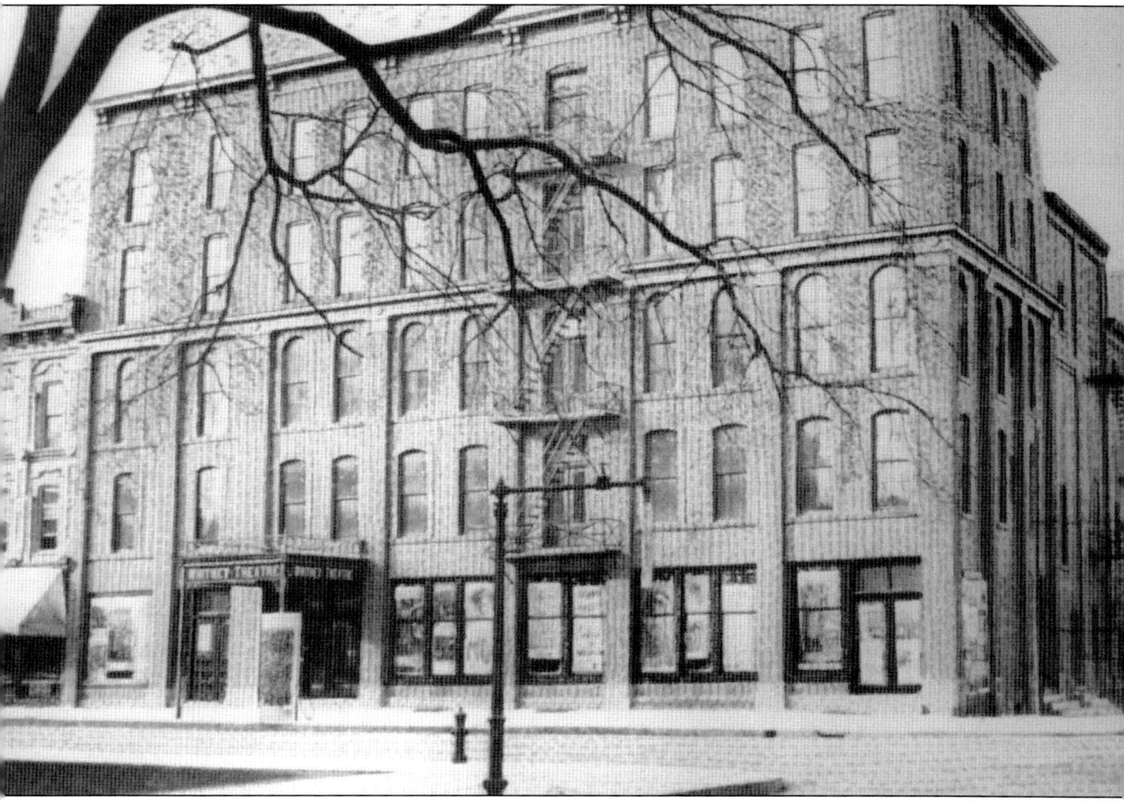

Townies often talk about former theaters that were turned into parking lots; this is just one example. The Whitney was located at the corner of Main and Ann Streets from 1908 to 1955. Previously, the space housed George D. Hill's opera house. B.C. Whitney purchased the space in 1908 and added two stories to the building. It could seat over 1,500 people in its auditorium and was for a time the largest theater in Michigan. Two balconies were hung above the main floor, and a gallery was located at the top. There was a special window on the second balcony through which people could buy tickets—as long as they were willing to climb the fire escape to reach it! The play *Knight for Day* opened the theater and included a 14-piece orchestra from Chicago as the musical accompaniment.

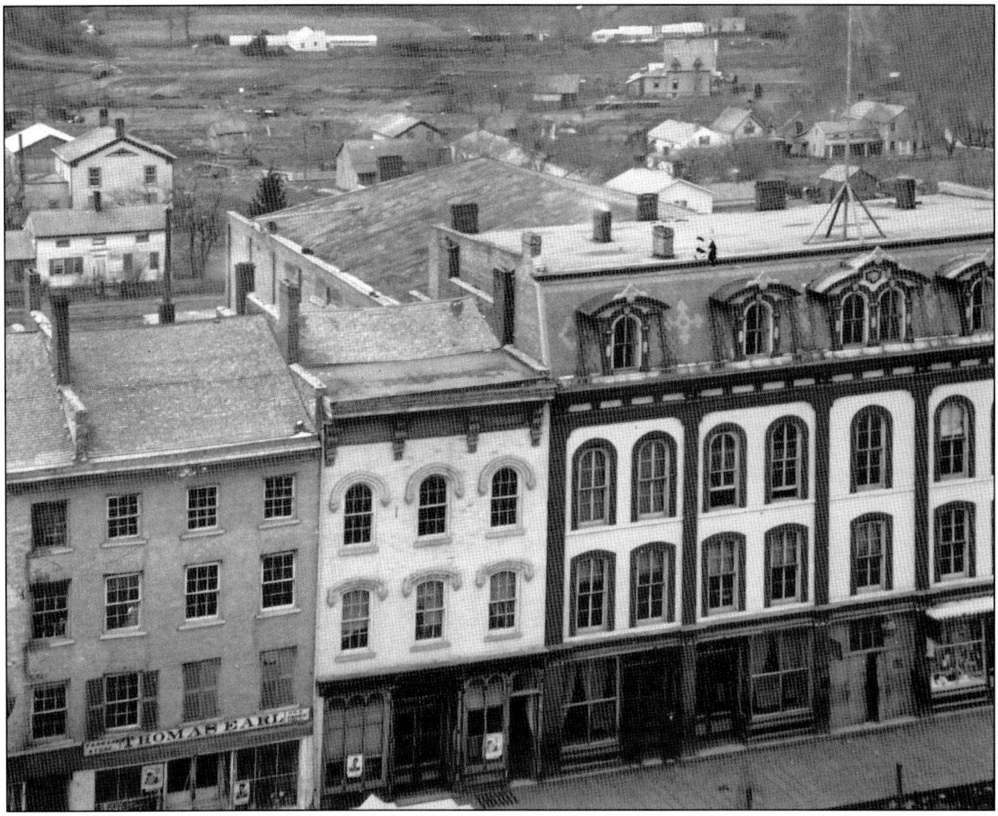

This aerial shot of Main Street was taken prior to 1882. Visible is a general store owned by Thomas Earl. Earl was an Irish immigrant who arrived in Ann Arbor in 1833. He purchased a home at 415 North Main Street with the original intent of doing business there; however, that location failed to meet his expectations. The Thomas Earl House remains standing on Main Street.

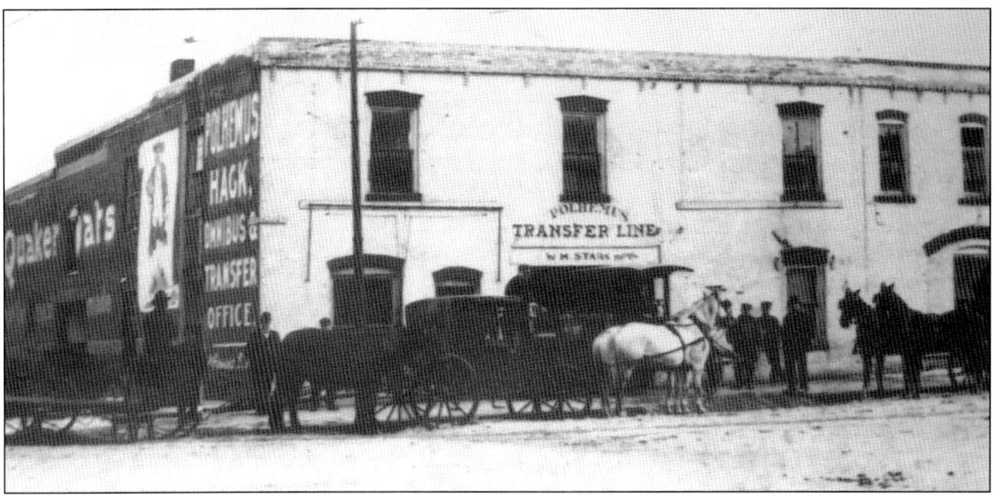

This photograph features the Polhemus Hack Omnibus and Transfer office, located at the southeast corner of Main and Catherine Streets. This livery billed itself as the "best and most extensive in the city" and the "only line which runs to night trains." The Washtenaw County Administration Building, formerly a post office building, now occupies this spot.

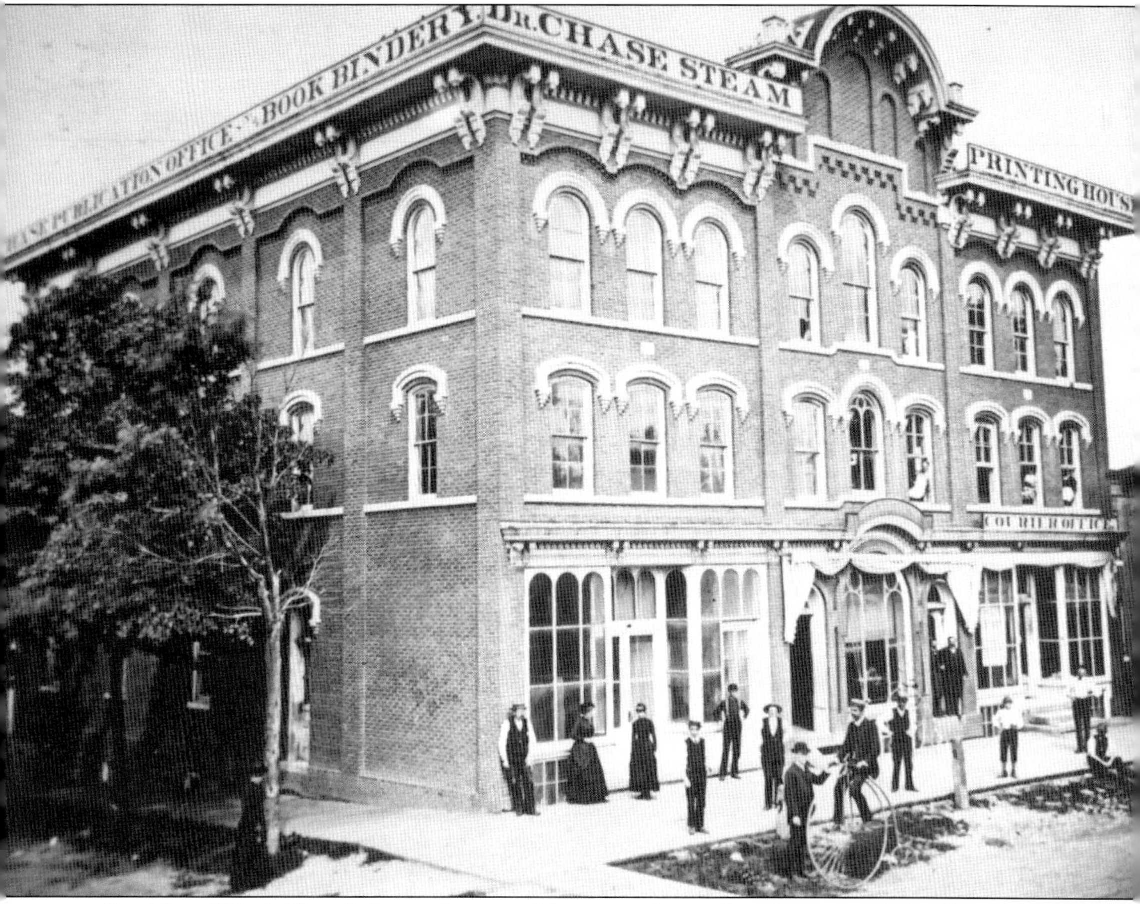

Dr. Alvin Wood Chase's Steam Printing House was located at the corner of Miller and Main Streets. According to an 1869 publication, this was the "finest printing office in the West," with a pressroom, counting room, job room, and bindery. Each of these rooms was 39 feet by 68 feet "in the clear, without a partition in any of them." Dr. Chase took great pains to prevent against fire. These measures included placing 100 feet of fire hose near the steam pump, as well as an additional 25 feet of fire hose in each of the other rooms. Dr. Chase was also the writer of books that were considered some of the most popular tomes of the 19th century, publishing dozens of editions in both English and German.

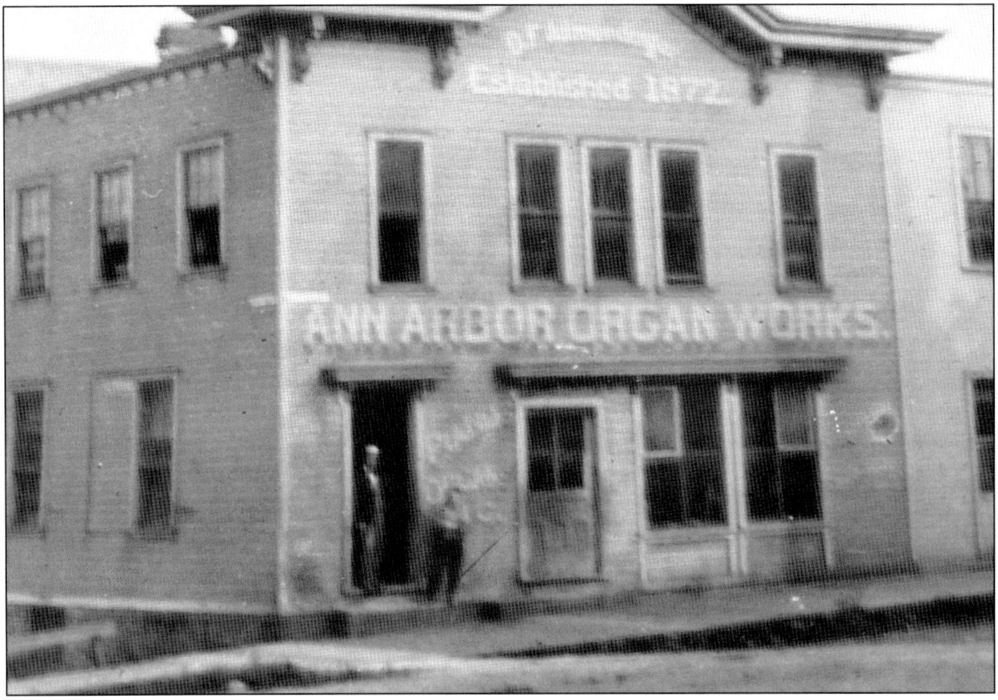

As noted earlier, David Allmendinger started making reed pump organs in the 1870s and had a successful business. The first factory was located at the northwest corner of First and Washington Streets, which was also the Allmendinger home.

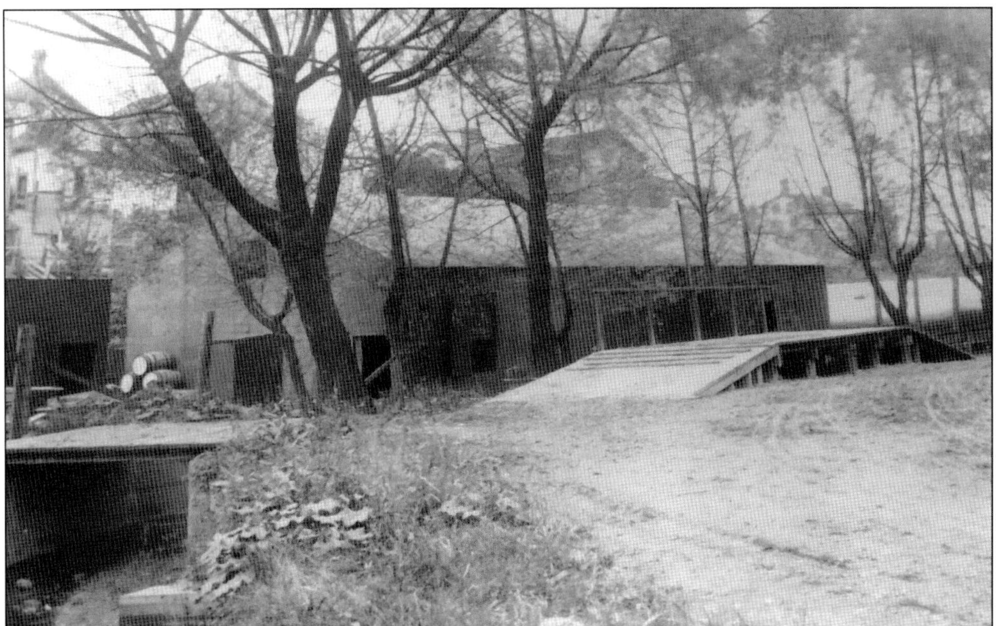

Buried since 1926, Allen Creek is visible in this c. 1900 photograph. Named after founder John Allen, the creek passed the site of the first dwelling in Annarbour village. This photograph was taken near the Ann Arbor Railroad tracks south of Liberty Street. Dean & Co.'s warehouse is on the right, facing First Street. The house at the upper left faces Ashley Street.

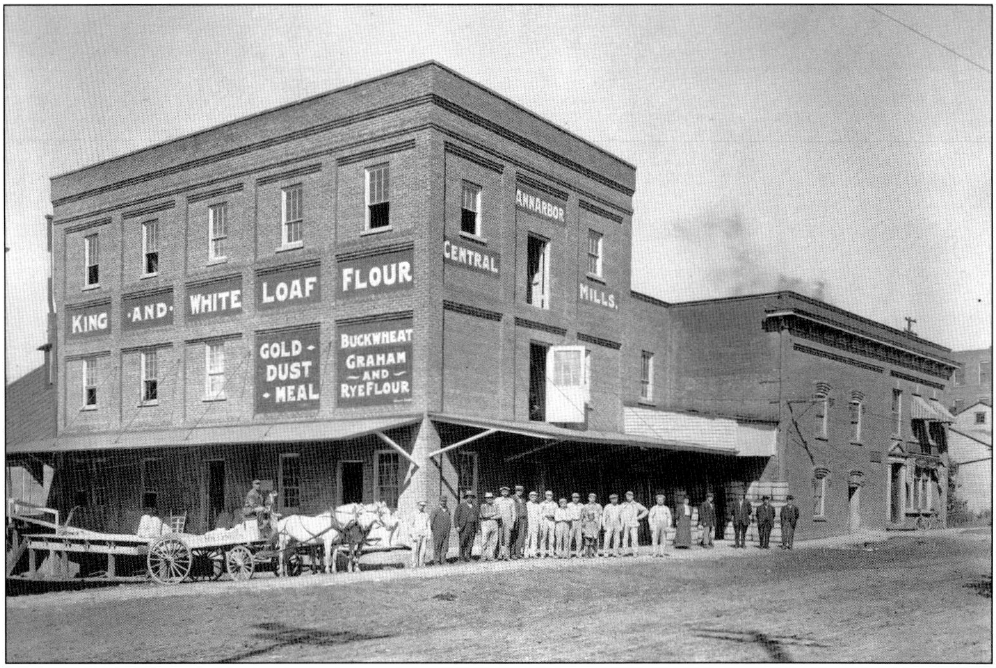

Ann Arbor Central Mills was at 206–222 South First Street between Liberty and Washington Streets. Located on Allen Creek, it was built specifically to be near the new Ann Arbor Railroad. The spot currently houses bars and nightclubs, but one can still see the old lettering on the building.

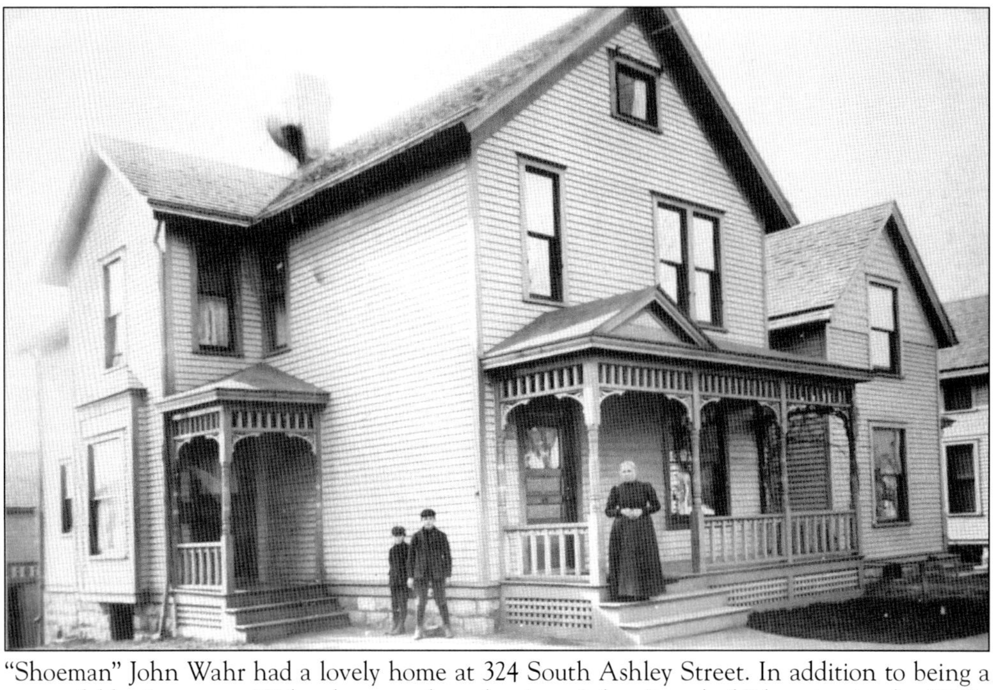

"Shoeman" John Wahr had a lovely home at 324 South Ashley Street. In addition to being a successful businessman, Wahr also served on the Ann Arbor Board of Education in the 1900s. Wahr passed away in 1916 and was buried in Forest Hill Cemetery.

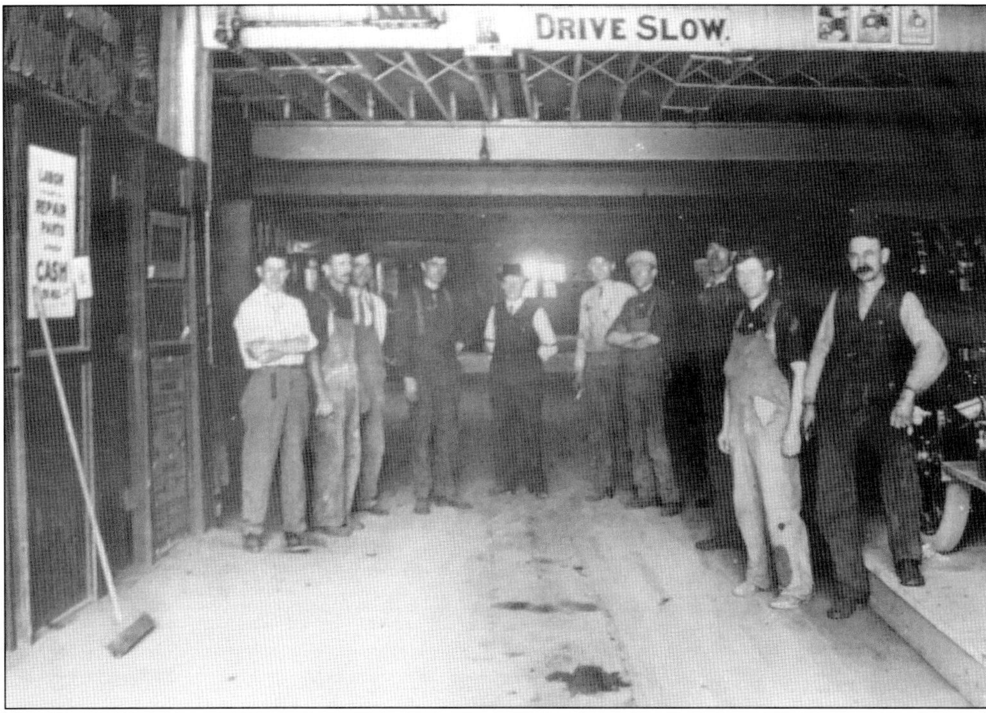

This image shows the interior of Andrew Hunter's Auto Tire Repair Company, located at 104 First Street at the corner of Huron Street. Hunter was also a dealer of Hudson-Essex automobiles. The Essex line, made by the Hudson Motor Car Company, is credited with beginning the trend away from open cars of the early years toward the enclosed passenger compartment.

A summertime photograph of Prochnow Grocery shows owner David Prochnow. Located at 208 South Ashley Street, this business sold everything from fresh produce to prepackaged items. Other members of the Prochnow family were busy in Ann Arbor as well. David's cousin Theodore operated Prochnow's Dairy Lunch on Huron Street, and another relative started the Ann Arbor Buick dealership.

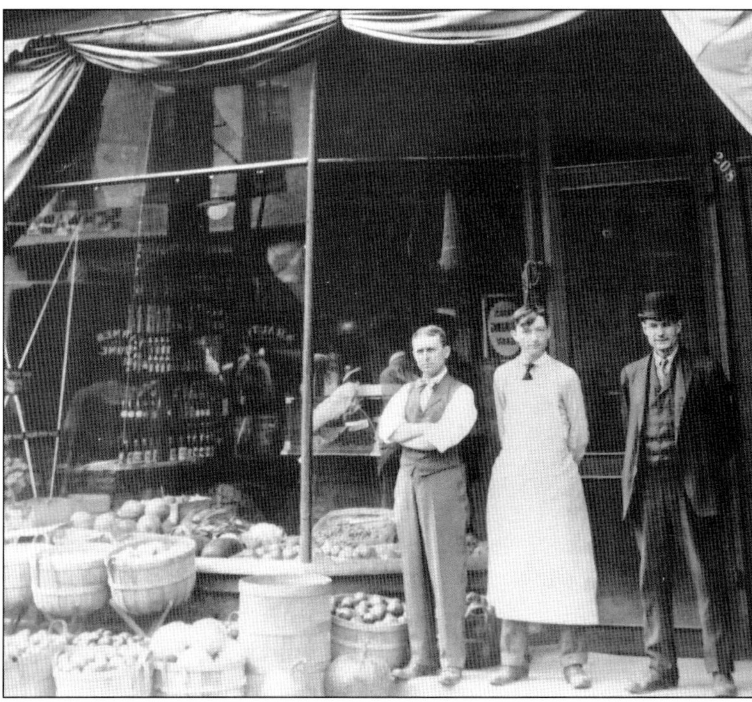

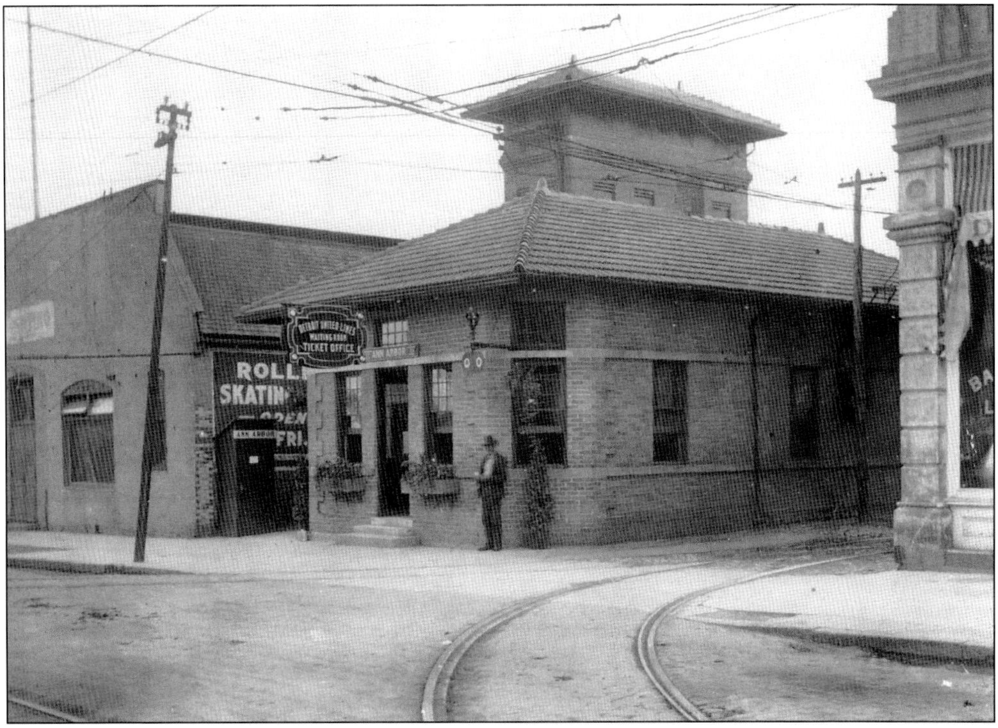

The ticket office of Detroit United Lines, facing Ashley Street, is shown here. Detroit United Railway operated more than 400 miles of interurban lines, including the Detroit-to-Jackson line. Next door to the ticket office was a roller-skating rink, which at one time was simply known as "the rink." Later, it became the local militia unit's meeting place until 1913.

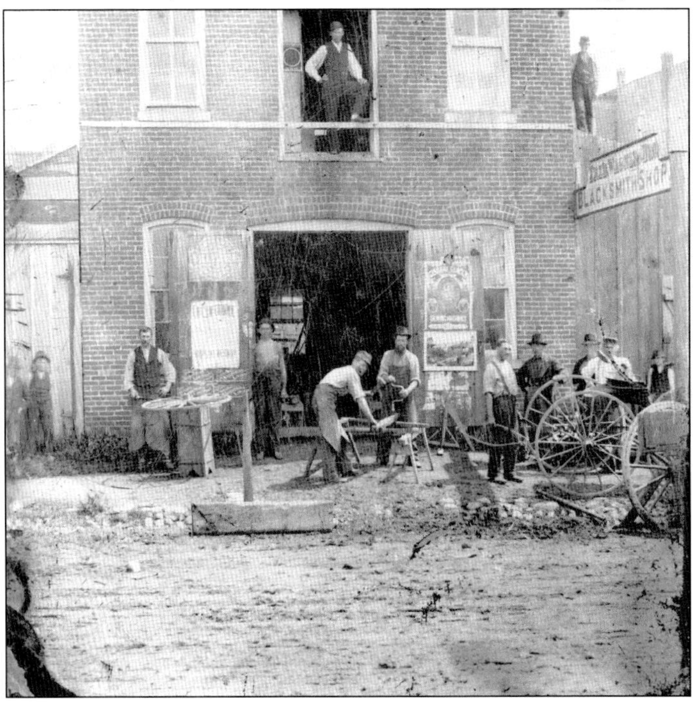

Before cars, horses and carriages ruled the streets of Ann Arbor. Like cars, they sometimes needed a bit of repair. One of the places where one could find help was Fred Wagner's blacksmith shop on Ashley Street. Wagner fixed wagons and carriages and also sold horseshoes.

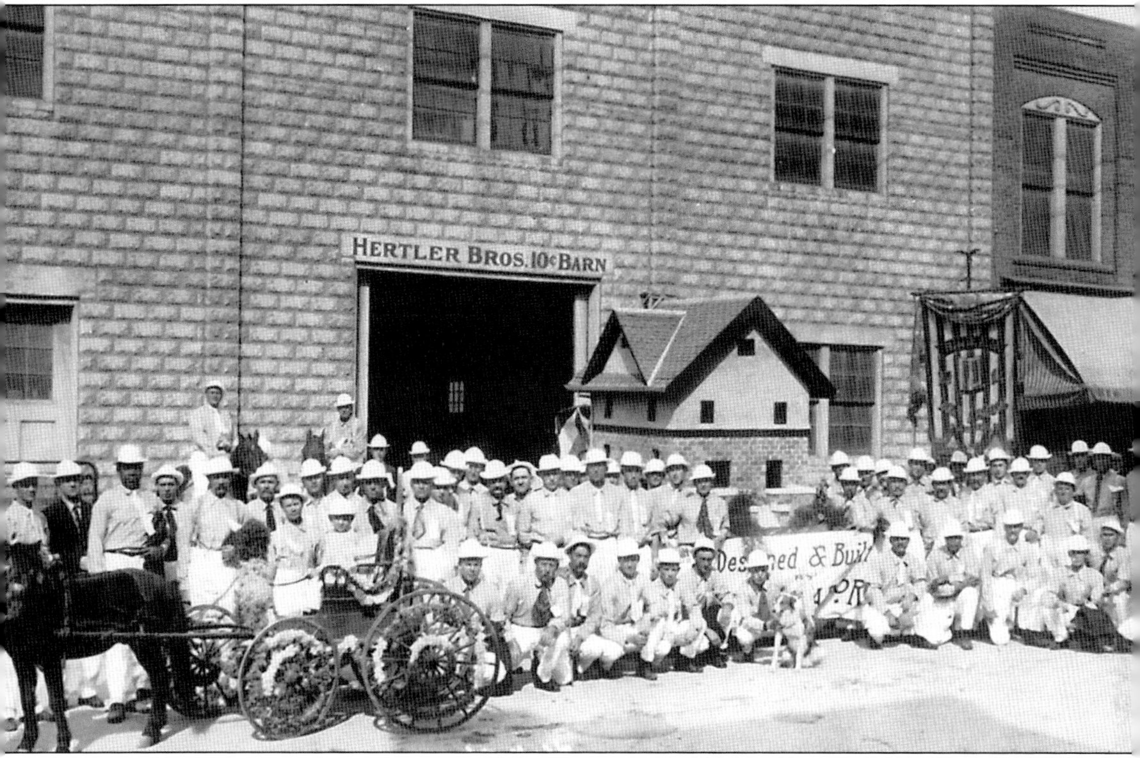

A 1916 Labor Day parade float is pictured in front of Hertler Bros. barn on Ashley Street. In addition to selling equipment, the Hertler family provided gardening and farming advice to interested customers. While inside or shopping around town, farmers could leave their horses at the business for only 10¢. Brothers Gotleib, Herman, and George, along with sister Emma, also hosted euchre games for friends and patrons. The building still stands and is the home of the very popular Downtown Home & Garden store. Its outdoor space also houses Mark's Carts and Bill's Beer Garden. When owner Mark Hodesh purchased the business in 1975, Emma Hertler was still running it; her brothers Herman and Gotleib were in the Huron View Nursing Home. Among other gems, the building contains the last horse stalls in downtown Ann Arbor. When asked if there are other photographs of the Hertler family, Mark Hodesh said that there are not many around because they did not like having their pictures taken—they would have rather been working!

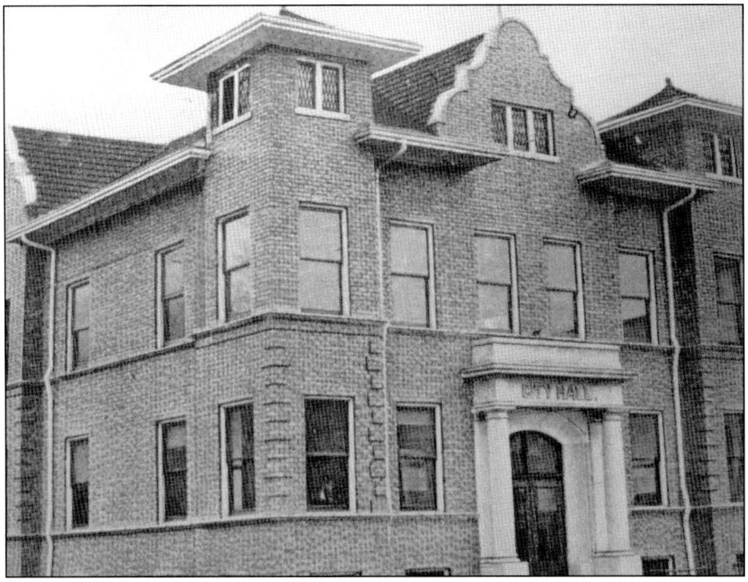

Ann Arbor's first city hall at the corner of Fifth Avenue and Huron Street was finished in 1907. Until its completion, much of the official business of Ann Arbor took place in the courthouse. As city services increased, so did the need for space. In 1895, a spot was rented in the city building on Fourth Avenue until city hall was completed.

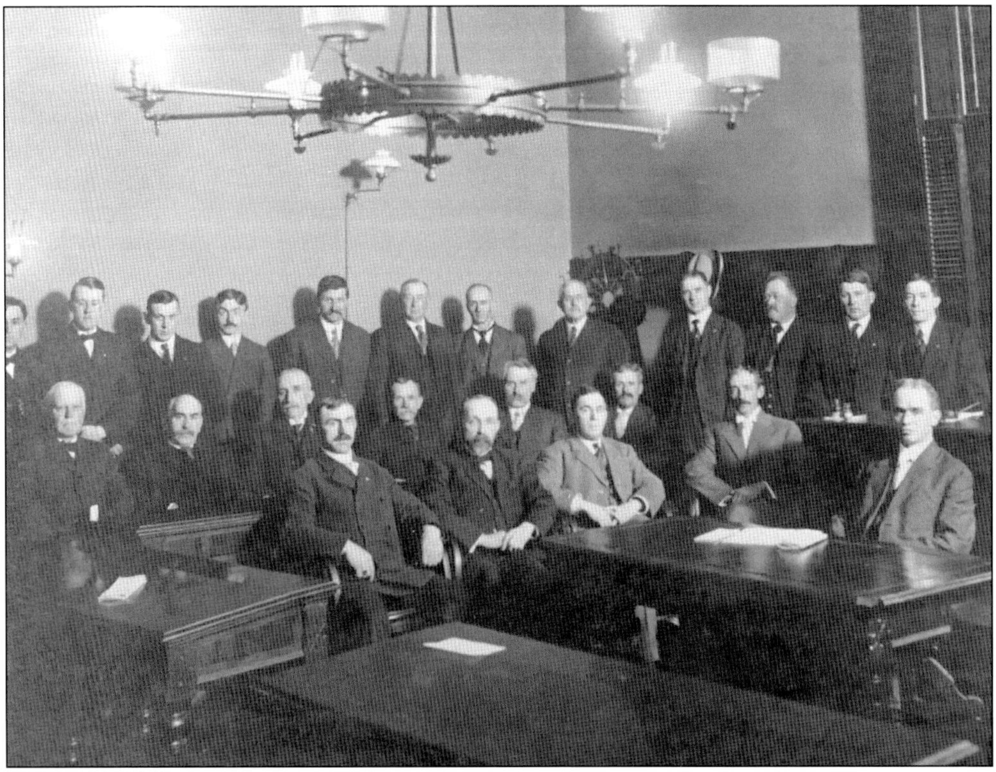

City council in 1909 looked very different from those of later years; Ann Arbor elected its first African American mayor, Albert H. Wheeler, in 1975 and its first female mayor, Elizabeth Brater, in 1991. Fluorescent lights have replaced the hanging lamps in the council chambers, and the tables are a far cry from the old polished wood of the early 20th century—but city business is still conducted efficiently today. Something else that did not exist in 1909 was the Internet and social media, such as Twitter; today, a dedicated group of volunteers live tweets council meetings.

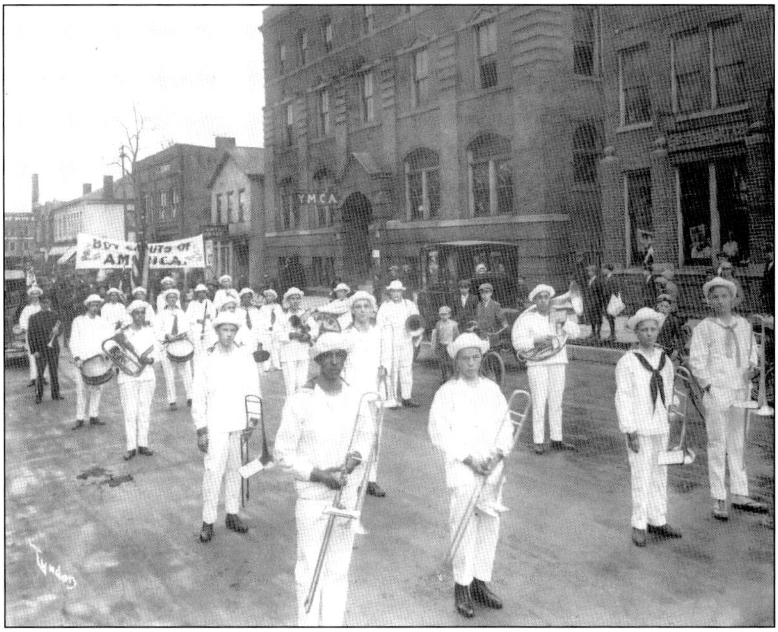

Van's Marine Band is shown here in 1916 at the 100 block of Fourth Avenue. Visible in the background is the YMCA building, which is now the courthouse annex. This block once housed the Goodrich House Hotel. Chauncey S. Goodrich ran the hotel from 1831 to 1842. In 1834, the first election of Ann Arbor trustees was held there.

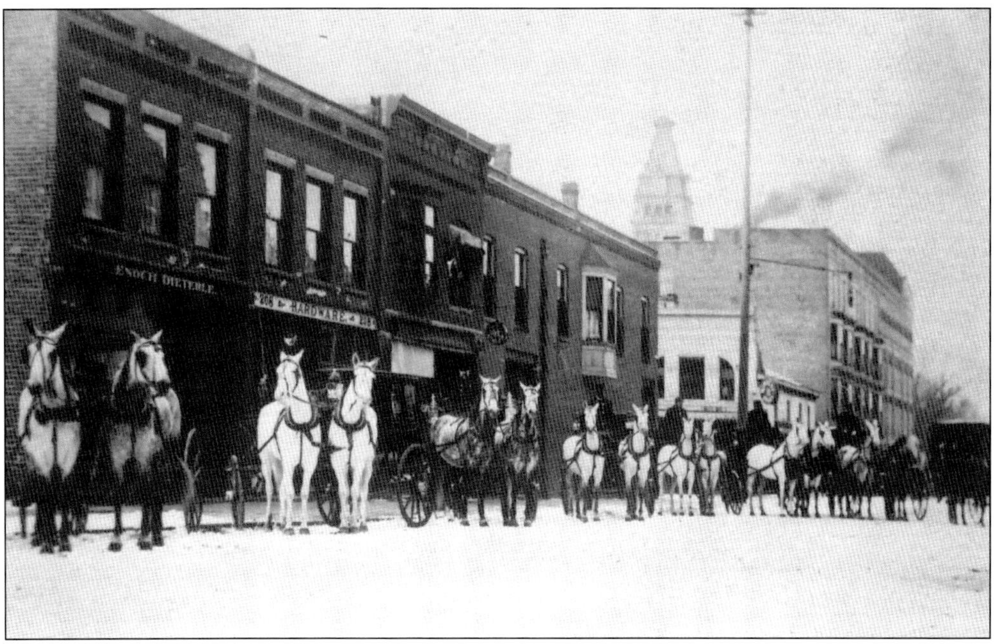

Funeral director Enoch Dieterle's horses and hearses are seen here outside of his Fourth Avenue business. The sharing of personal information did not begin with social media; two separate advertisements in the *Argus* offered his home address. Dieterle promised calls were "attended day or night." Dieterle passed away in 1929 at age 64.

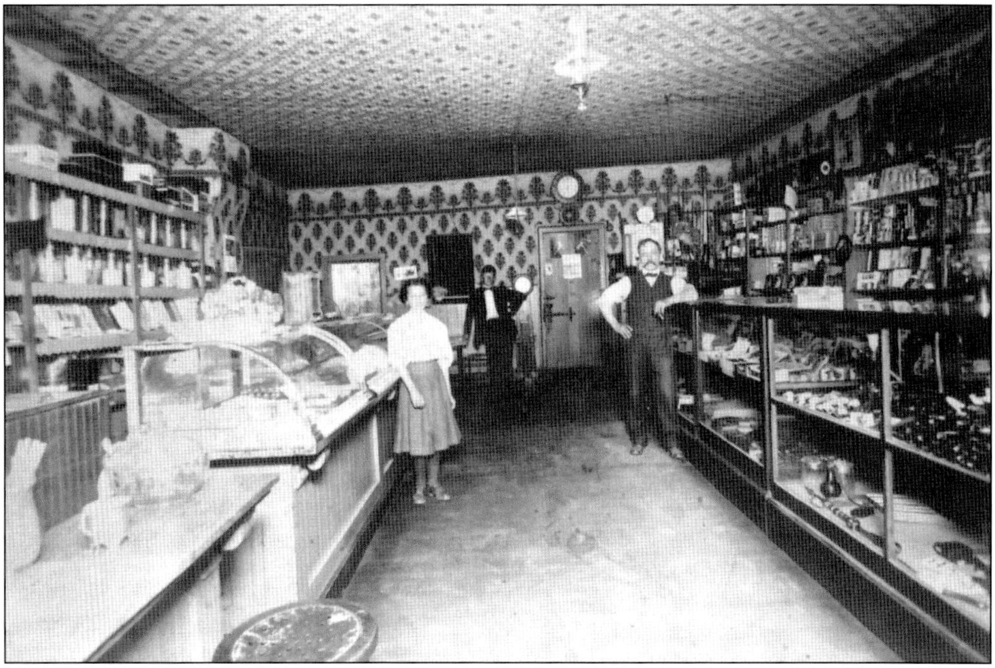

Malloy's harness shop, pictured here, was one of many such businesses in Ann Arbor. As car-repair shops are needed now, so were harness-repair shops in that era. Another early harness shop was operated by Solon Cook, who opened his store in 1830 on the southwest corner of Main and Huron Streets. Cook eventually bought property on the southwest corner of Fourth Avenue and Huron, where he had several businesses, including Cook's Hotel.

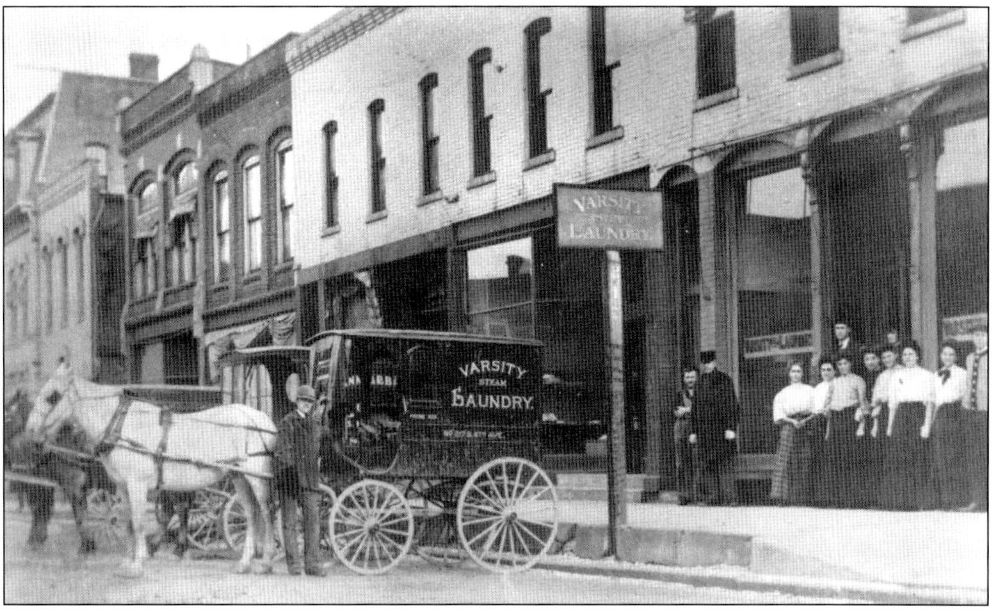

Traditionally, laundry was a laborious chore that was done in the home, but in the 1870s commercial laundries began to advertise their services. Varsity Steam Laundry was one of Ann Arbor's laundries, and it was located at 215–217 South Fourth Avenue. Owners H.B. Tenny and Fred Lantz are in the doorway.

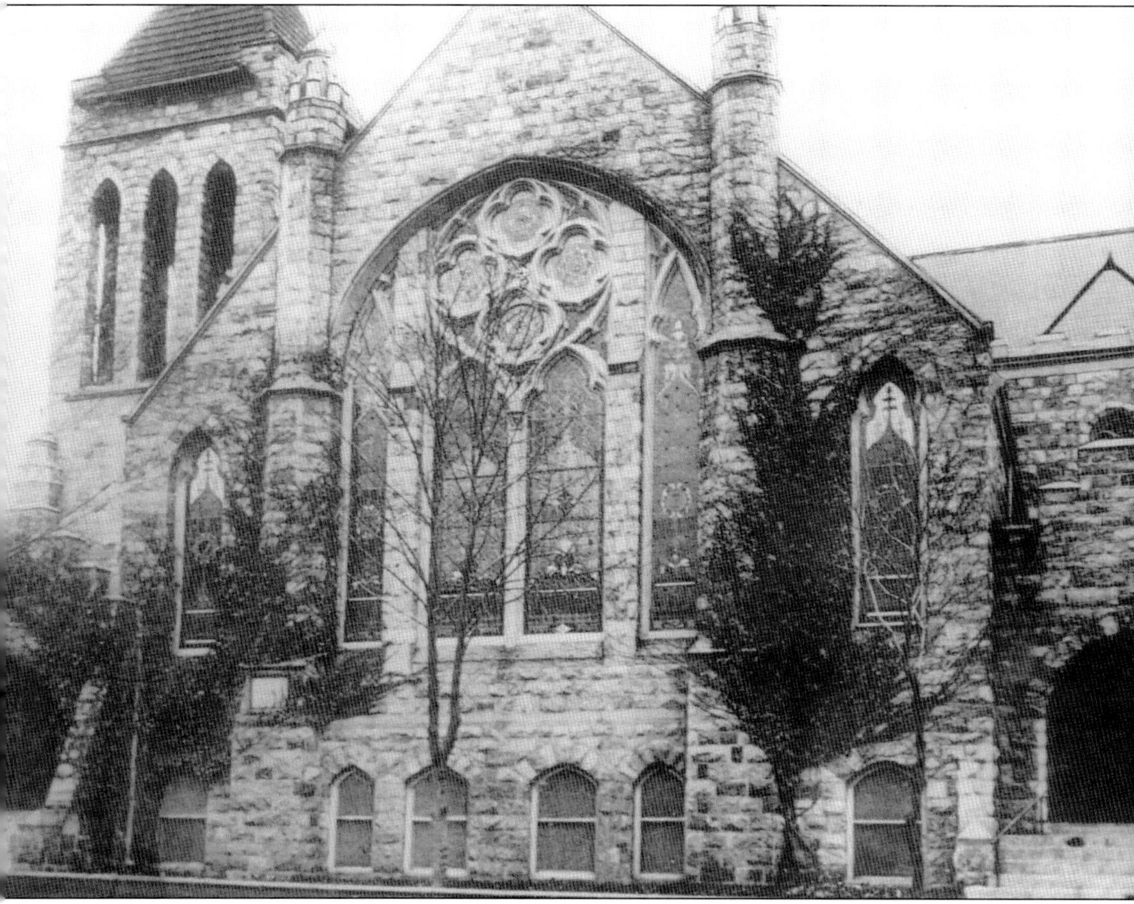

In 1833, Pastor Friedrich Schmid organized the first German congregation in the state. The original church was on Jackson Road, where the Bethlehem Cemetery is now located. The congregation moved to the downtown area in 1849. The church outgrew that location and dedicated a new building at 423 South Fourth Avenue in 1894; the Bethlehem United Church of Christ continues there to this day. Like many churches, it strives to do good work. In 1968, the *Ann Arbor News* featured photographs of volunteers renovating the shelter at Island Park. They continue their good deeds through work with the Alpha House, Peace Neighborhood Center, and Food Gatherers, among many others. There are two groups that make and sell delicious homemade soft pretzels: the Holy Rollers and Parking Lot Pretzels. These are for sale on some Fridays and Saturdays.

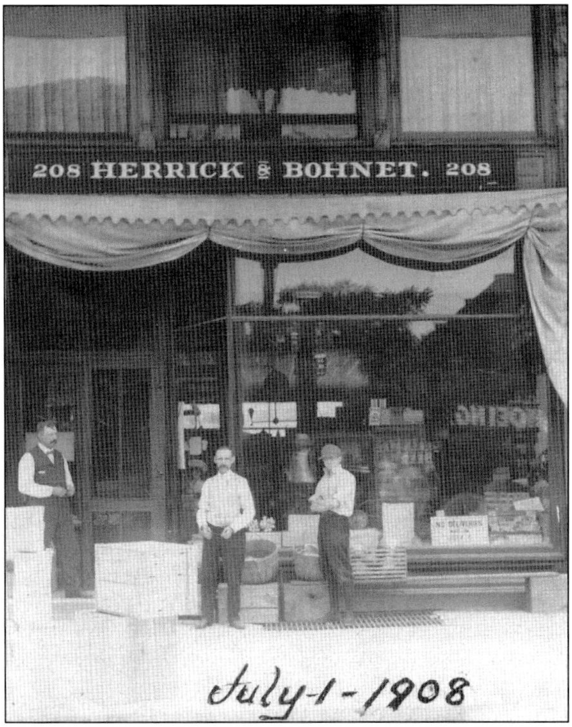

Herrick and Bohnet, a grocery store located at 208 North Fourth Avenue, is shown here on July 1, 1908. The seeds for sale are indicative of the fact that many homcowners in the city had their own private gardens. This block is still home to a number of businesses, including bookstores, the Tea Haus, and People's Food Co-Op.

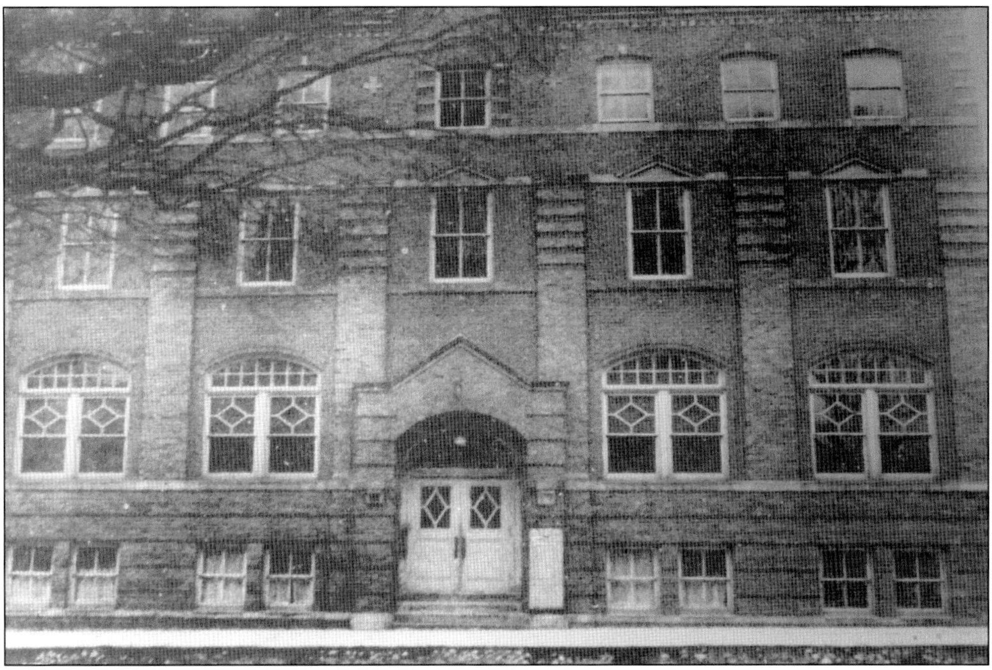

Ann Arbor's YMCA was built at 110 North Fourth Avenue in 1904. By the 1950s, the YMCA was placed in a building that faced Fifth Avenue, William Street, and Fourth Avenue. That facility also included housing for low-income residents in the form of "single room only" occupancies. The current YMCA on West Washington Street opened in 2005. The original building is now used as the courthouse annex, and the second building the YMCA used was demolished.

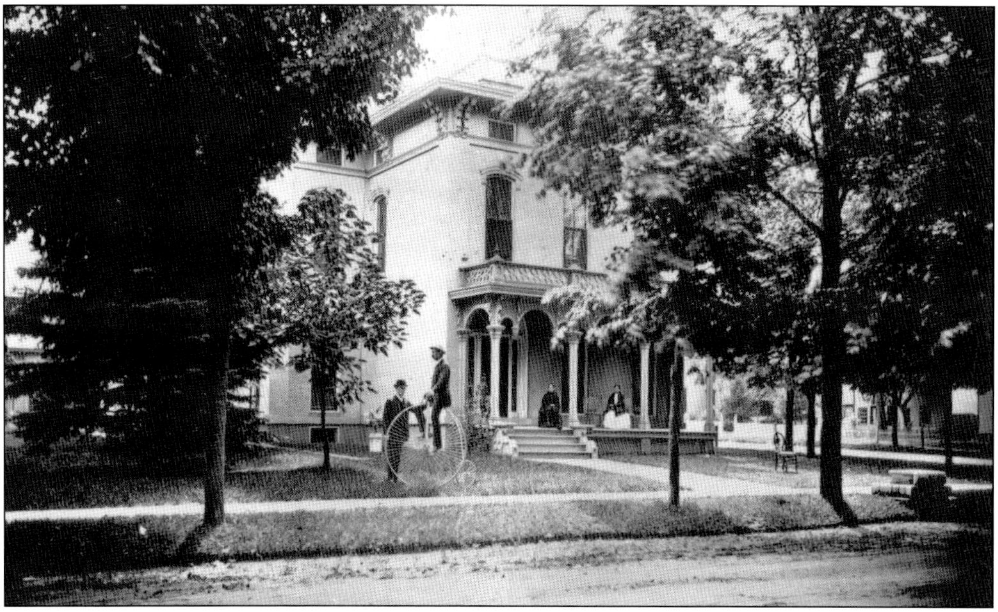

This is the elegant family home of Junius Beal at Fifth Avenue and William Street, where the public library now stands. Junius was a prominent citizen in the city, serving as a regent of the university as well as the publisher of the weekly *Ann Arbor Courier*. Beal's father purchased the home, and when Junius resided there it became "the center of true social life and hospitality." In 1956, the house was demolished to make room for the public library.

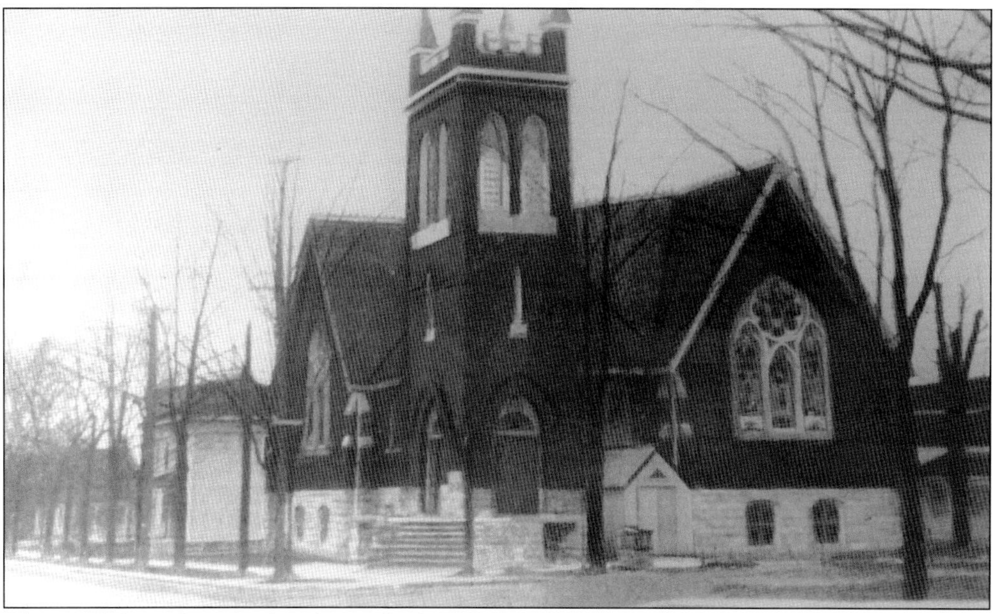

The English Lutheran Church was built in 1895 at the corner of Fifth Avenue and William Street. Two years prior, the *Ann Arbor Argus* quoted a report from the *Lutheran Observer* that Rev. Dr. M.W. Hamma had decided to "run over" to Ann Arbor to see this new settlement. After spending some time with members and their pastor, Rev. W.L. Tedrow, he was pleased with their enthusiasm over the future church. The church is now Trinity Lutheran, which has a building on West Stadium Boulevard.

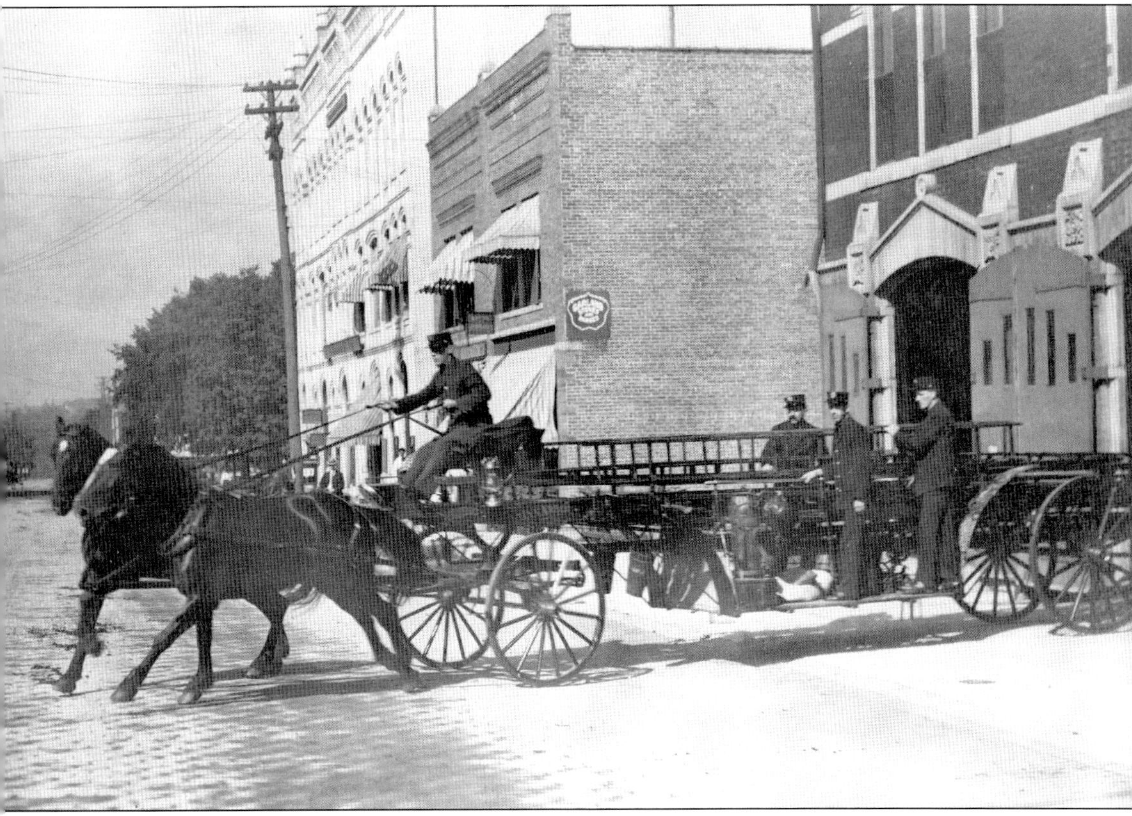

Ann Arbor firefighters are on the move from the firehouse on Fifth Avenue and Huron Street. Fire was a constant danger in early Ann Arbor, as buildings and sidewalks were all made of wood; thus, just 12 years after the village's founding, Ann Arbor's "ordinance relating to a fire department" passed. Approved on December 12, 1836, the ordinance ran seven pages long and appointed fire wardens in the town's wards. Shortly thereafter, volunteer firefighting teams were organized. A small, two-story wooden fireman's hall was constructed but eventually proved insufficient to meet the needs of the growing town. The volunteer firemen lobbied successfully for a new fireman's hall, and the result was a hall that, at the time, was the most elegant and expensive city-owned building. Opening in 1882, the new hall had a second floor for meetings and social events, a first floor to store hooks and ladders, and a bell tower to summon the volunteer firefighters. The building would house the fire department for 96 years.

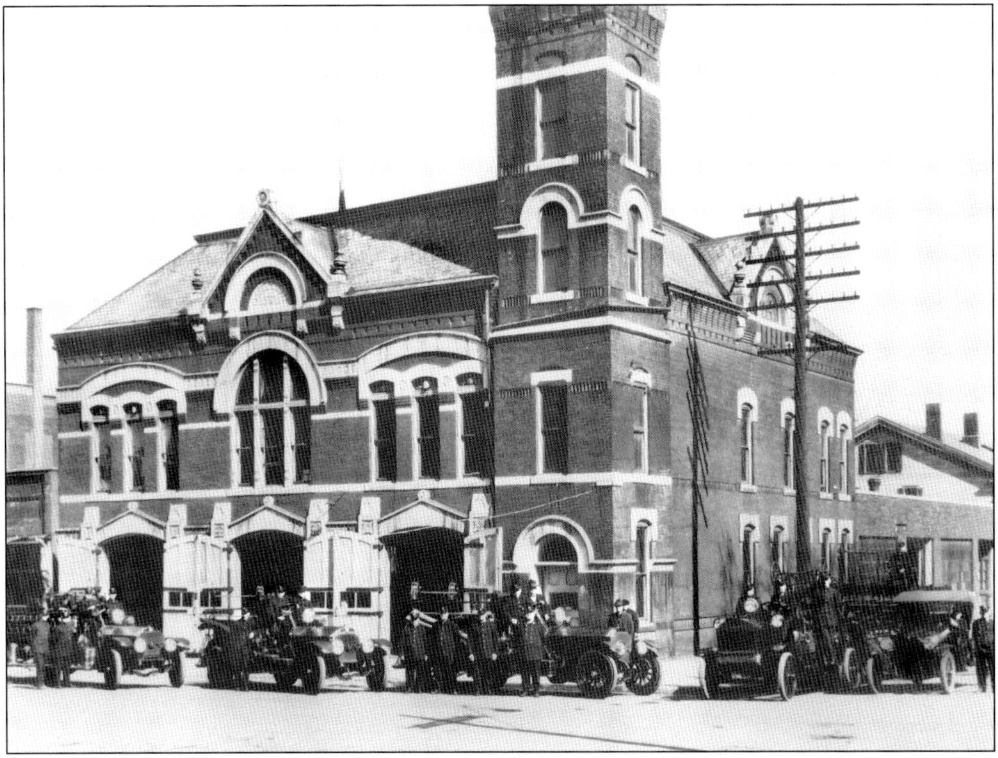

The building seen here is the main firehouse that was constructed in 1882. In 1978, the department moved to a new building just north of this location. Part of the 1882 structure still exists as the Hands-on Museum, a popular destination for old and young alike.

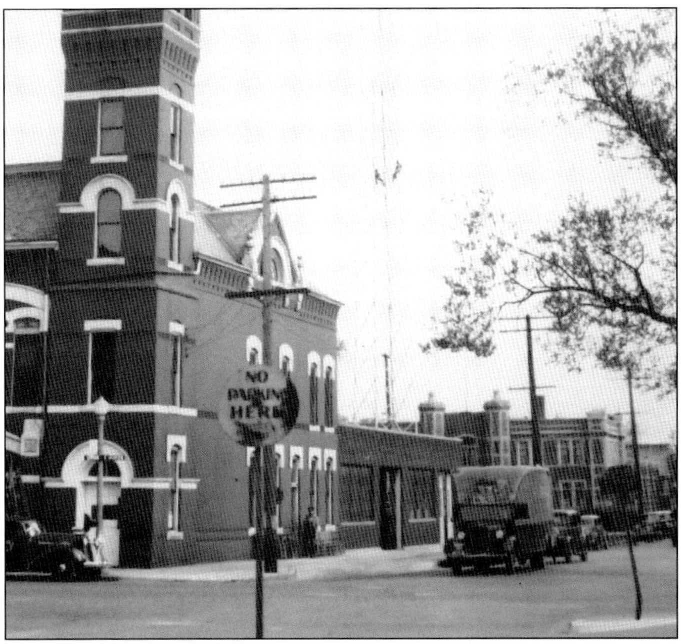

In 1941, a city-county radio tower was installed behind the fire station. The *Ann Arbor News* reported that the tower was 180 feet tall, and with the addition of extra piping, it topped out at 198 feet above ground. The system provided the police and sheriff departments with two-way radio communication. The total cost of the tower was $1,005.

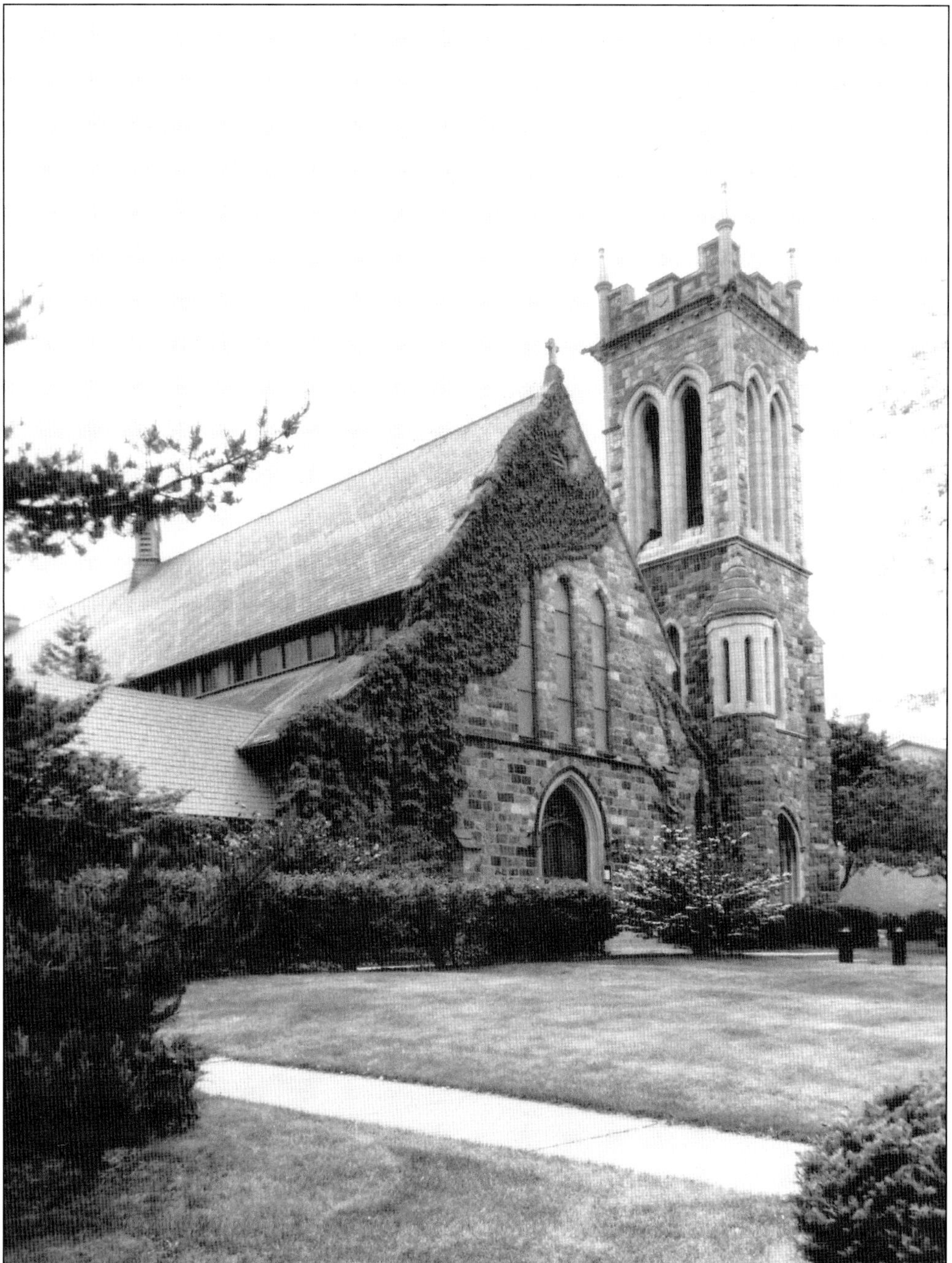

St. Andrew's Episcopal Church still stands at 306 North Division Street. This beautiful church was established in 1828, and the first building was constructed in 1839 thanks to a land donation from George Corselius. It expanded in 1856, and the present building was erected in the late 1860s. The church currently has a congregation of over 1,300 parishioners. The Breakfast at St. Andrew's program has offered a daily, free, volunteer-run breakfast for over 30 years.

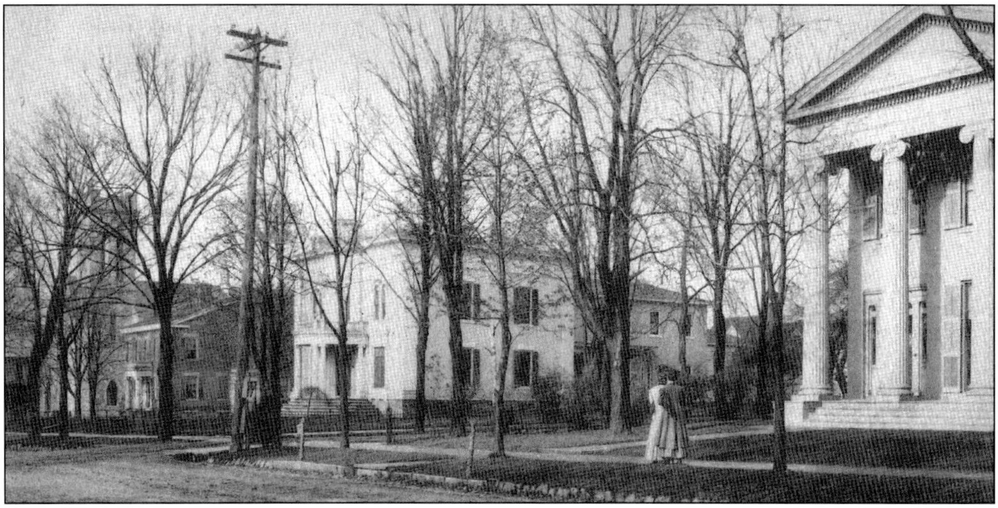

Here is another view of the magnificent St. Andrew's Church (back left). It was built in the English Gothic style and made with hand-selected granite field boulders. Dressed with different shades of slate, the roof supports a stone Greek cross. The tower is over 80 feet high and contains stairs that lead to a balcony and belfry. The interior is graced with many gifts, including a walnut eagle lectern from 1875. The beautiful John Maynard House, Ebenezer Wells House, and Judge Roberts Wilson House in this photograph are still standing today.

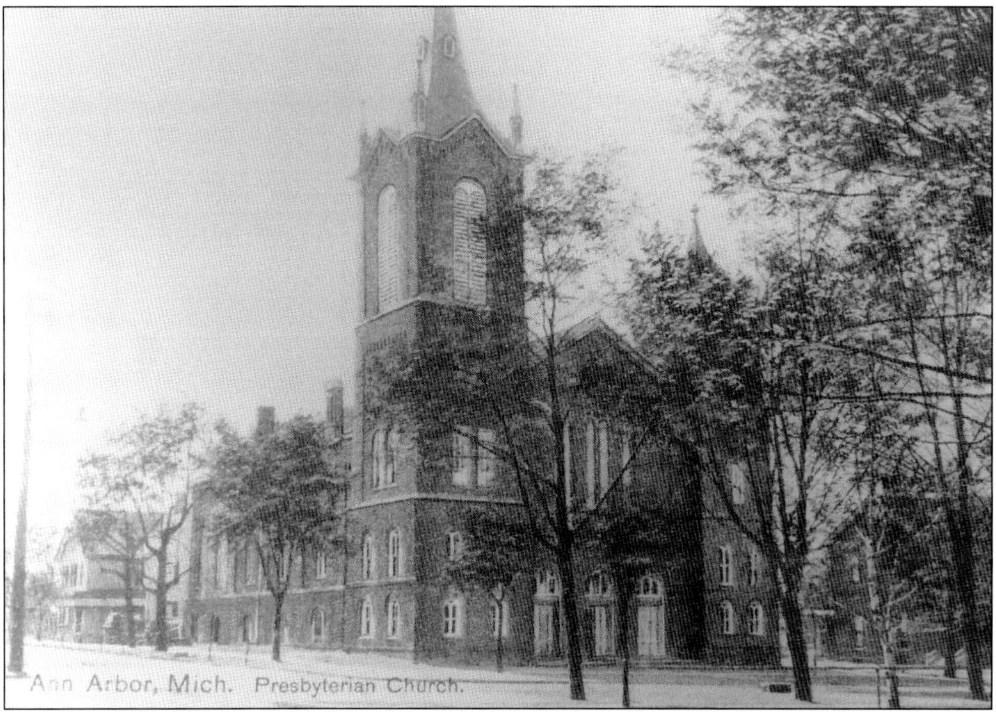

The house of worship seen here in 1910 is the First Presbyterian Church, located at the southwest corner of Division and Huron Streets. Ann Arbor Presbyterians founded the Presbyterian Society in 1826, and just a year later they were planning to construct their first church building. Two other churches were ultimately erected at Division and Huron. The current church is on Washtenaw Avenue.

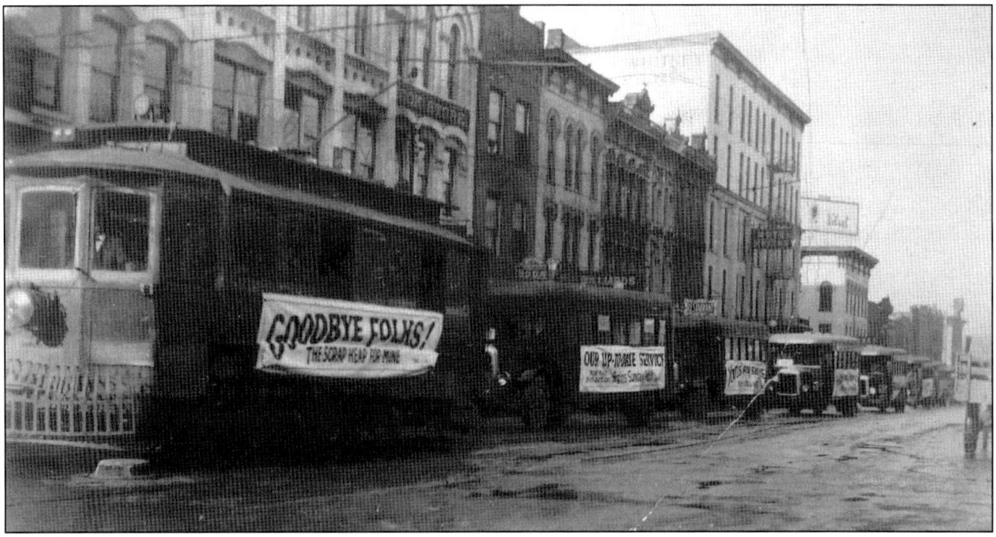

Trolleys were a popular mode of transportation in Ann Arbor, but they did not last forever. As seen in the image above, the trolley is rolling up Main Street, saying goodbye to the city. The photograph below depicts the subsequent mode of transportation: the bus. These women are exchanging tickets at the Greyhound bus station, which opened in 1940. The original style of the station was Streamline Modern and was the last such styled building left in the downtown area. Some trolley tracks are still visible today, especially on roads that have suffered wear and tear of harsh winters, but the trolleys themselves are only visible in photographs.

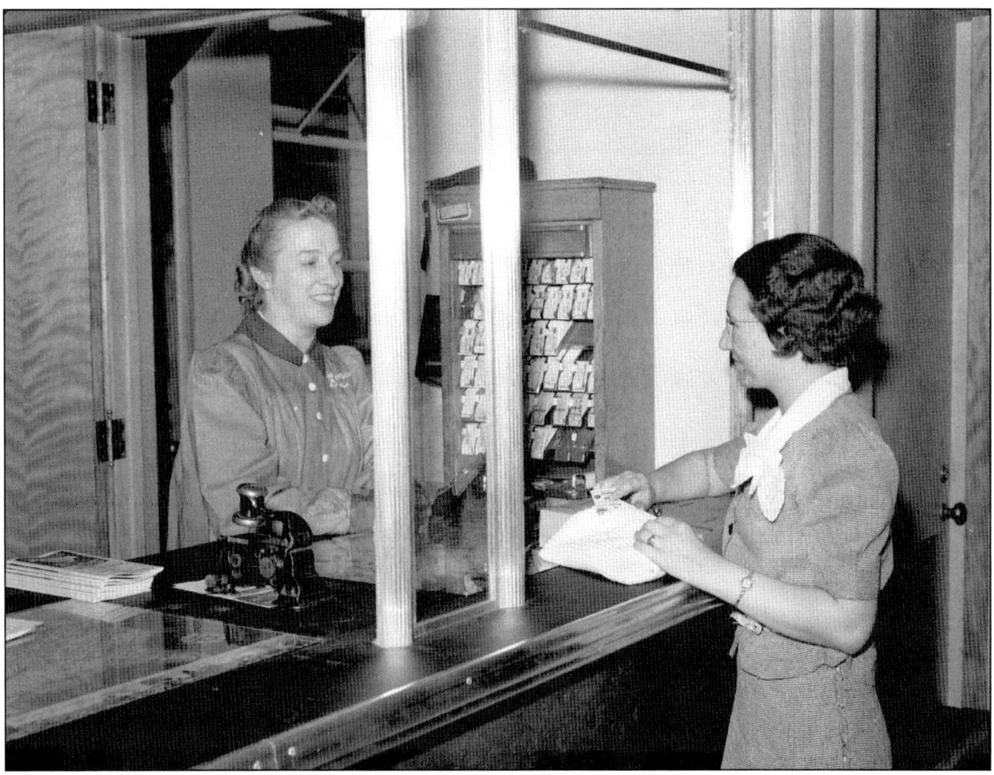

Two

East-West Streets

Allen and Rumsey divided Annarbour east to west using Huron Street as the dividing line. Rumsey named his streets Washington, Liberty, and William, while Allen named his Ann, Catherine, and North. Now named Kingsley, North Street was originally the northern edge of the town.

These streets still thrive. Huron Street remains a major thoroughfare through downtown as it passes the courthouse and then heads west, where it turns into Jackson Avenue. Heading east, it turns into Washtenaw Avenue. William Street does not end with an "s," but some accounts indicate that it was known as Williams Street on older maps. It starts at the University of Michigan Diag and travels all the way to the Old West Side, where it dead-ends into Fourth Street. Liberty Street dead-ends into the State Theater, but along the way it passes by restaurants, bars, and shops. Washington Street also features a number of outstanding restaurants and is home to three brewpubs: Arbor Brewing Company, Grizzly Peak Brewing Company, and the Blue Tractor.

In the beginning of Annarbour village, Rumsey donated half a square block on Liberty Street (between Fourth and Fifth Streets, now Avenues) for the purposes of a county jail. The county jail is no longer in downtown, and its former space is now home to the federal courthouse and post office. Allen set aside a square block on his side of Huron Street at Fifth Avenue for use as public space for a courthouse, which became known as the courthouse square. There is a courthouse on this spot today.

The courthouse square was truly the heart of the community and its nerve center. When the Civil War broke out, it was there that residents received their news. Visiting dignitaries spoke on the steps, and ordinary citizens posed there for photographs. The tour of Ann Arbor's east-west streets could start in no better place.

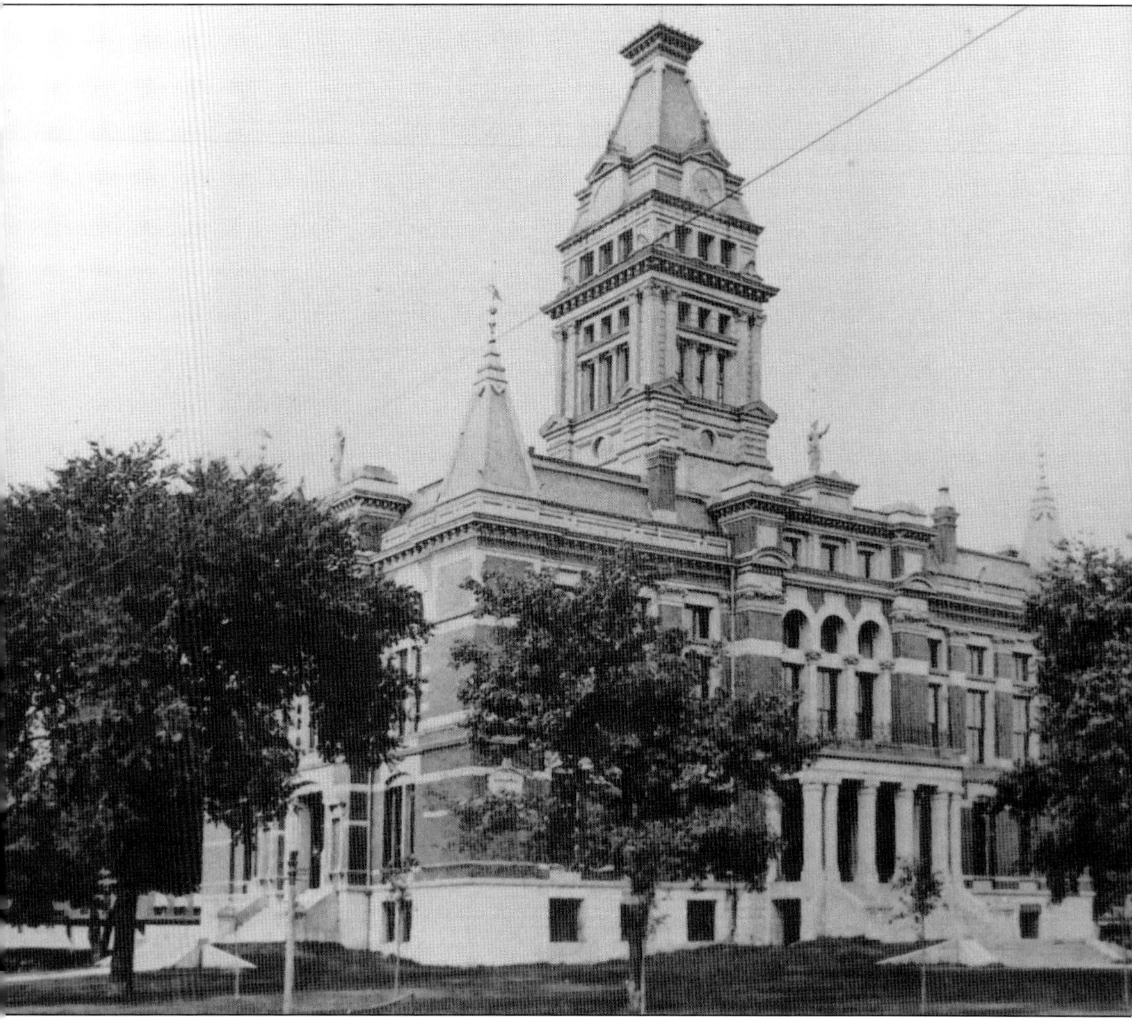

The first courthouse was located on Ann Street in the courthouse square. After acquiring the land that would become Ann Arbor, John Allen and Elisha Rumsey plotted out streets. One of the more prominent areas they planned for was the courthouse square in the area bounded by Huron Street, Main Street, Fourth Avenue, and Ann Street. In 1831, the village of Annarbour had six attorneys; by 1843, it had 22. Courthouses of yesteryear, however, were used for much more than attorneys and legal matters; people gathered on the square for rallies and to hear important news. Construction on the current courthouse began in 1954. Its parking lot occupies the space taken up by the courthouse in this photograph.

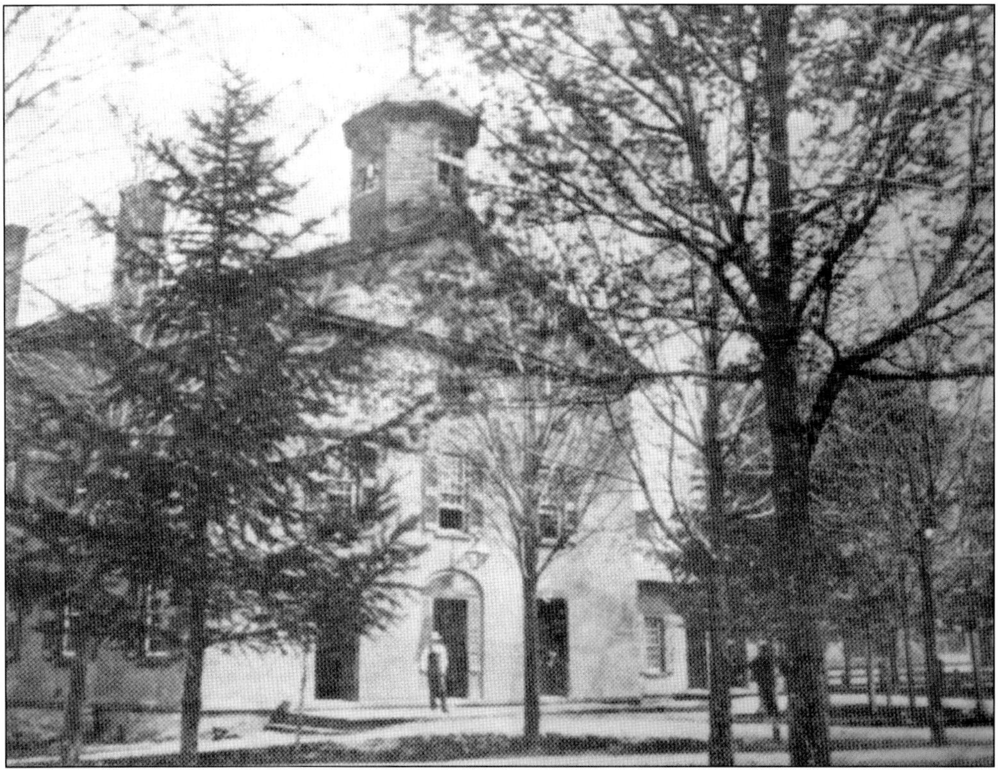

Here is the Washtenaw County Courthouse around 1892. The first courthouse was built in 1834 for a little over $5,000. It was far more modest than the one pictured. Voters rejected a new courthouse in 1866 but approved the building shown here 11 years later at a cost of $88,000.

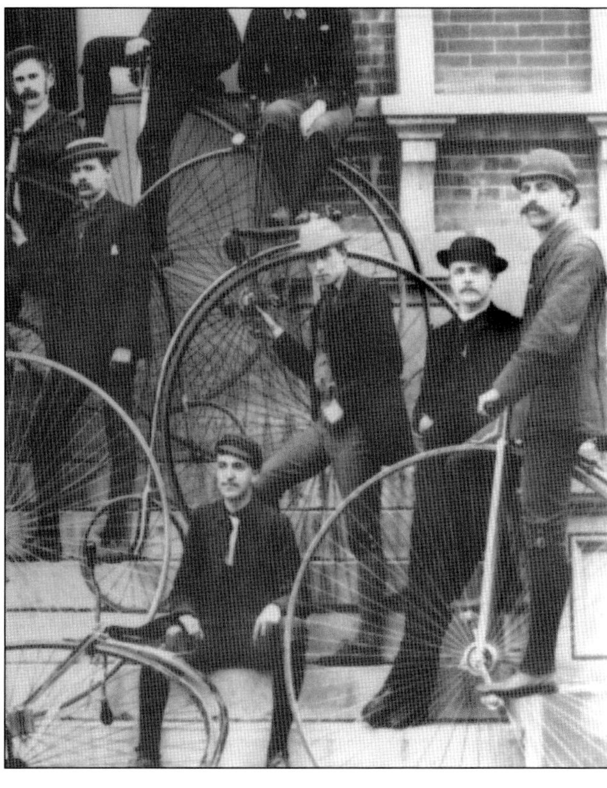

Bicycling became popular in the 1880s, particularly when safer bicycles were introduced to the public. The Ann Arbor Men's Bicycle Club is posing here on the courthouse steps in 1880. In 1886, Junius Beal's *Ann Arbor Courier* announced that the "Bicycle Club" opened up two "fine club rooms" on the Masonic Block, where members and their friends could meet. Beal, a leader of the cyclists, owned the Masonic Block.

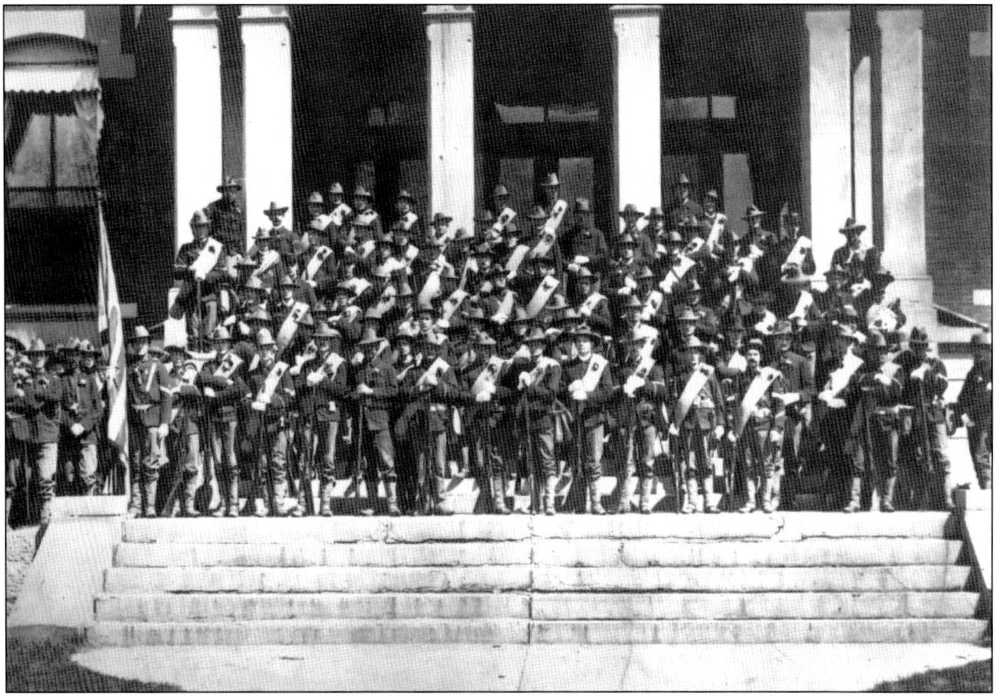

Members of Company A, 1st Infantry of the Michigan National Guard pose for this photograph on the courthouse steps. On April 26, 1898, the battleship *Maine* had been sunk, and the company was preparing to ship out to the Spanish-American War. When the company returned to Ann Arbor the following year, members were greeted as heroes. Money was raised toward the purchase of a local armory and for medals for all who served.

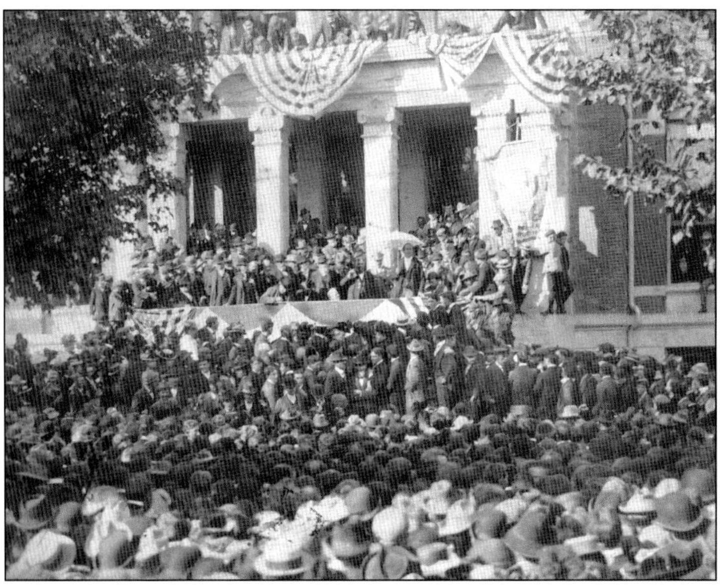

Here is another view of the courthouse steps, but this time William Jennings Bryan, who ran for president on the Democratic ticket in 1896, 1900, and 1908, is pictured. Unfortunately, hecklers prevented "The Great Commoner" from delivering his speech that day in 1900. Bryan later spoke at the Cook House during his 1908 presidential campaign.

The Luick Lumber Company, located in what is now the Kerrytown area, sold a variety of lumber and materials for homes and new construction work. This image shows the Luick Lumber crew hard at work; in the background is the courthouse.

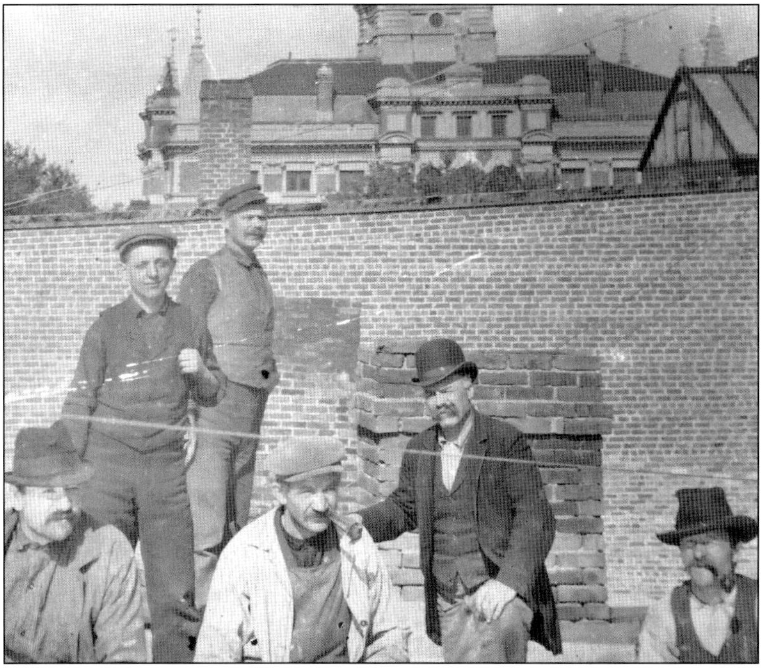

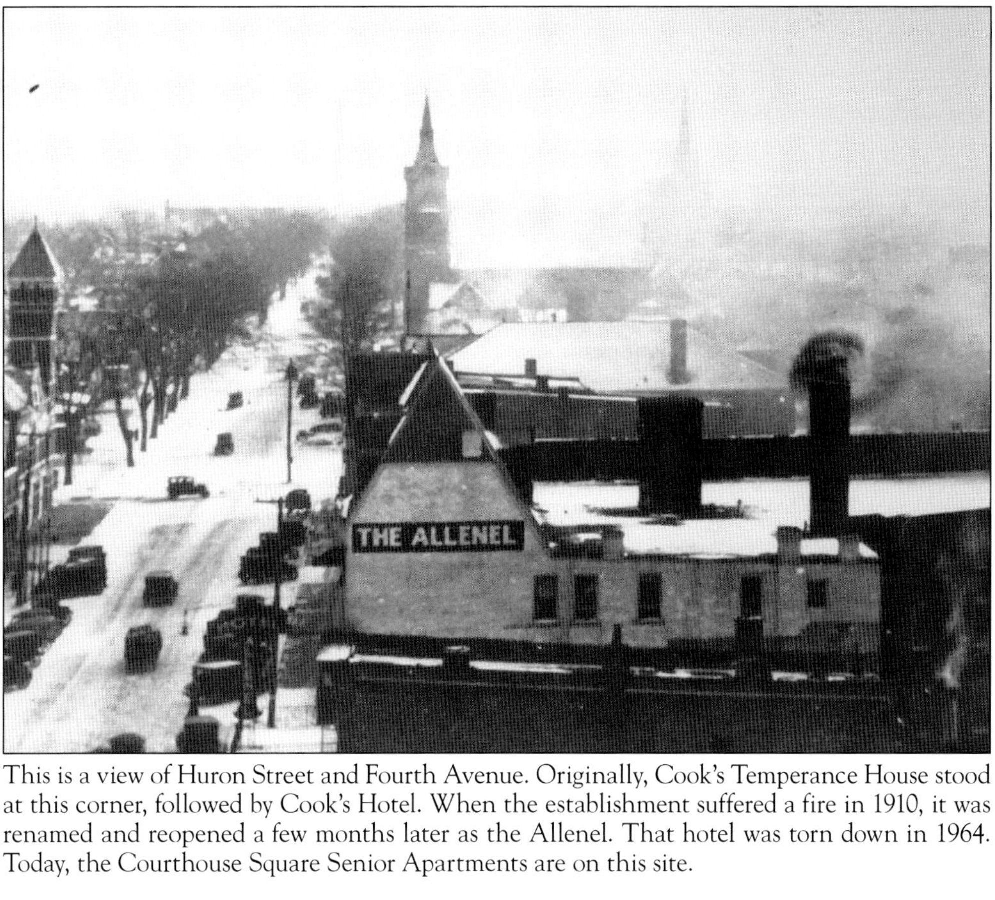

This is a view of Huron Street and Fourth Avenue. Originally, Cook's Temperance House stood at this corner, followed by Cook's Hotel. When the establishment suffered a fire in 1910, it was renamed and reopened a few months later as the Allenel. That hotel was torn down in 1964. Today, the Courthouse Square Senior Apartments are on this site.

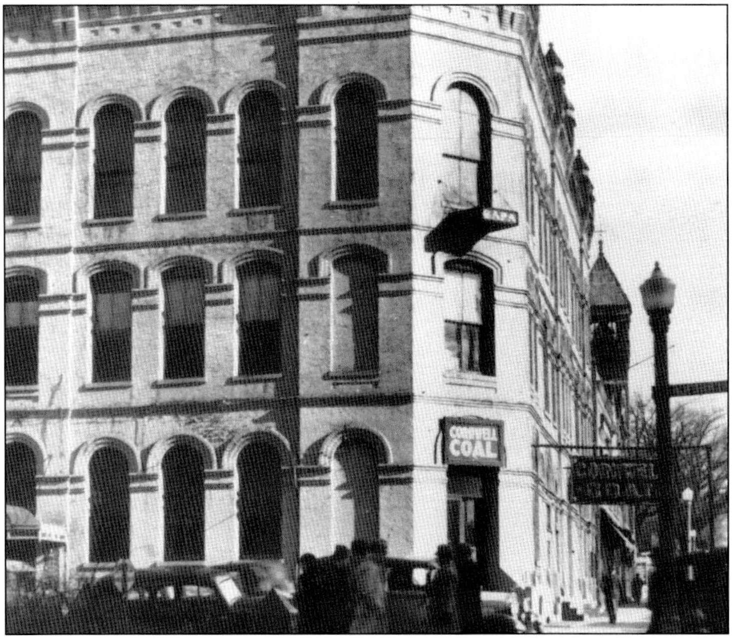

Another view of Fourth Avenue and Huron Street shows the Cornwell Building, which was erected in 1885. Frank Cornwell started a coal-supply business and sold it to two of his employees in the 1940s. When coal fell out of favor as a method of heating homes, the coal suppliers in town suffered. The last one in Ann Arbor to close was Cornwell.

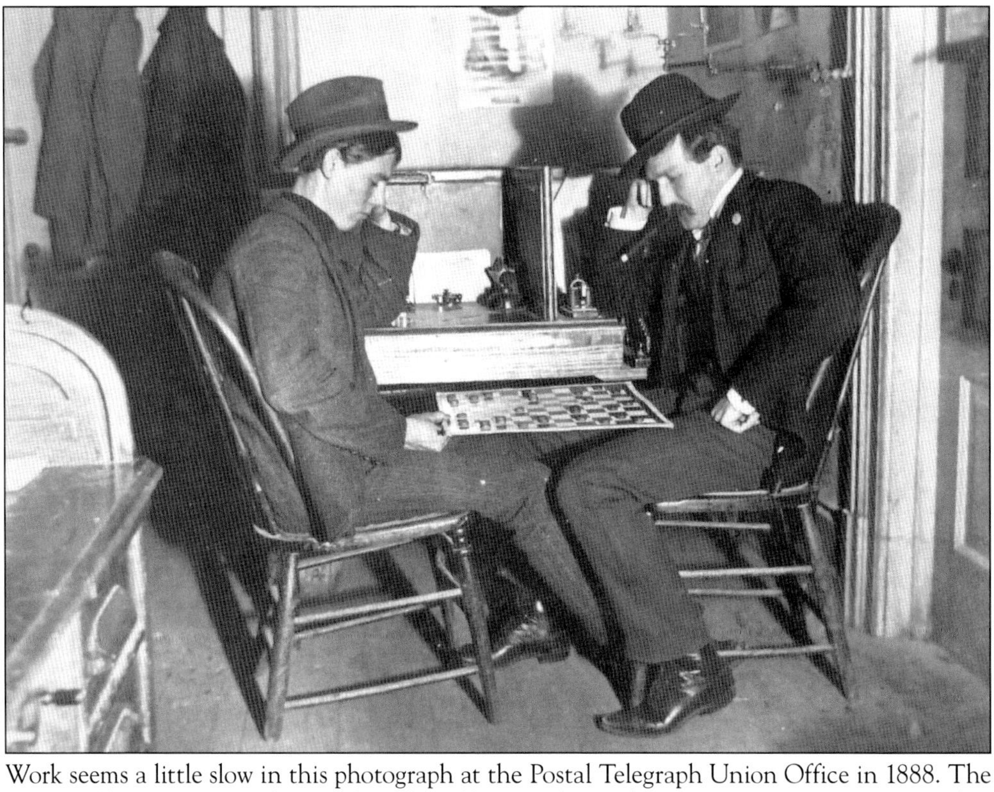

Work seems a little slow in this photograph at the Postal Telegraph Union Office in 1888. The 1908 "Polk Directory" indicates that this office was located at 112 East Huron Street, with a Western Union office located a few blocks away at 106 West Huron Street. Even though telephones were available (the directory also listed two telephone companies), one did not have to go far for telegraph services.

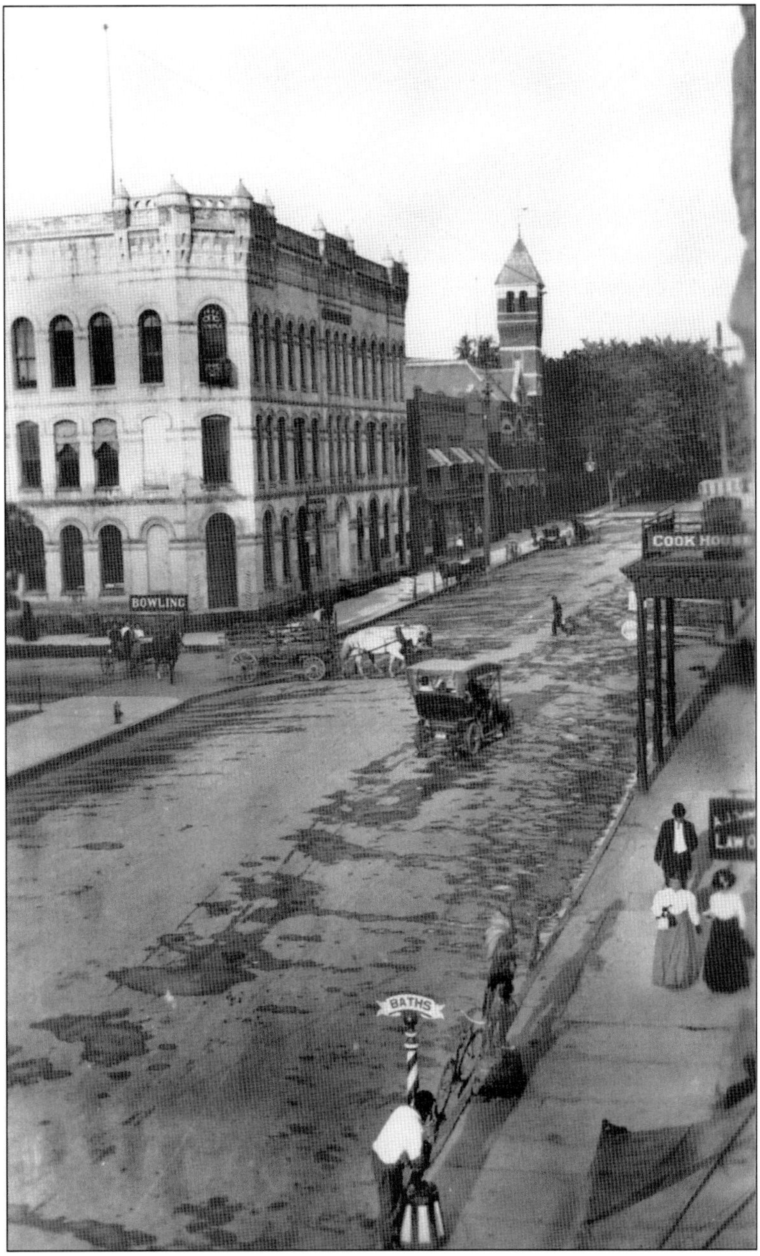

The Postal Telegraph Cable Company (or Postal Telegraph Union Office), located in the Cornwell Building at East Huron Street and North Fourth Avenue, is pictured here. This image of the building is from the mid- to late 1890s. At the time, there were numerous telegraph offices located around the courthouse square, and while it is not known if they all employed primarily female operators, it is known that this was one of the jobs available to women at that time. Women took over operator jobs when male operators left for the Civil War, but after the war ended the men came home to reclaim their positions; however, some of the women wanted to keep those jobs. As a result, in 1869, Western Union opened a telegraph school for women and began to employ women in large numbers. Unfortunately, women's wages were often lower than those of men who performed the same jobs. By 1920, approximately 20 percent of operators were women.

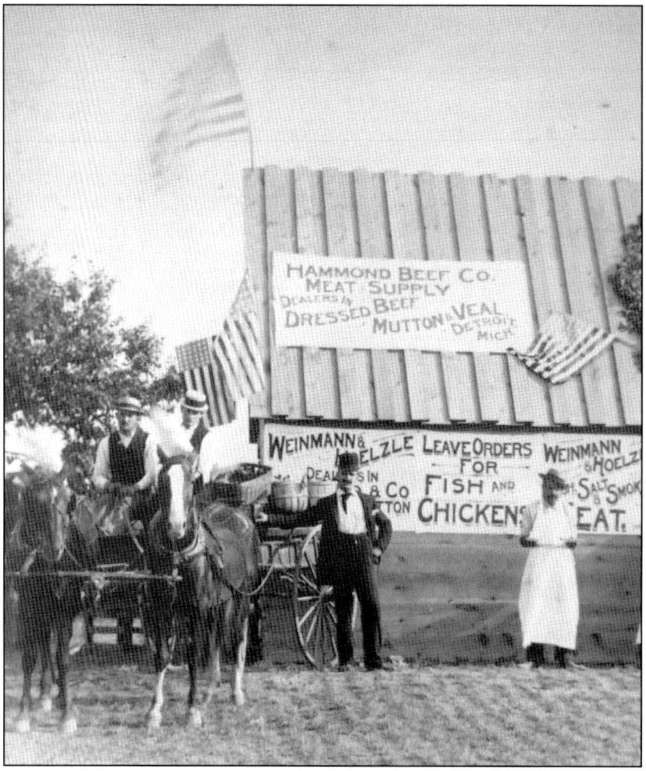

This photograph appears to have been taken around Flag Day, or perhaps butchers Weinmann & Hoelzle were patriotic year-round. J. Fred Hoelzle arrived in Ann Arbor in the 1870s and promptly began work as a butcher. Hoelzle eventually opened his own shop on the corner of Washington Street and Fourth Avenue, where business flourished.

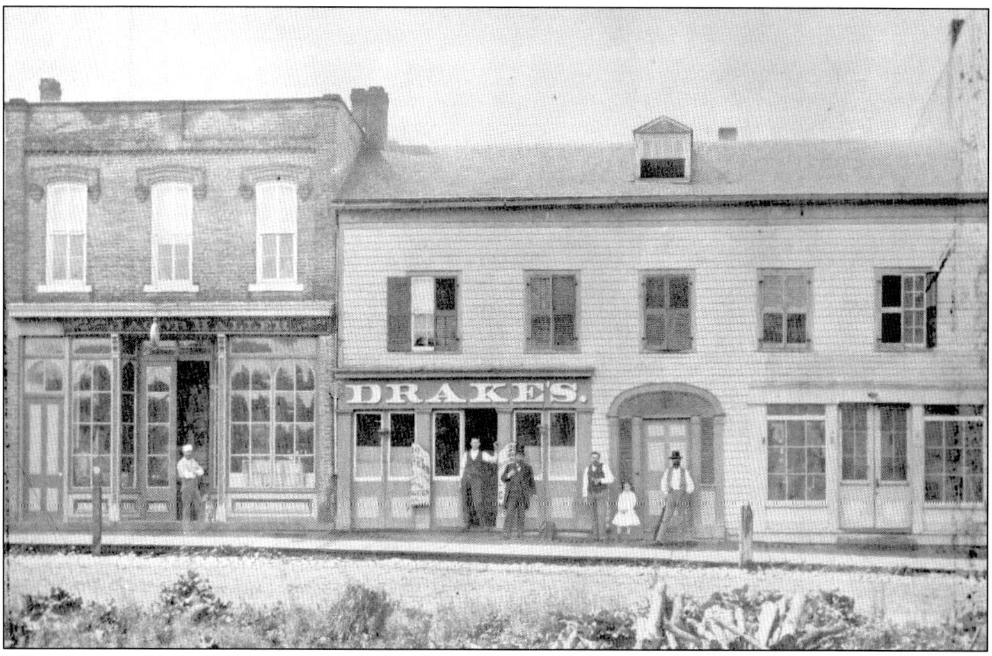

When most Ann Arbor townies talk about Drake's, they are referring to the much-missed sandwich shop on North University. But, the Drake's seen here had a different focus: it was a saloon across from the courthouse on Huron Street in the 1870s. Jacob Haller's Jewelry Store was located next door.

Part of the Washtenaw County Savings Bank on Washington Street, the offices of L.D. Hale had originally been located in Grass Lake, a town located about 25 miles west of Ann Arbor. According to the *History of Washtenaw County*, Hale was born in Massachusetts and made his way to Michigan in the late 1830s. He stopped in Grass Lake one Sunday, found a good spot for a business, and "opened the first store of any consequence." In 1861, he came to Ann Arbor to deal in bonds and mortgages.

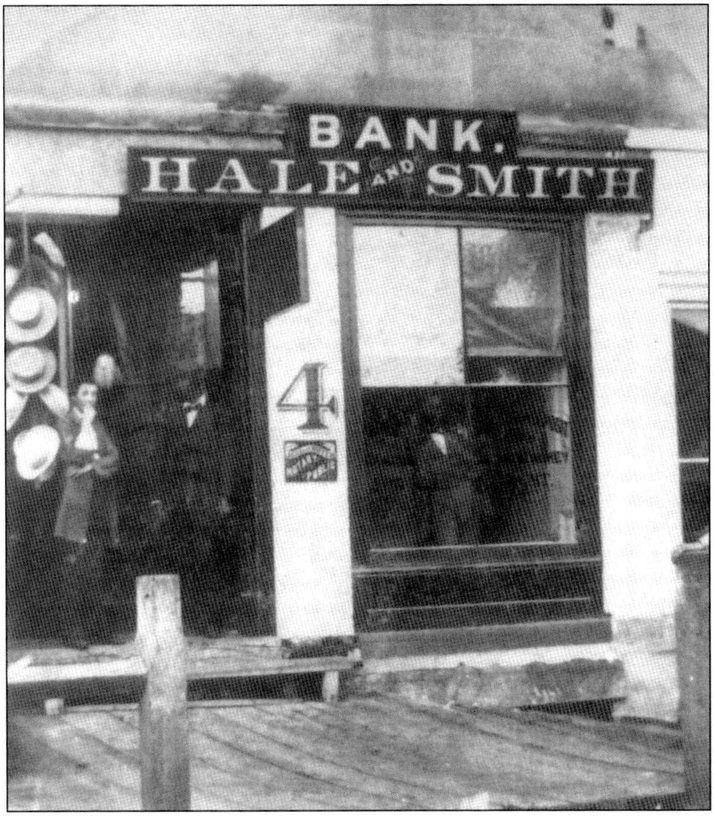

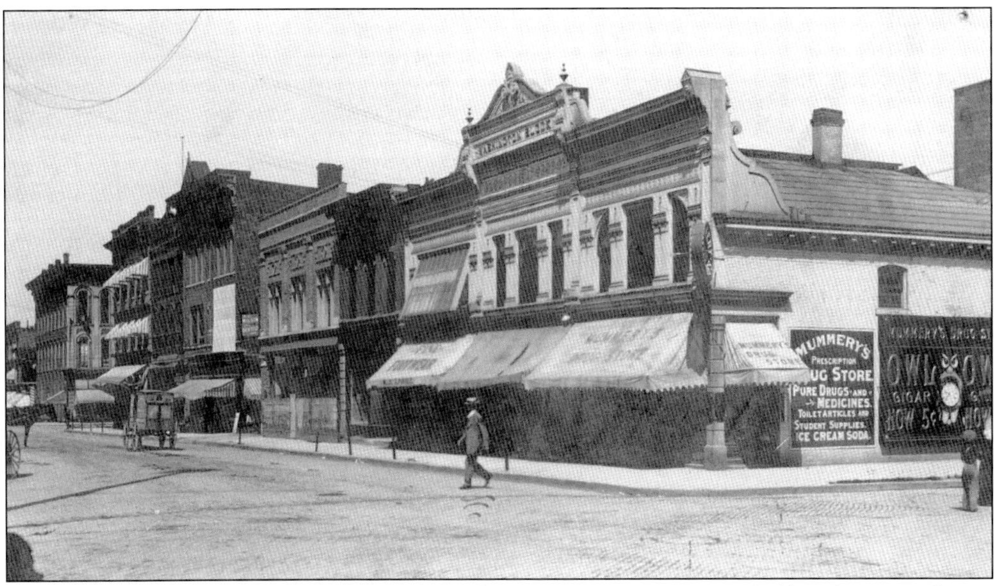

According to *Michigan Alumnus* magazine, Arthur E. Mummery was awarded his pharmacy degree in 1885. This is a photograph of Mummery's Drugstore on the corner of East Washington Street and South Fourth Avenue around 1910. The building was known as the Washington Block. A parking garage is located in this space now, the construction of which inspired the nearby Arbor Brewing Company to name one of its beers Jackhammer.

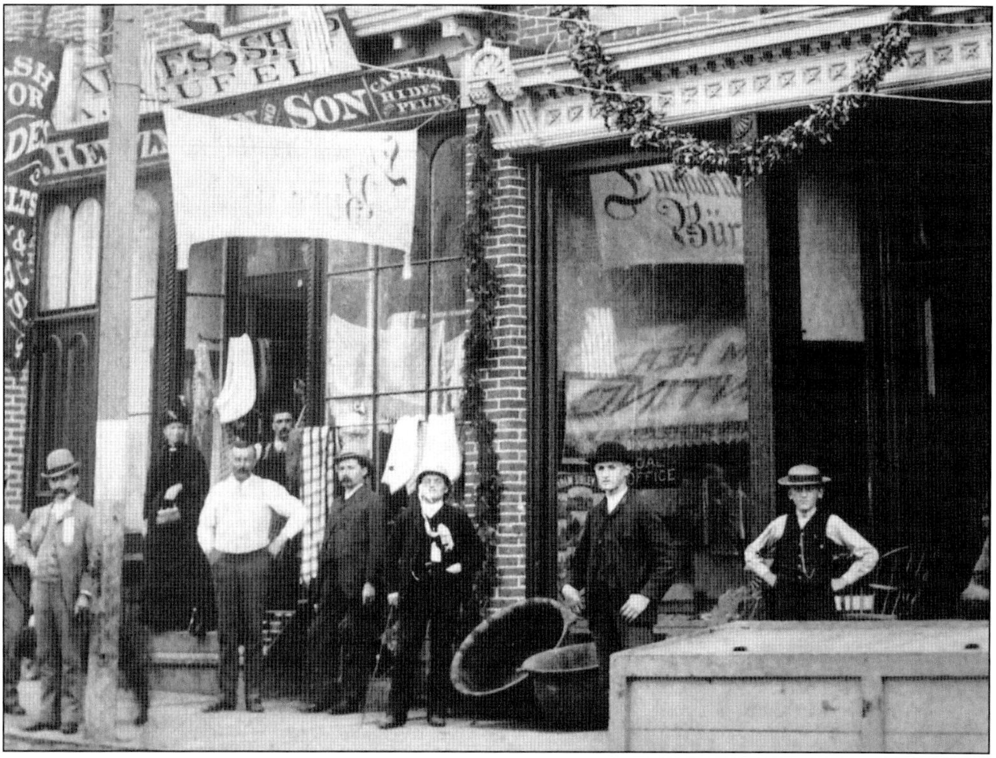

Gene Heinzmann & Sons Harness Shop was located at 114 or 117 West Washington Street. The shop offered cash for hides and pelts but was primarily involved with the making of harness leather.

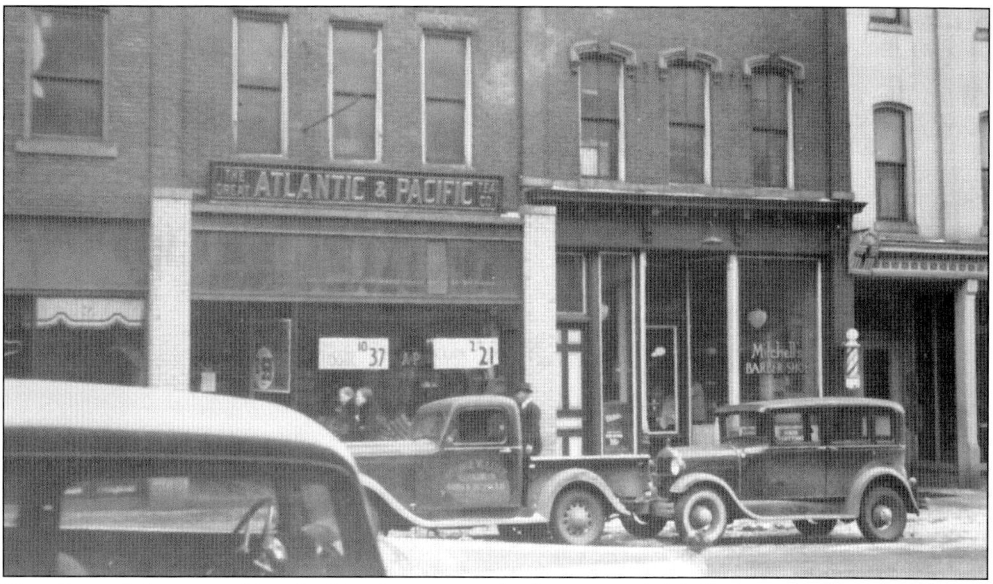

The Great Atlantic and Pacific Tea Company, also known as A&P, had a store at 115–117 West Washington Street. The company began as a mail-order tea business in 1859, but by the turn of the century there were 20 stores in the A&P chain. In its heyday, the company had thousands of markets all over the country. Great food can still be found at this location in Ann Arbor; the Logan Restaurant and Frita Batidos now occupy the spot.

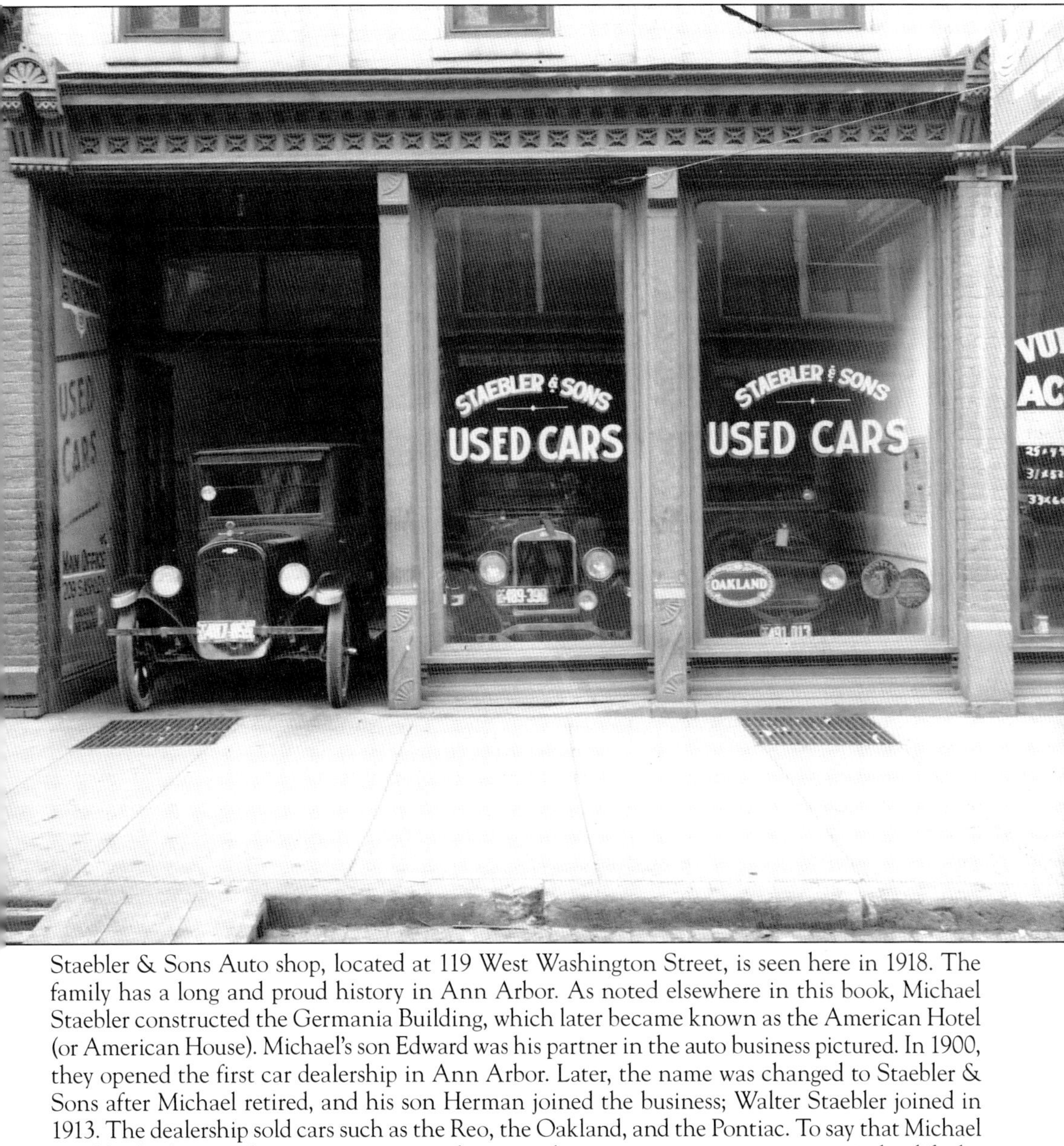

Staebler & Sons Auto shop, located at 119 West Washington Street, is seen here in 1918. The family has a long and proud history in Ann Arbor. As noted elsewhere in this book, Michael Staebler constructed the Germania Building, which later became known as the American Hotel (or American House). Michael's son Edward was his partner in the auto business pictured. In 1900, they opened the first car dealership in Ann Arbor. Later, the name was changed to Staebler & Sons after Michael retired, and his son Herman joined the business; Walter Staebler joined in 1913. The dealership sold cars such as the Reo, the Oakland, and the Pontiac. To say that Michael Staebler had many diverse interests may be an understatement; at various times in his life, he sold coal, farm machinery, and bicycles. In his late 40s, he belonged to the firm of Staebler and Elmer, which manufactured speed carts. Michael passed away in 1929.

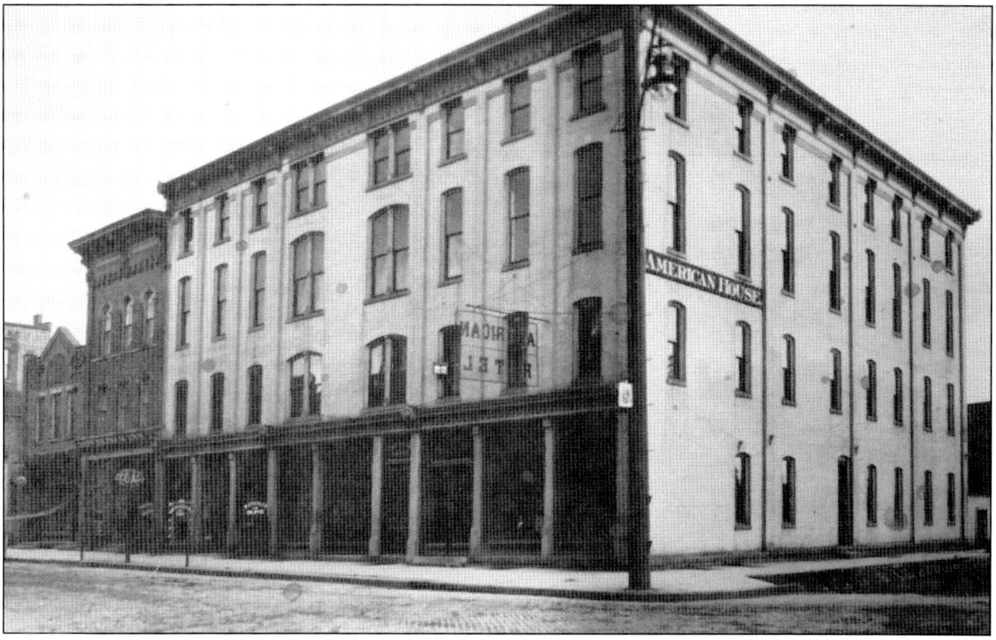

Michael Staebler constructed the building on Washington Street that now houses the Earle restaurant. It began life with the name Germania and was used as a hotel. The third story, which was at one time the top floor, was the ballroom where concerts, lectures, and other social meetings were held. In 1895, the family divided the ballroom into more guest rooms, built out the fourth story, and changed the name to the American House.

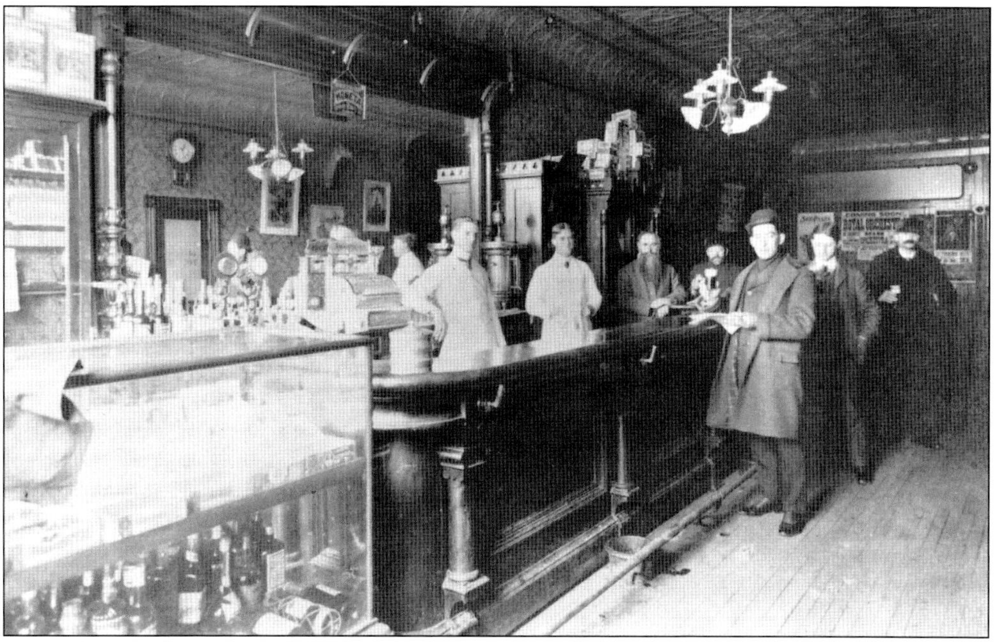

Pictured in 1905 is the bar at the American House, with bartenders Corson and Frazier posing for the camera. Traveling salesmen, actors, performers, and other kinds of visitors stayed in the hotel, which was located at 123 West Washington Street. During Prohibition, visitors to the saloon had to settle for soft drinks. The Earle is located in this building's basement today.

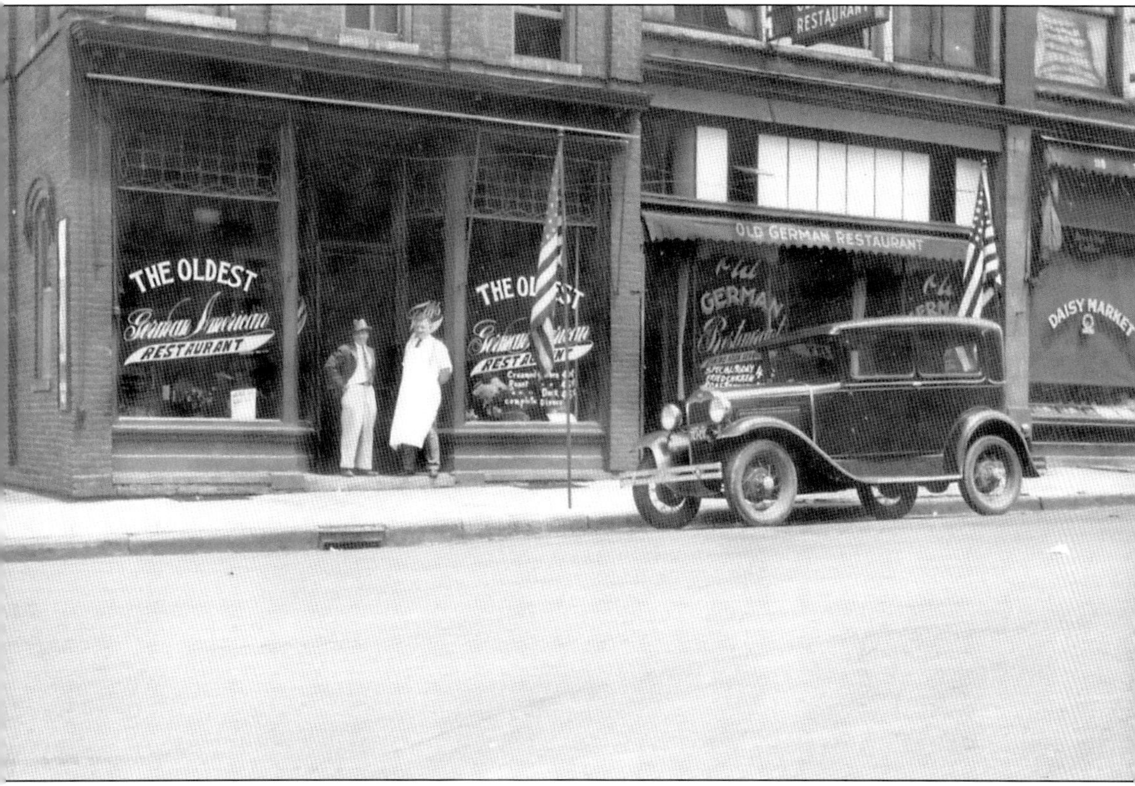

Metzger's German American Restaurant was opened by the Metzger and Kuhn families in 1928. Wilhelm and Marie Metzger and their children, along with their partner Christian Kuhn, rented the space from the Flautz family and named their original restaurant the German American. Mr. Metzger (right) and Mr. Kuhn are shown here in 1928. Today, the third and fourth generations of Metzgers, including John Metzger, continue the tradition of excellent service and delicious German food. In 1946, Wilhem's brother Fritz Metzger bought the Old German Restaurant next door. (Courtesy of John Metzger.)

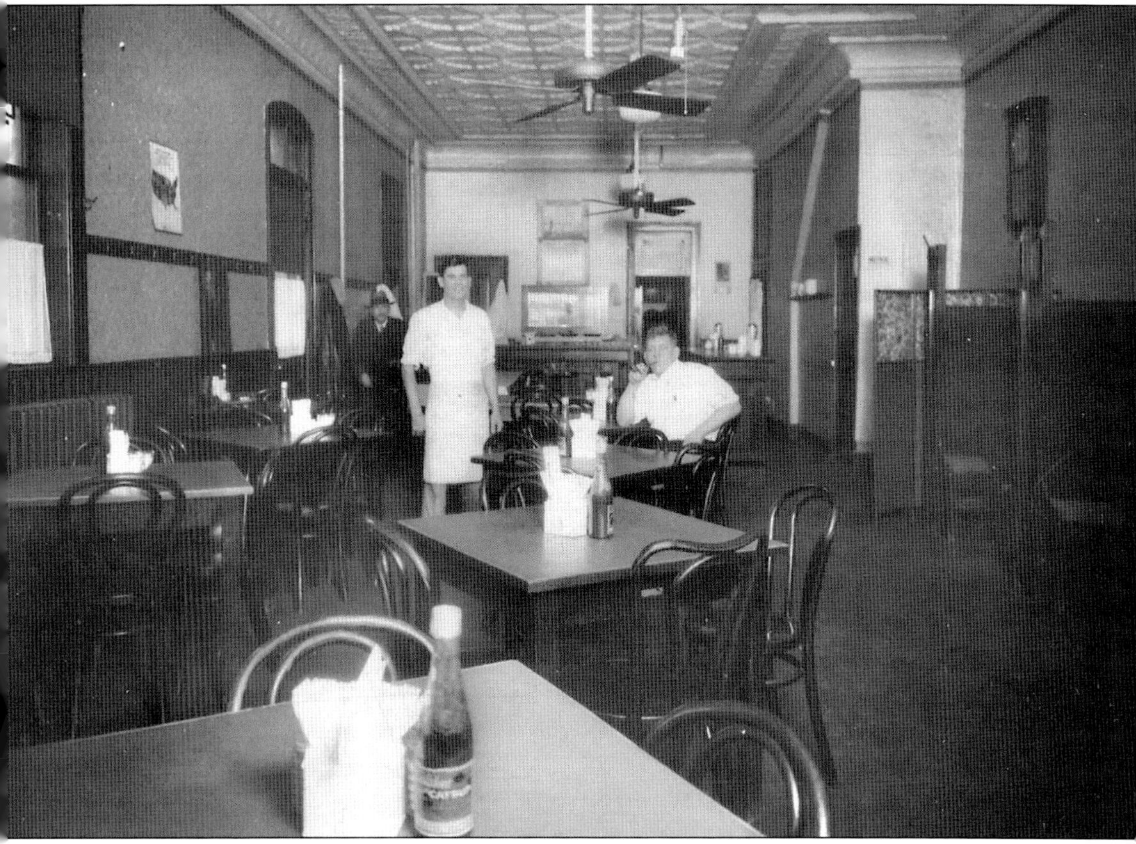

This is an interior shot of the restaurant, featuring Wilhelm Metzger (sitting down) and partner Christian Kuhn. Metzger's restaurant resided at the Ashley Street/Washington Street location until 1936, when it moved to Fourth Avenue and Washington Street (near where the Arena Bar is today). The Metzger's restaurant currently carries on in nearby Scio Township; meanwhile, a new version of the Old German restaurant opened on Washington in 2013. The new bar, while unaffiliated with the Metzger family, features an Old German sign as well as a table from the original restaurant. (Courtesy of John Metzger.)

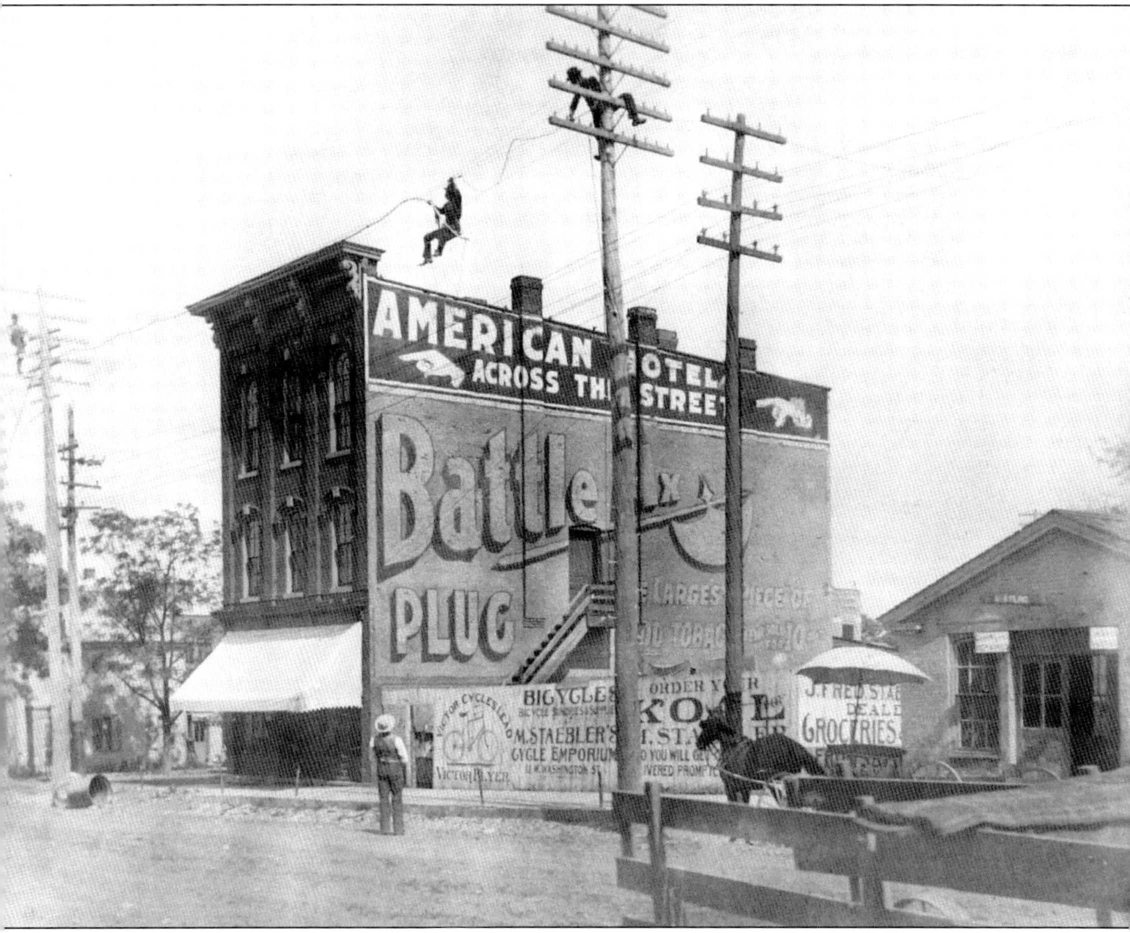

An advertisement for the American Hotel is seen here on the building that had once been John J. Wagner Jr.'s carriage and blacksmith shop. Wagner Jr. constructed the shop in 1869, carrying on a blacksmithing tradition started by his father, who arrived from Germany in 1837. Under the awning is Oswald Dietz's saloon, which operated after 1895. Washington Street at Ashley Street has long hosted bars and saloons, including the Barrell House, Flautz's, Metzger's, the Del Rio, and its current occupant, the Den, which is part of the adjoining Grizzly Peak Brewing Company.

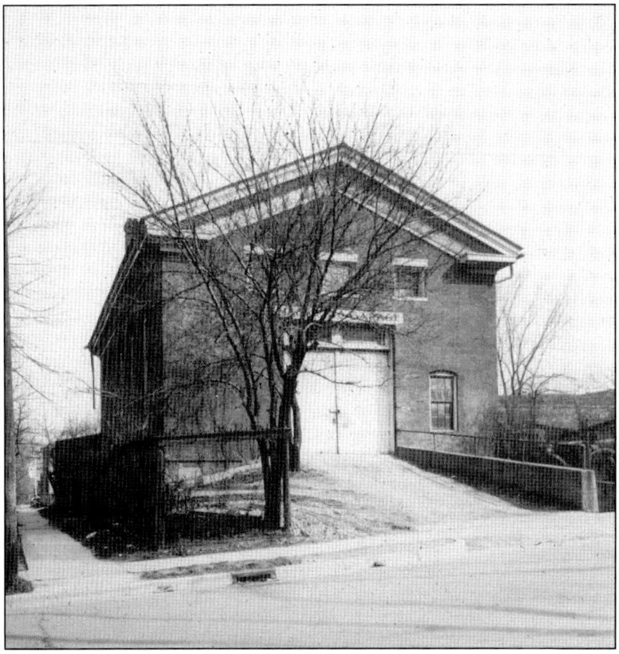

At one time, the Mack & Co. department store was the largest store in downtown Ann Arbor. Its delivery wagons and trucks were kept off site at a barn located on West Washington and South First Streets. This was originally the oldest German church in town. The site later became part of a Chevrolet dealership.

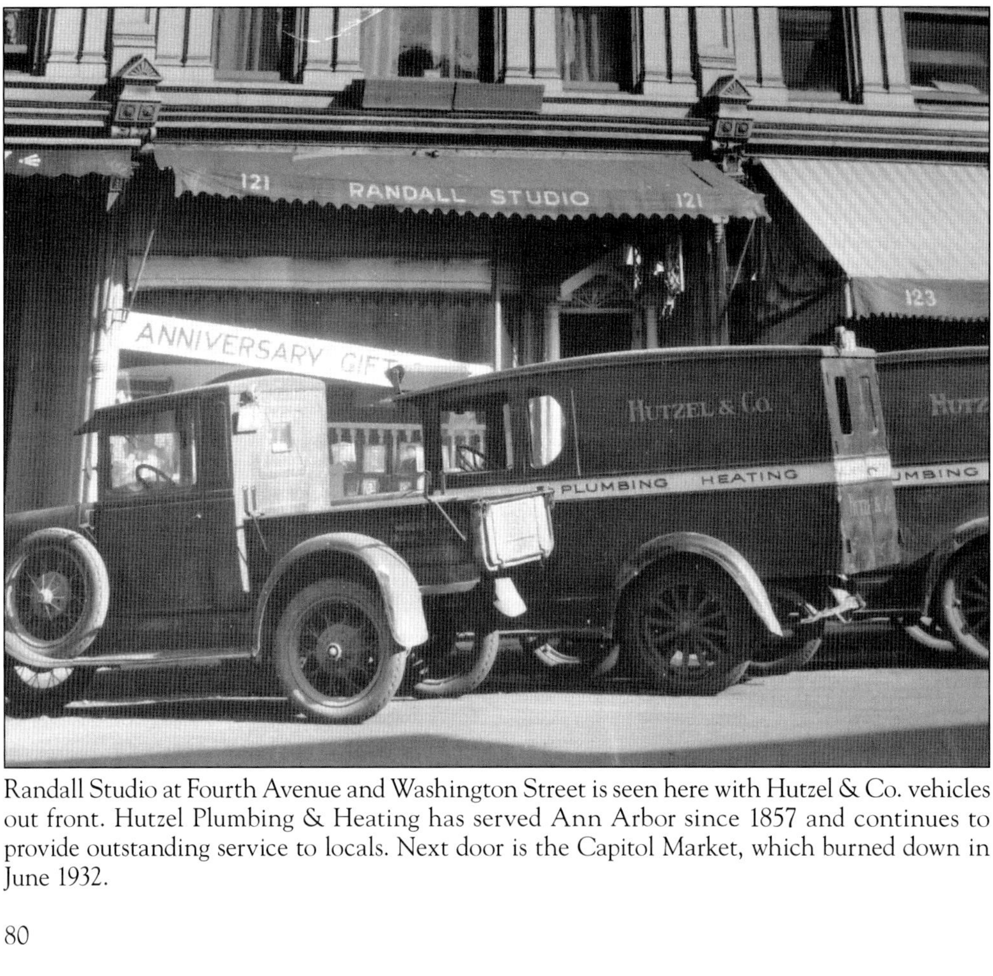

Randall Studio at Fourth Avenue and Washington Street is seen here with Hutzel & Co. vehicles out front. Hutzel Plumbing & Heating has served Ann Arbor since 1857 and continues to provide outstanding service to locals. Next door is the Capitol Market, which burned down in June 1932.

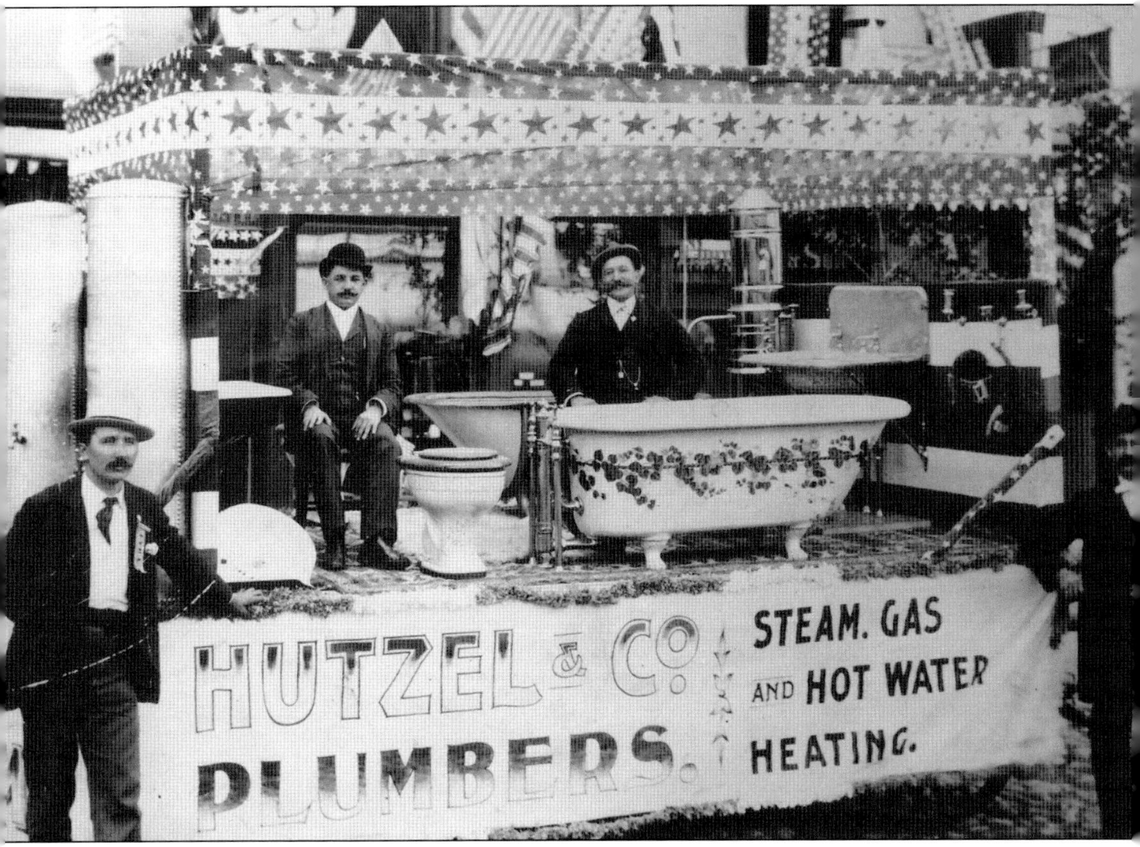

This is a photograph of a parade float from Hutzel & Co., which moved from Main Street to 119 East Washington Street in 1919. After the move, two of August's sons, Hermann and Titus, later joined the business. Titus learned the plumbing trade, and with this knowledge he steered the company to become what it is today. Water closets, steam and hot-water systems, and claw-foot bathtubs were in demand, and Hutzel & Co. was there to fill those needs. The business was also the contractor for the city's new waterworks. The privately held Ann Arbor Waterworks Company provided Hutzel & Co. with the opportunity to lay miles of cast-iron water pipe under the streets of Ann Arbor during the late 1880s. The company continued to grow as a second August Hutzel (son of Titus) joined his father and Uncle Hermann in the business in 1915. Titus's son August retired in 1953, and a new partnership was formed. Even though the Hutzel family is no longer directly involved with the business, the company continues in business to this day.

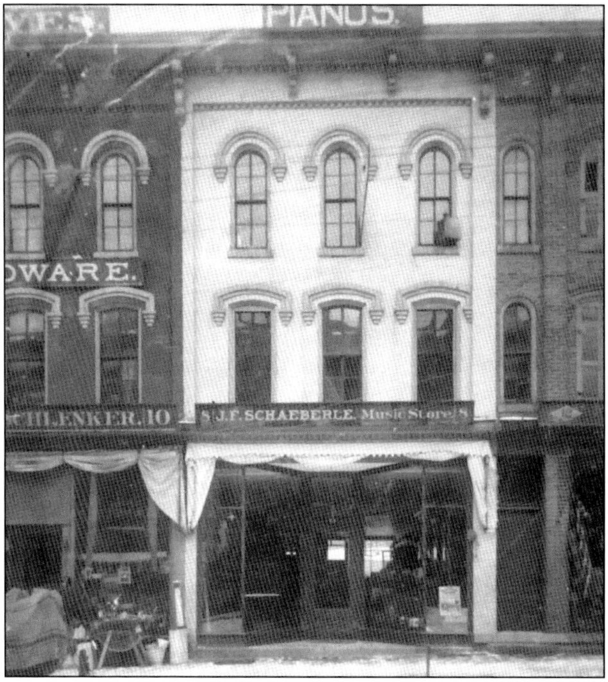

In August 1896, J.F. Schaeberle opened his music store at 114 West Liberty Street, pictured here. In a little over a decade, he outgrew the space and moved to 110 South Main Street. During that time, he also took his son Ernest on as a partner. Schaeberle & Son carried pianos, along with "everything that you might expect to find in an up-to-date music store." Today, the Pacific Rim restaurant is in this location and is joined by a number of restaurants, including the Grange, the Alley Bar, the West End Grill, and the Old Town tavern.

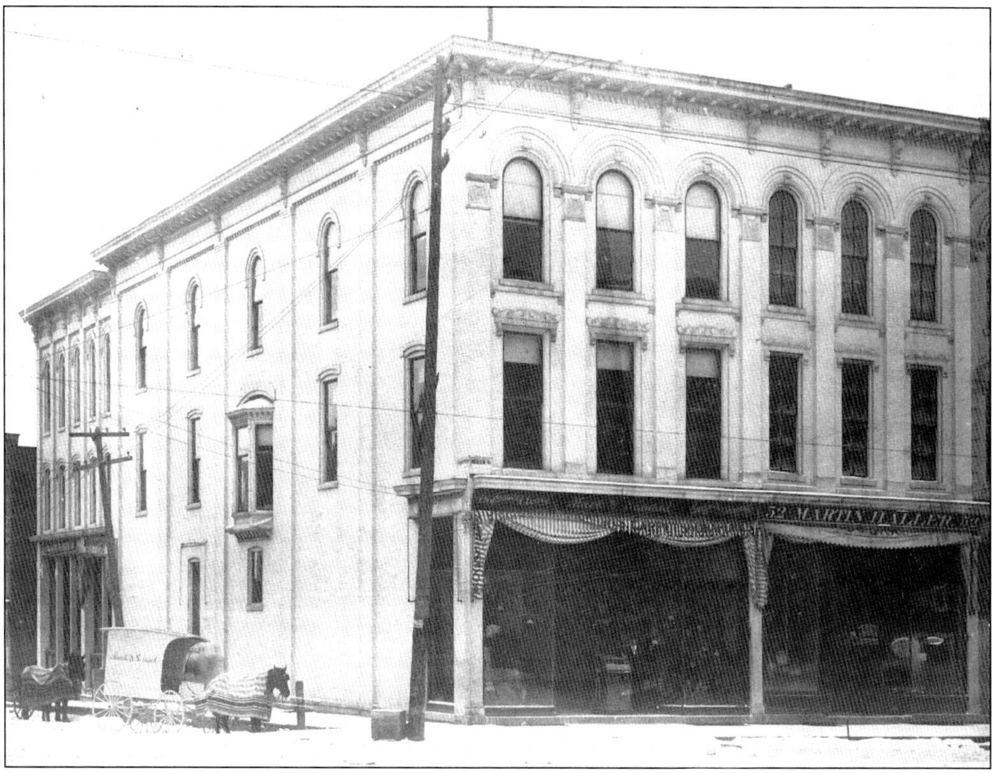

Liberty Street was home to the businesses of Mack & Schmid and Martin Haller, with the latter selling furniture. A 1969 fire ruined the Haller Building, and it was later torn down. Damages were estimated upwards of $1 million.

A brewery wagon makes a beer delivery in this 1898 photograph. With a large population of German immigrants, Ann Arbor had many breweries; sadly, most did not survive the Prohibition. Also seen here is the Kurtz saloon, located at 120 West Liberty Street, which is now home to the Old Town Tavern and the West End Grill. Note the steep drop-off from the sidewalk.

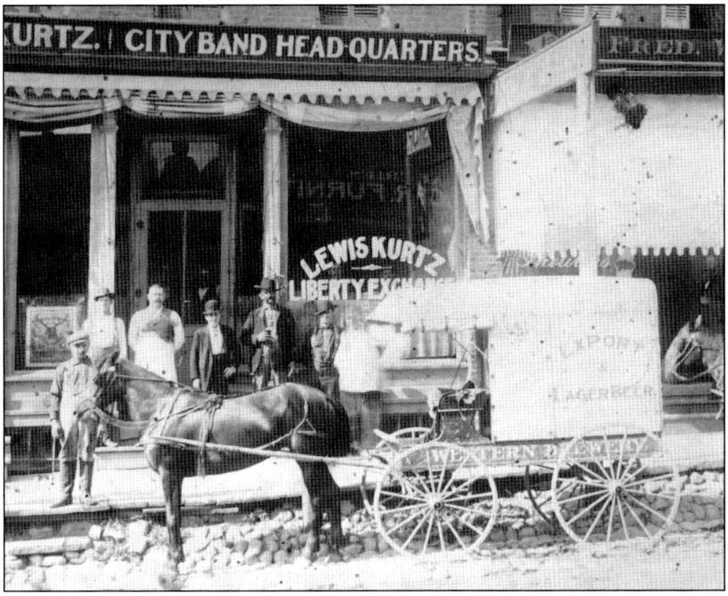

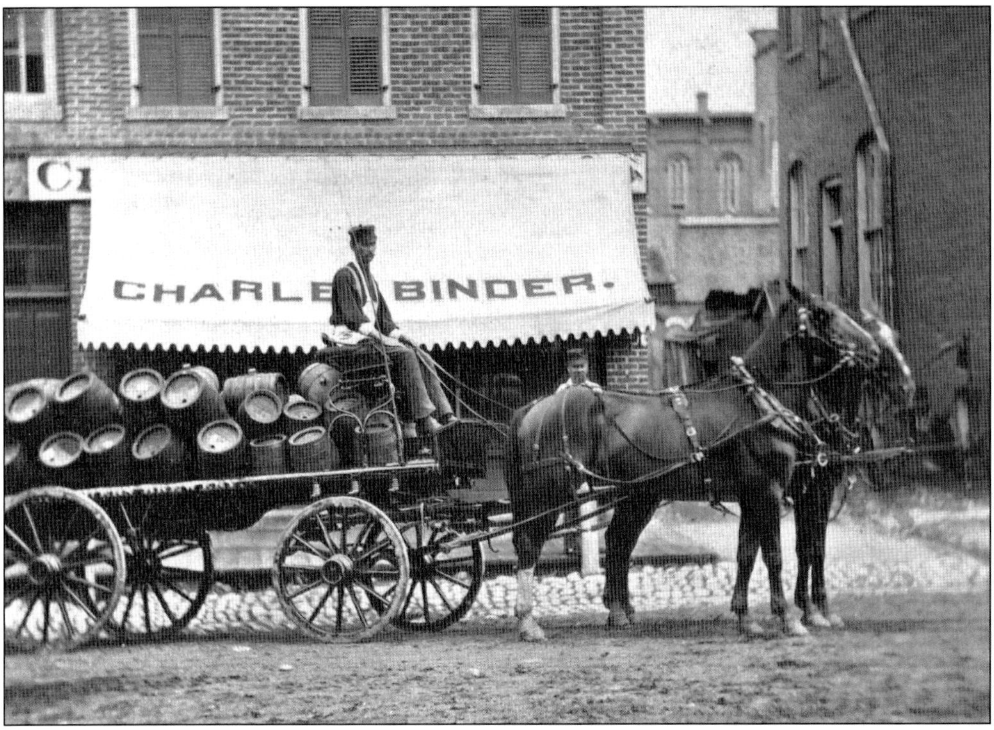

Charles Binder was a German emigrant from Wuertemberg. After working for Henry Binder for two years, Charles opened his own saloon. Located on Liberty Street, at what is now the Alley Bar, the saloon went out of business in 1897 due to of Charles's poor health. He passed away at the age of 52, just a week after moving from 208 West Liberty to West Jefferson Street.

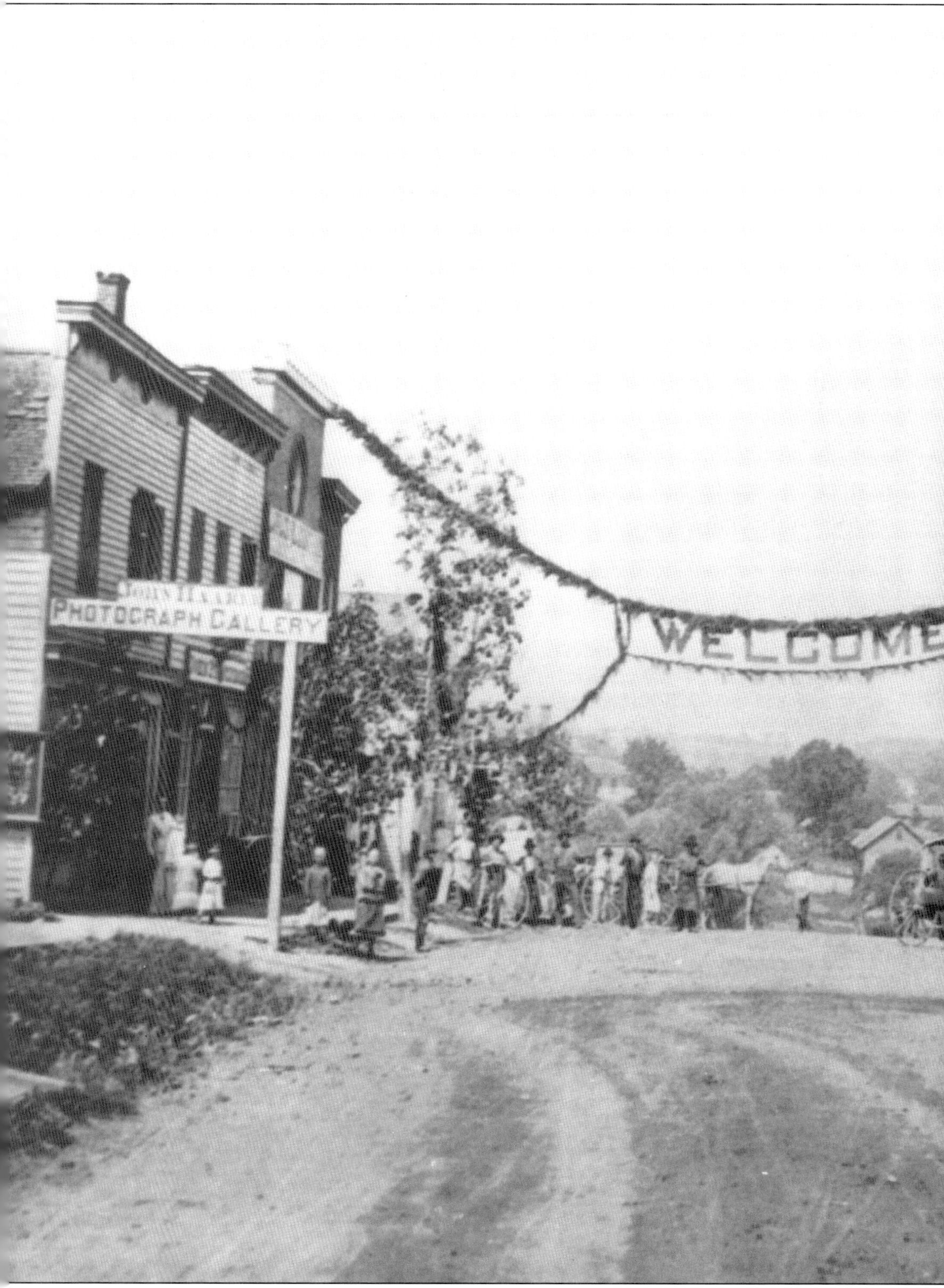
PHOTOGRAPH GALLERY
WELCOME

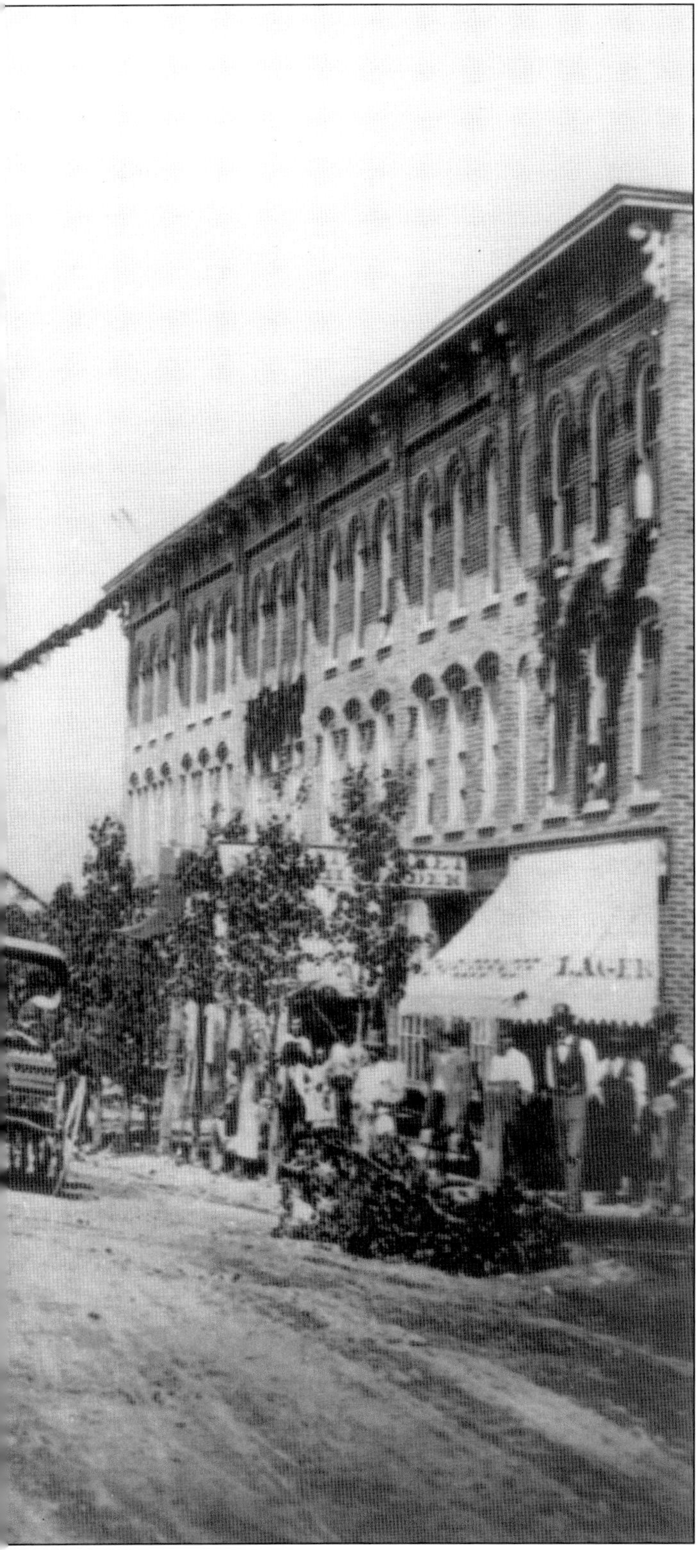

Ann Arbor's large German American population found many ways to celebrate its culture. In this 1870s image is a large banner hanging on Liberty Street celebrating German American Day. Germans began arriving in Ann Arbor as early as 1829, and a third of Ann Arbor's population was German or of "German extraction" by 1880. Most lived in what is now called the Old West Side. Germans brought many things to town, only one of which was their love of good beer. Germans brought their knowledge of how to make the beverage, along with the tradition of including it at every possible social function. Beer was central to the German culture and was used in such diverse events as entering contracts, ending disputes, or formalizing wedding arrangements.

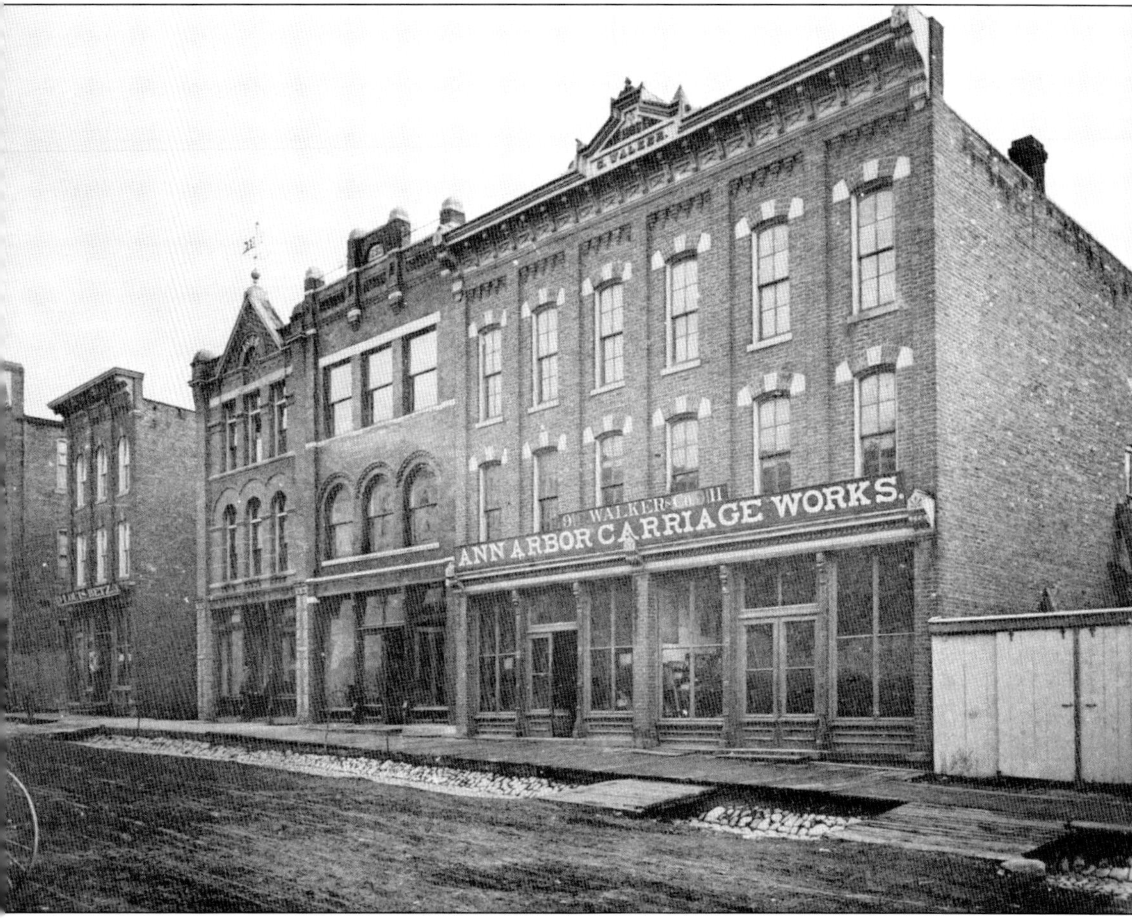

This corner of West Liberty and Ashley Streets was home to Christian Walker's Ann Arbor Carriage Works. Proud artisans built custom carriages at this business. Carpenters, blacksmiths, and upholsterers worked in the space years ago, but the tradition of artists carries on to this day as the space now houses the Ann Arbor Art Center. The carriage trade thrived until the 1920s, when more automobiles were being built and serviced. Workers did not have to worry about what to do on their lunch breaks, as there were a fair number of saloons in the vicinity that catered to the men who worked in the area. Workingmen were often seen carrying beer by the bucket at lunchtime.

This property at 326 West Liberty Street was the home of Peter Brehm, founder of the Western Brewery. The brewery, established in 1861, was located at 416 Fourth Street. Brehm named it after its location in the heart of the German neighborhood, today's Old West Side.

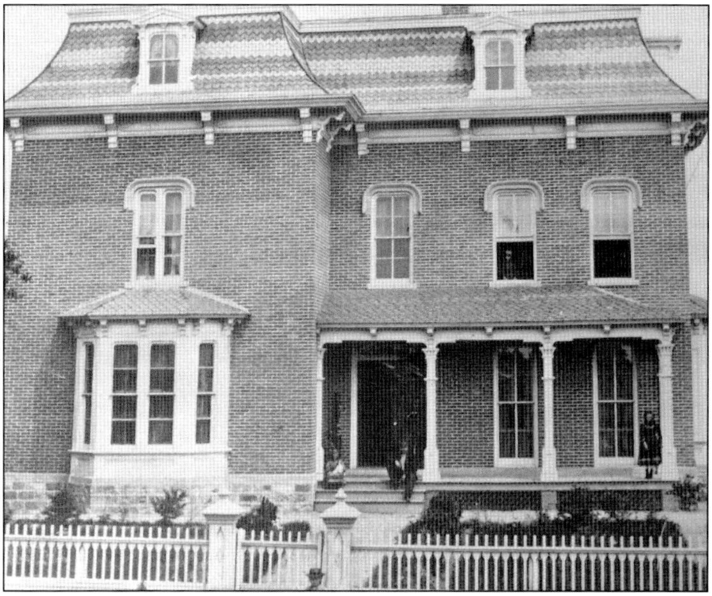

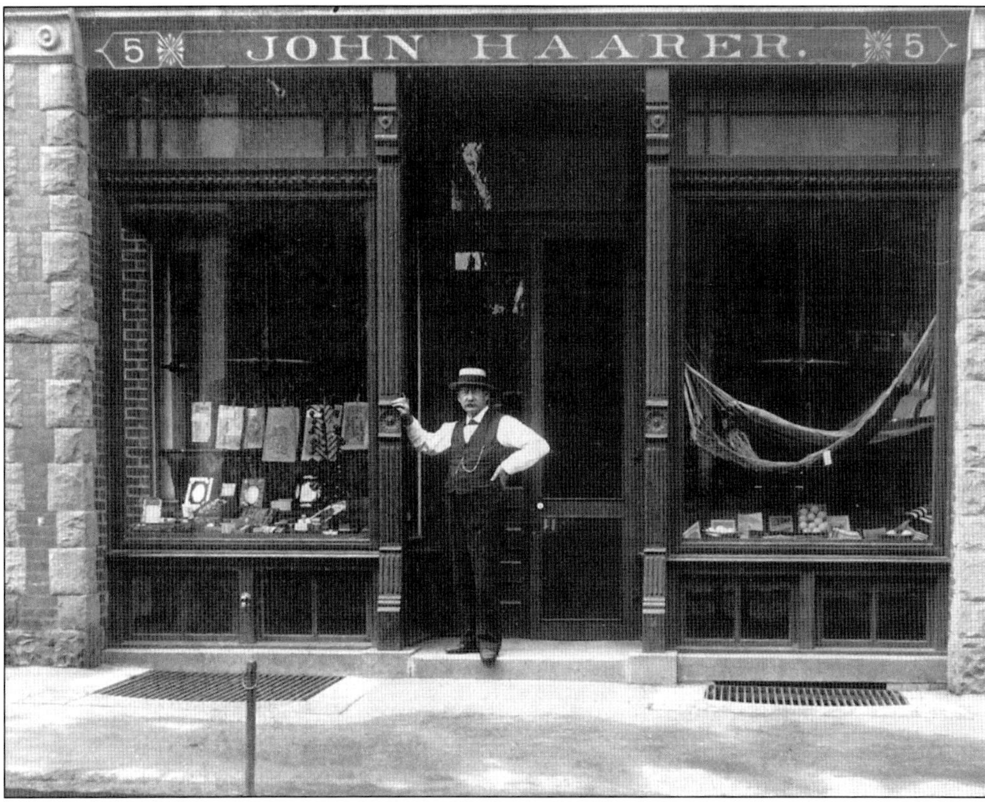

Built in 1888, the John Haarer Building boasted the city's first plateglass storefront window. Haarer, a photographer by trade, also sold books and insurance from this store. Haarer and his family lived upstairs, and his studio and darkroom were in the back of the store. The building survived an attempt at demolition in the 1960s and now houses the West Side Book Shop. The bookstore's restroom is where the darkroom used to be located.

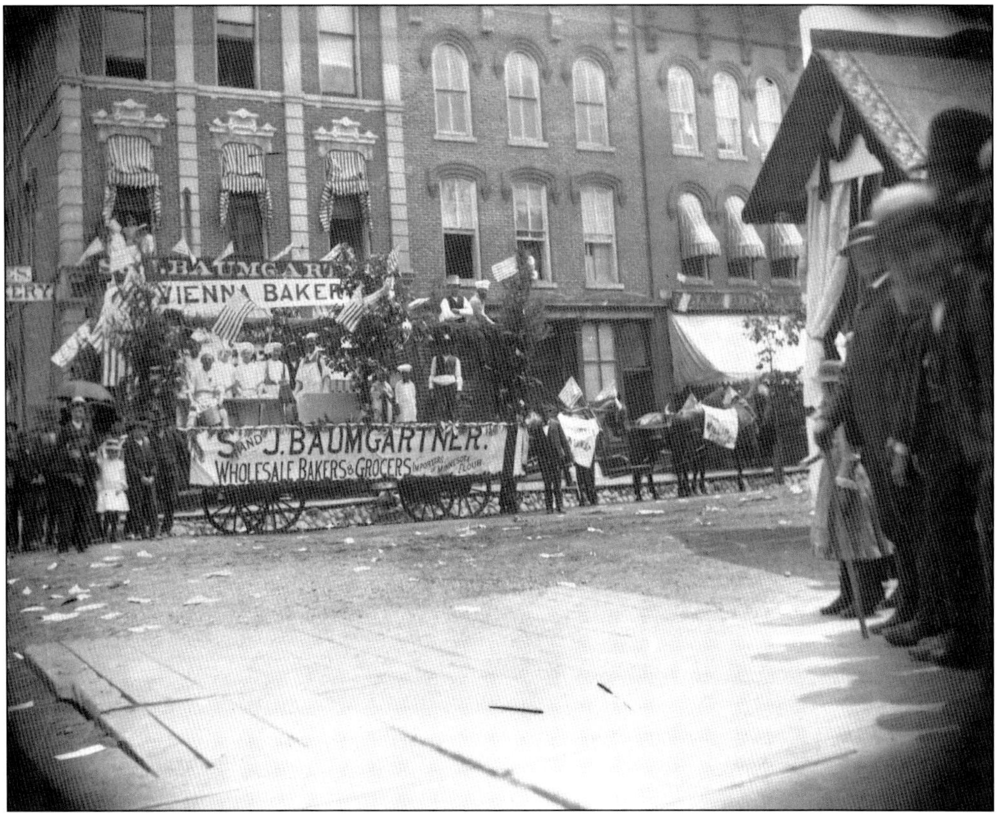

Mr. Baumgartner advertised baked goods from his shop at Liberty and Main Streets. An 1893 article in the *Ann Arbor Argus* called his shop "the center of retail grocery and bakery trade of Ann Arbor." The business began in 1878 and employed eight men as bakers and clerks plus three delivery wagons. Further, the *Argus* boasted that "Mr. B" possessed the qualities necessary to succeed as a merchant and enjoyed the "fullest confidence" of the people of Ann Arbor. This photograph is from a parade on Liberty Street.

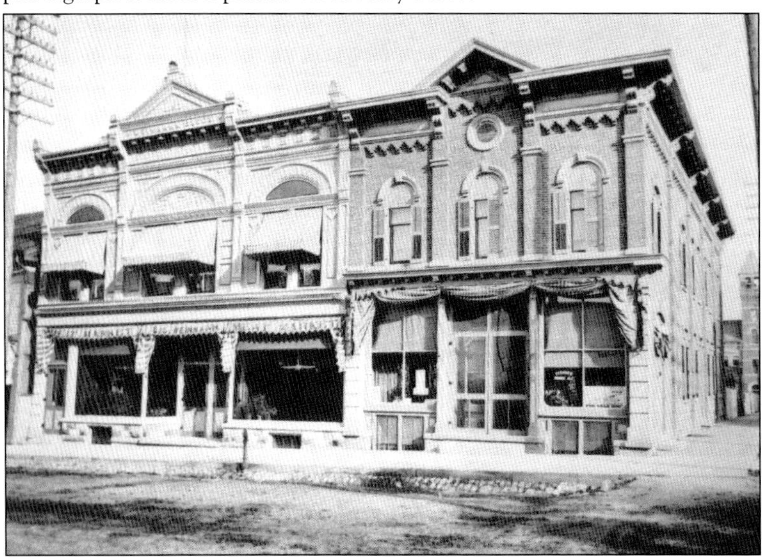

The Weinmann Block, located at East Washington Street and South Fifth Avenue, is currently home to the Blue Nile restaurant. The meat market included a sign advertising Vernors Ale, which is still a popular drink around Michigan.

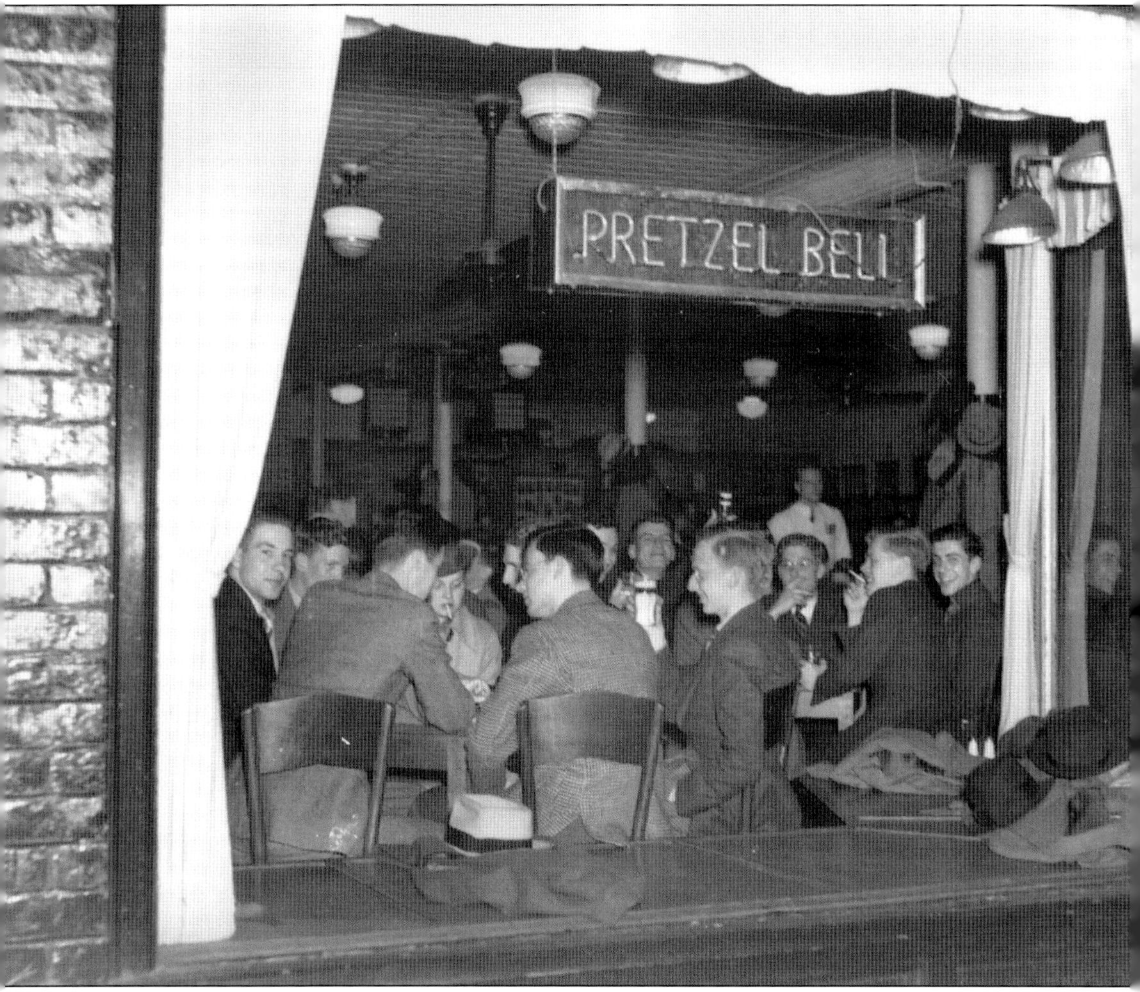

Many longtime residents of Ann Arbor still bemoan the loss of the Pretzel Bell restaurant, which was located on Liberty Street at Fourth Avenue. Some called it the preferred place to drink when one "turned of age." Others remembered it as the place of choice for the *Michigan Daily* staff and the Men's Glee Club. "Chug a lug" contests were held in which students stood on the tables and drank while the Bell's bell tolled. A 1965 *Sports Illustrated* article reported that hundreds of students could be found at the bar on an "ordinary midweek night" and that on average they consumed seven and a half kegs of beer each night. Clint Castor and his family owned the restaurant/bar from 1934 until it closed in 1985. The building is still known as the "Pretzel Bell Building" and has housed several restaurants since the closing of the Bell.

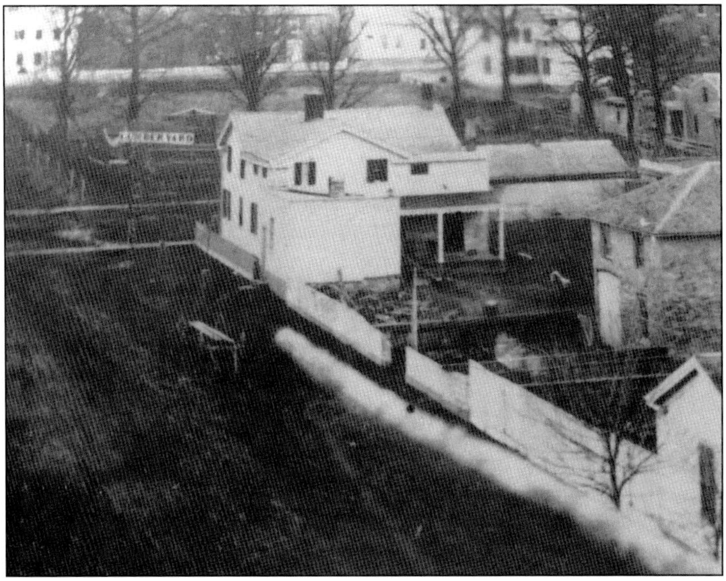

This photograph of Liberty and Main Streets was taken in 1875. The lumberyard in the background is now the location of the Ann Arbor Federal Building, and the dirt road is now paved and is often busy with traffic. In addition to a post office, the Ann Arbor Federal Building houses various federal government offices and part of the US District Court for the Eastern District of Michigan.

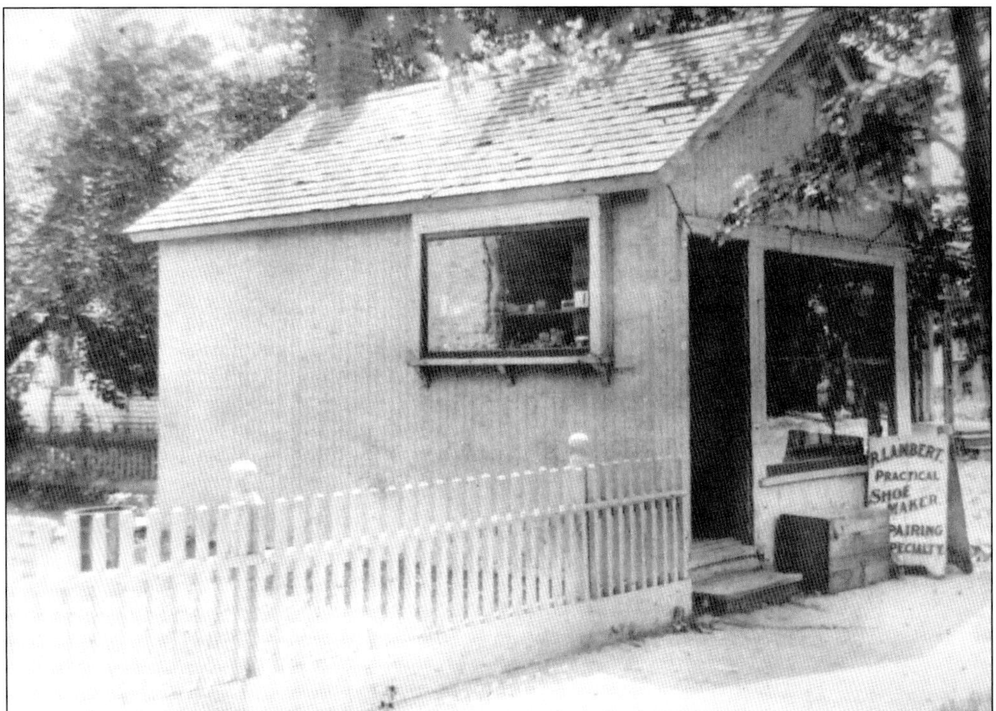

R. Lambert's "practical" shoe-making business was on East Liberty Street. This location later became the home of the much-loved Jacobson's department store. After Jacobson's closed, the space was leased to Borders, which occupied the space until 2011. The space is currently occupied by the second location of the locally owned Knight's Steakhouse, Sweetwater's coffeehouse, and the Chicago-based Slurping Turtle.

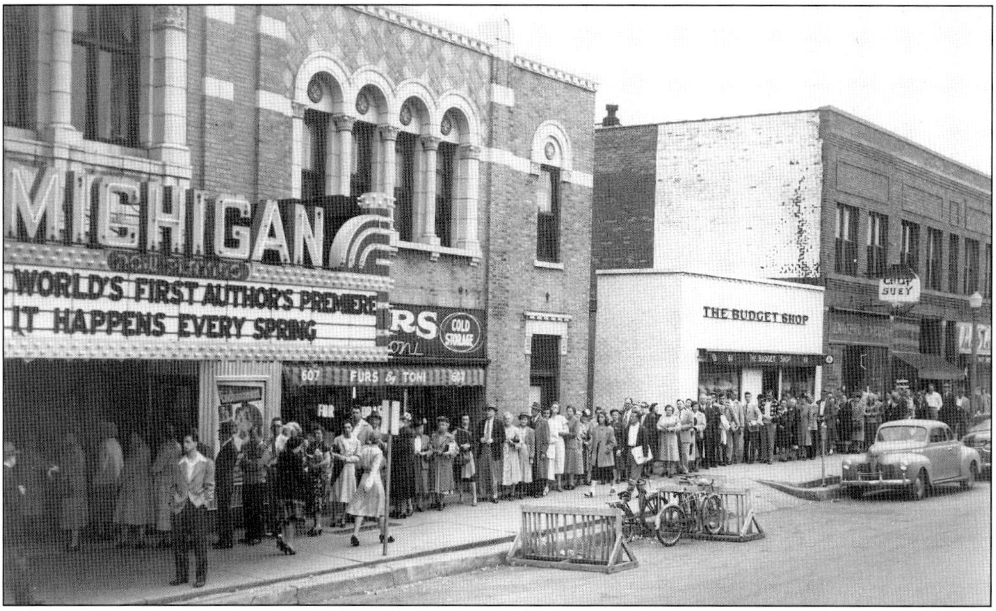

Opened in 1928, the Michigan Theater remains as a thriving local art house theater. The main theater auditorium seats 1,700 people and features beautiful architectural details. For a brief time, the theater showed vaudeville acts, but it quickly embraced silent and talkie movies. Like many other theaters, it suffered from the advent of television and other modern distractions. In 1979, the building's future was uncertain. Fortunately, members of the Motor City Theater Organ Society, philanthropist Margaret D. Towsley, and organist Henry Aldridge urged people to take action and to save the theater. It not only was saved, but it also underwent a renovation to restore the original design. The theater hosts independent movies, film series, silent films, live performances, and many other special events throughout the year. Two of the many annual highlights are the long-standing Ann Arbor Film Festival and the more recently created Cinetopia festival, which screens films in the early summer and has proven to be a hit with local audiences.

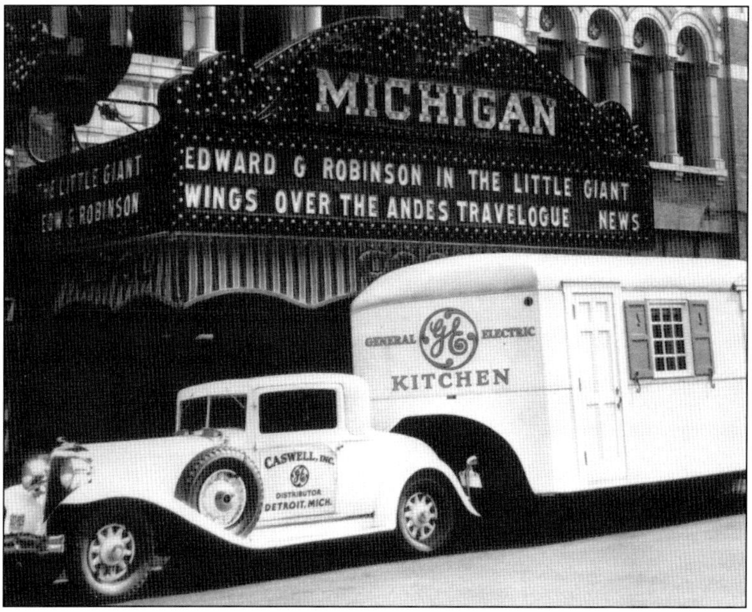

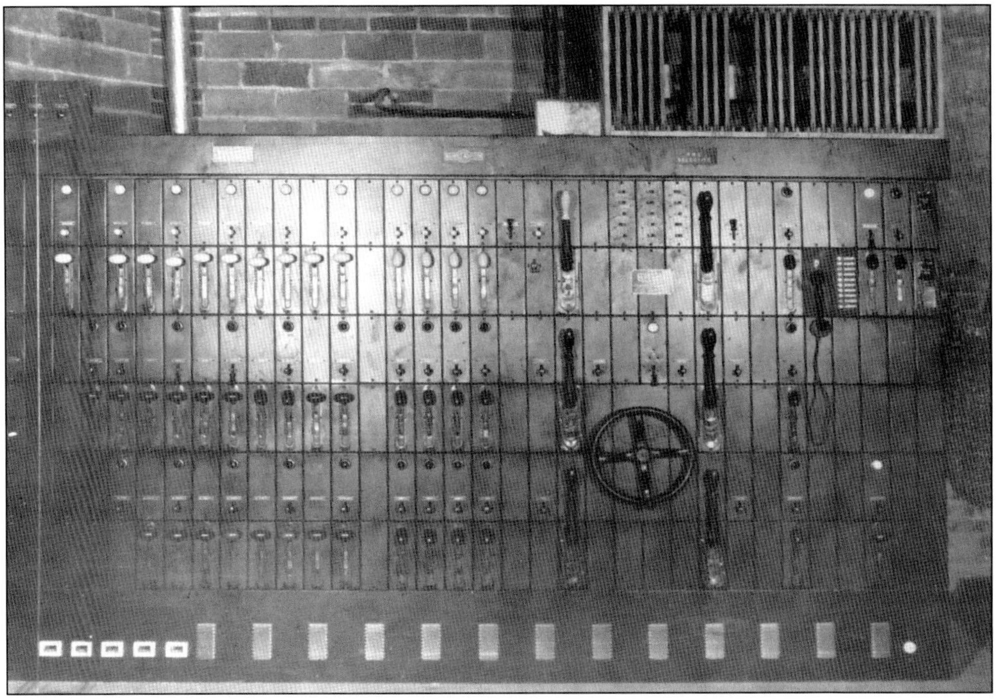

At one time, this was the main control board for the Michigan Theater, but modern updates have since been installed. One thing that has not changed is the Barton Theater Pipe Organ, installed before the theater opened. The organ was specifically designed to accompany silent movies and vaudeville acts. It was one of 7,000 such organs installed in movie palaces throughout the country and is one of the few that remains in its original home. In the photograph below, the pit orchestra readies itself for a performance. Today, the Ann Arbor Symphony Orchestra and the Ann Arbor Concert Band continue the tradition of live music at the theater.

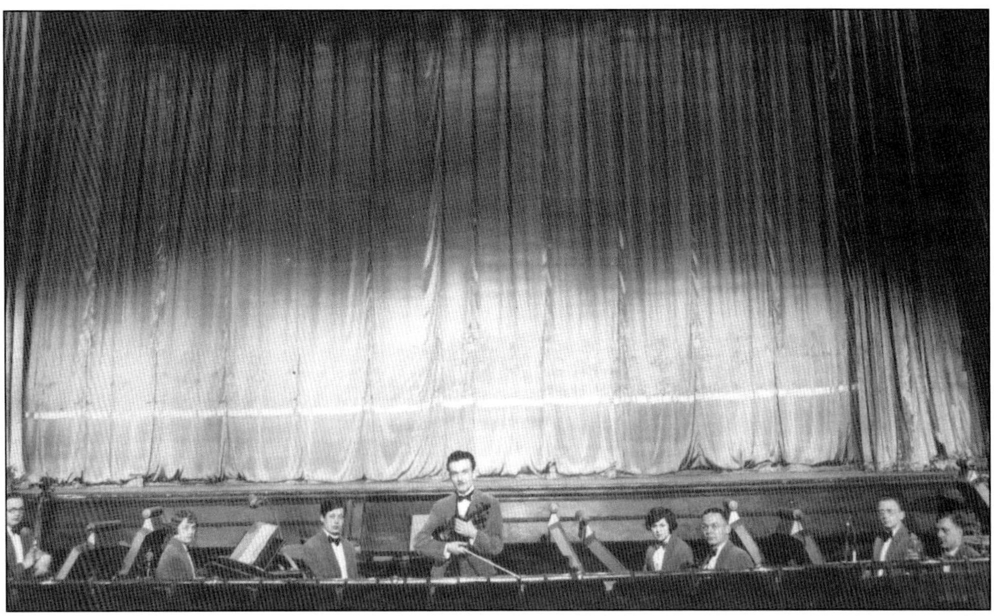

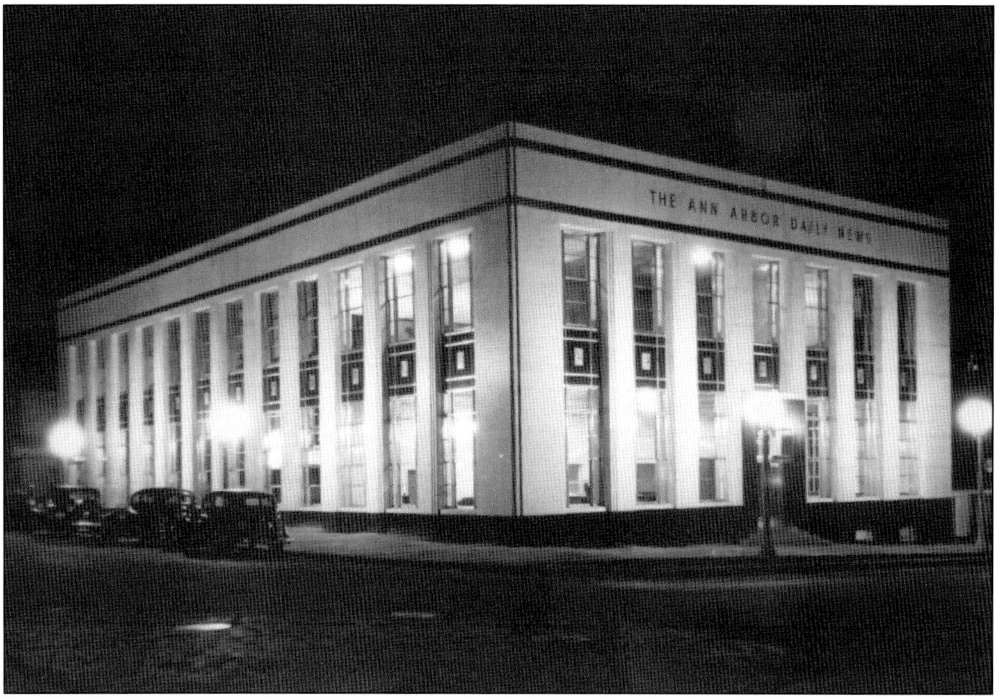

The Ann Arbor News Building at Huron Street and Division Street is seen in an undated photograph. The building remains standing, but the daily printed newspaper is gone. After 174 years, the *Ann Arbor News* ceased publication in 2009. AnnArbor.com became the daily paper for the city, existing online and in Thursday and Sunday print editions. AnnArbor.com rechristened itself the *Ann Arbor News* in 2013.

The Ladies Library Association Building was located on the south side of Huron Street between Fifth Avenue and Division Street. The association first met in 1866 in the basement of a church, and for the next two decades the women hosted speeches, presented papers, and held fundraisers. The fundraisers proved successful enough that, in 1880, they were able to purchase land on which to construct a permanent building. This 1885 image shows the result of those efforts.

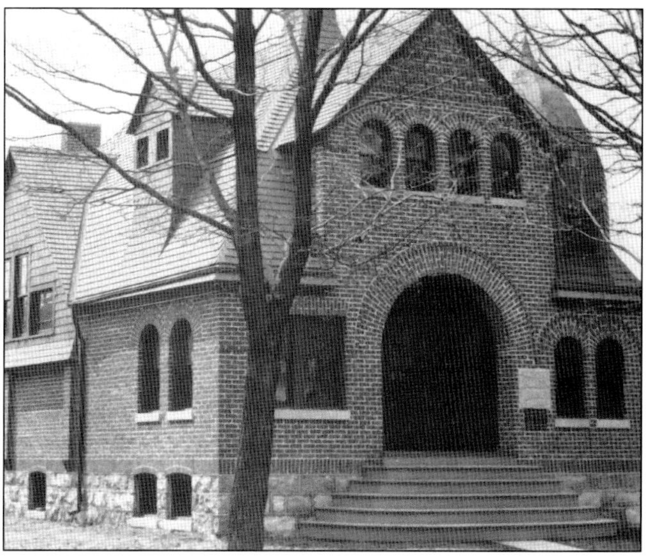

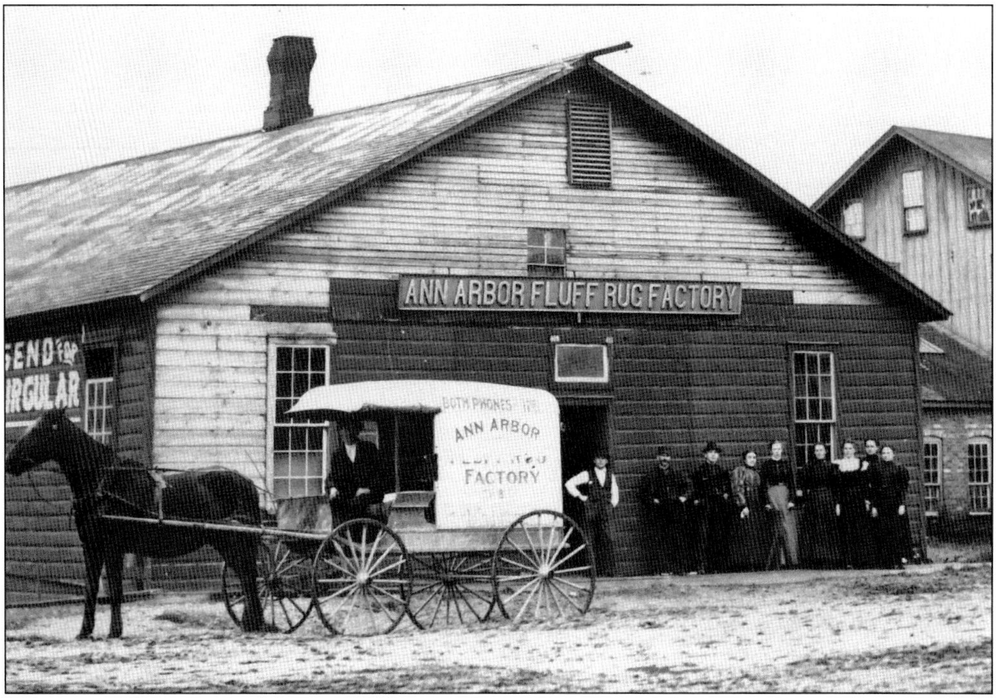

The Ann Arbor Fluff Rug Factory was once located in the Germania Hall on Second Street. When it outgrew that location, it moved to 409–421 West Huron Street. At one time, it was the largest rug manufacturer in the country. George and Henry Schlemmer owned the business.

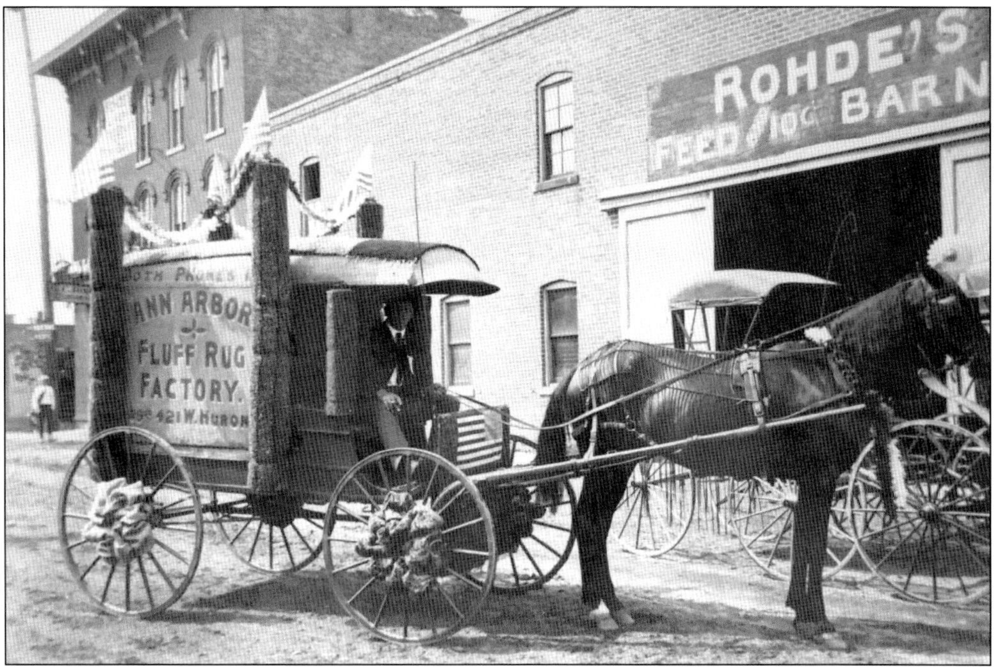

Here is a horse-drawn cart of the rug factory. Buying a new rug was more expensive than recycling, so many people opted for the latter option. Recycled rugs ended up being softer, but not necessarily fluffier, than the originals.

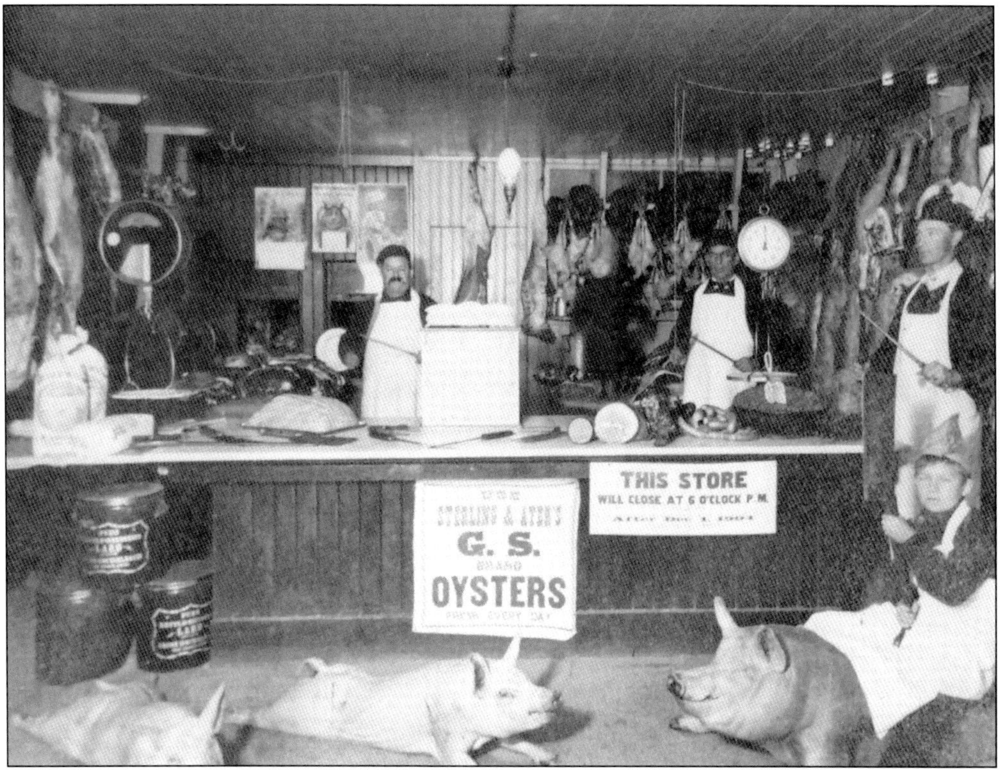

The Eschelbach Meat Market was located at 202 East Huron Street, as seen in this 1907 image. Note the very fresh meat hanging all over the store. Butcher and owner Jacob Eschelbach was known as "Jake" to customers and was in business for 41 years. He passed away in 1943 and was interred in Forest Hill Cemetery.

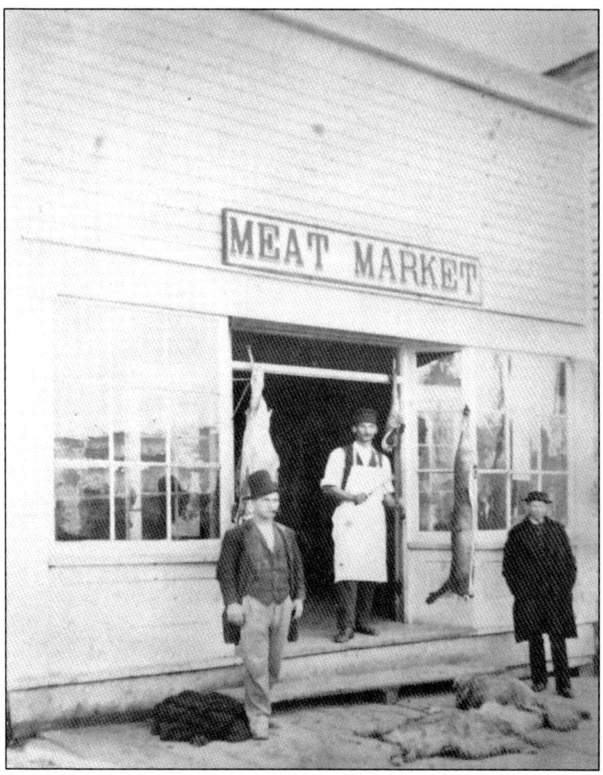

Several members of the Vogel family owned meat markets in Ann Arbor. Louis Vogel ran one at Huron Street and Fifth Avenue, as shown here in the mid-1880s. Louis and his brother Martin (also in the meat business) are pictured. Charles Vogel opened his meat market at 115 East Ann Street around 1900.

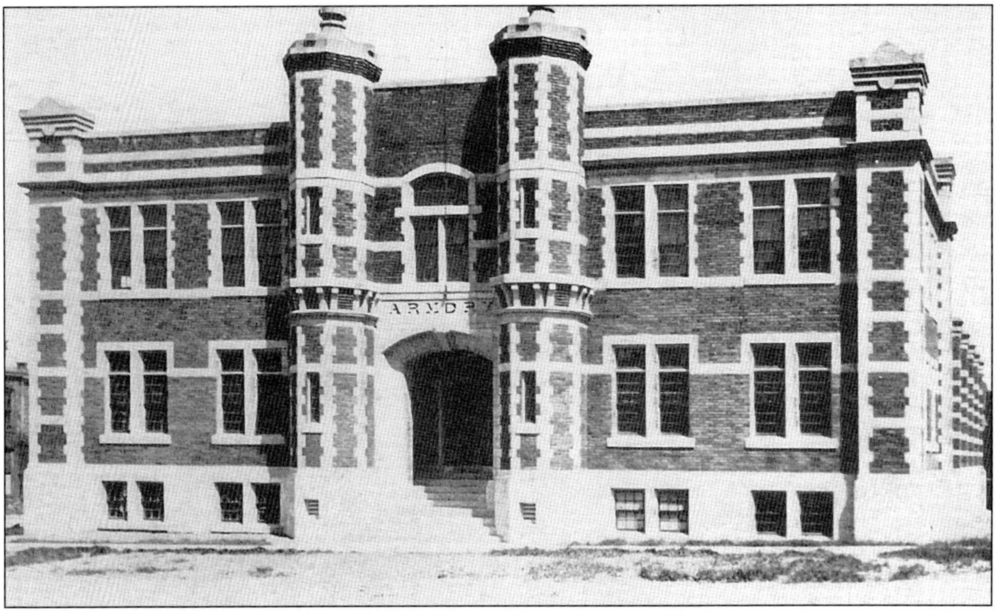

Built in 1913, the armory remains standing on Ann Street. Once housing classrooms, offices, and other activities of the local militia, it has since been converted into condominiums. It also contained a large hall that was open for public use. This was the first armory built in the city and the third built in the state.

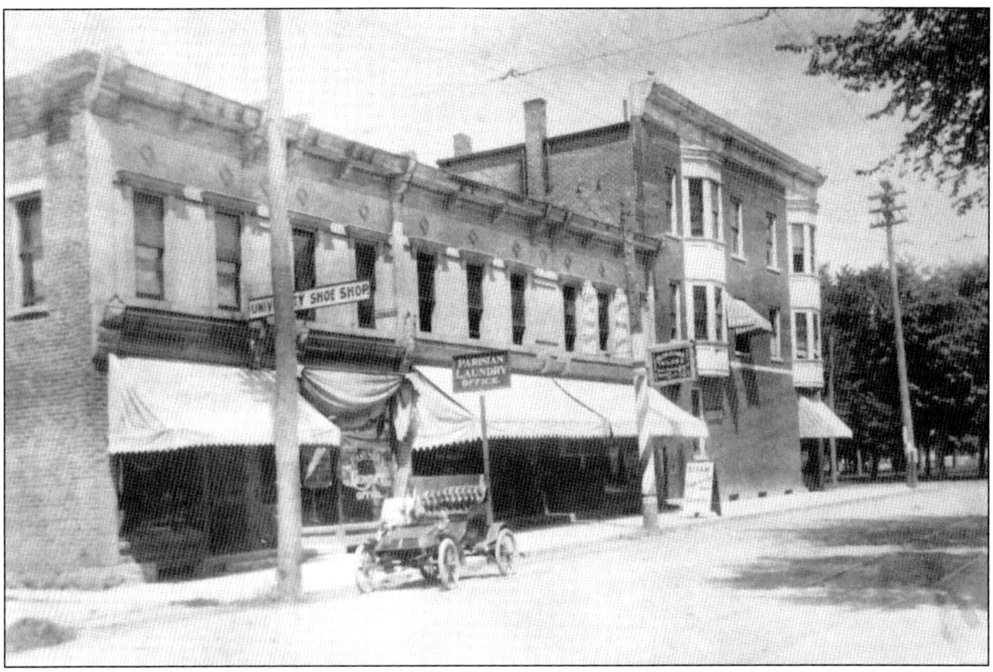

This 1908 photograph shows Lambert's University Shoe Shop, located at 613 East William Street, as well as a nearby laundry and tailor shop. According to the May 1, 1899, *Argus-Democrat*, Sterling Bullock sold the business to Eugene Lambert before moving out to a farm.

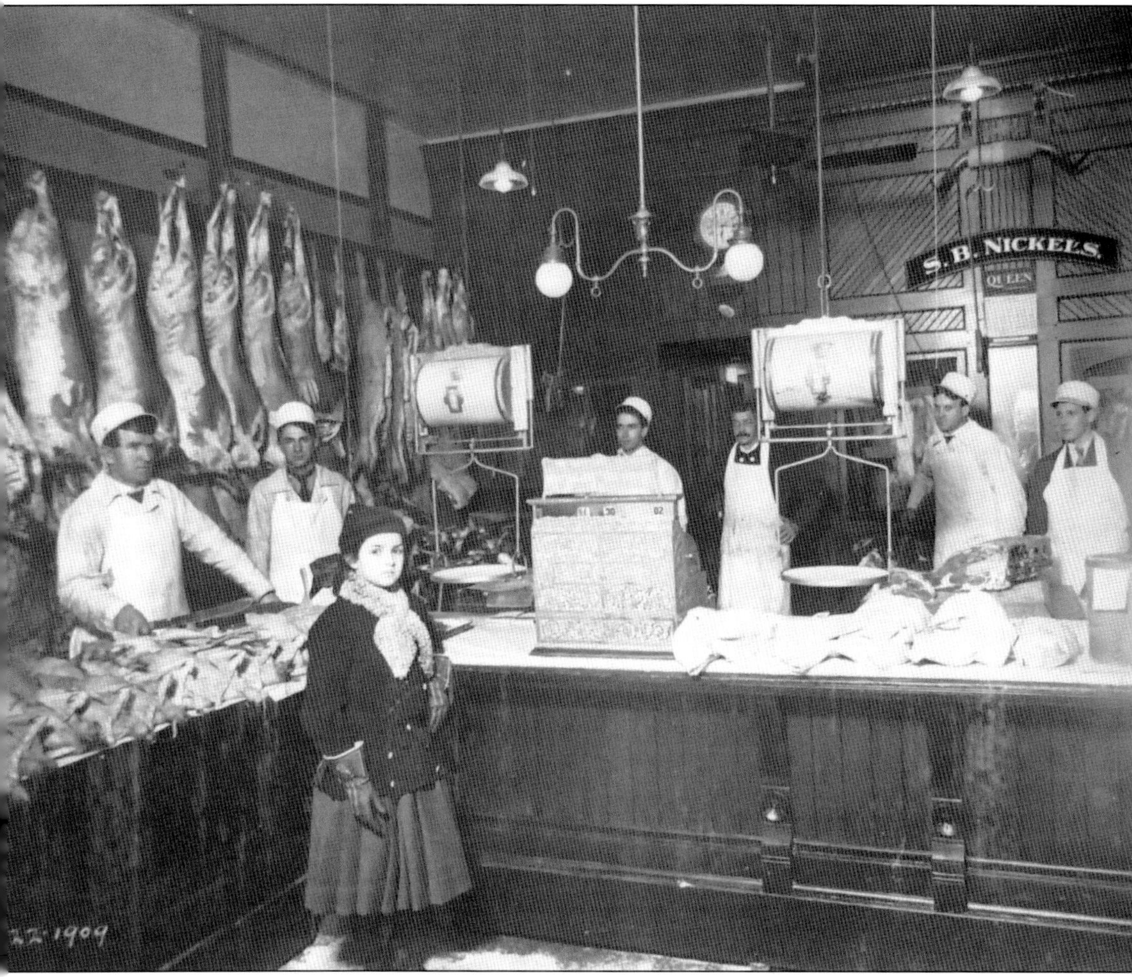

This is the Stafford B. Nickels Meat Market at 607 East William Street in 1909. An ad in the 1911 *Michiganensian* yearbook promised the best poultry, meat, and fish around. The 1890–1891 "Polk Directory" indicated that S.B. Nickels worked as a butcher at Thomas E. Nickel's meat market, located on State Street; John H. Nickels, father of Thomas, also ran a butcher shop. Thomas went to on to tear down the market and build Nickels Arcade, which stands to this day and houses a variety of small businesses and offices. An 1896 issue of the *Argus* announced that S.B. Nickels was retiring from the meat business to focus on his ice business.

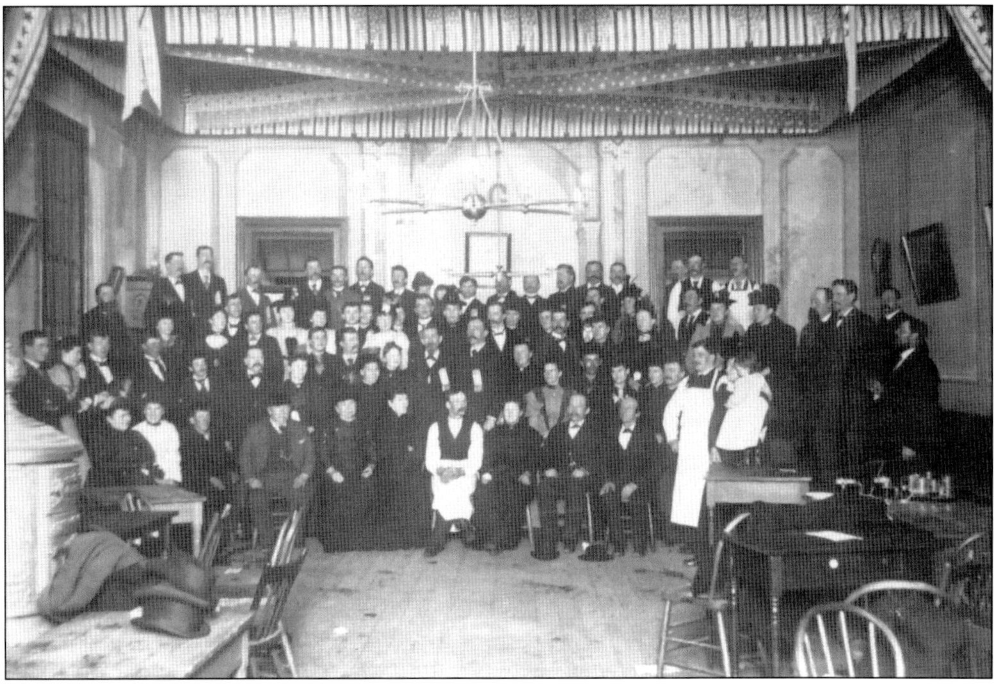

Located at the corner of Second and William Streets, the Germania Hall was dedicated in 1897. The *Argus* detailed the celebration as a "good time for all." The hall was a two-story building with a large basement. The ground floor held a reception room and a dining room, while the second floor had a "neat little stage." At the dedication ceremony, clothiers Lindenschmitt-Apfel & Co. presented an American flag that was 12 feet by 20 feet and was suggested by the *Argus* to be one of the biggest—if not the biggest—flags in the city. A parade, headed by Otto's Band, was also held that day. After a welcome address by Mayor Charles Hiscock, the concert program began. A grand "Festball" was also held, featuring music by the Ann Arbor Orchestra. Refreshments were served, and it sounded like a good time was had by all.

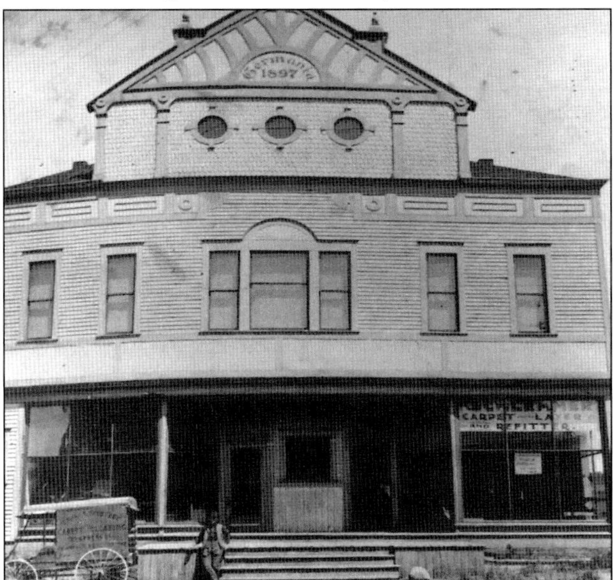

Three

Kerrytown, Lower Town, and Near Downtown

Part of the original village of Annarbour, Kerrytown is named after County Kerry in Ireland. According to Ann Arbor historian Wystan Stevens, the late Ann Arbor lawyer Art Carpenter named Kerrytown. The exact boundaries of Kerrytown have been described in different ways. One such definition is Huron Street to Huron River, and Main Street to the main hospital. For the purpose of this book, the definition includes locations that are not in the described downtown area but are in close enough proximity to be considered worthy of inclusion. For example, the beautiful train depot is located on the edge of the area that is often considered Kerrytown. The very popular Zingerman's Deli can also be found in this area, along with a concert house; Braun Court, which includes a cluster of houses converted into businesses, restaurants, and bars; and a farmers' market.

Many festivals and other activities take place at various times throughout the year in the Kerrytown farmers' market space. The HomeGrown Festival takes place in early September and features local food tastings combined with other events highlighting the local growers. The Kerrytown Book Fest and Kindlefest take place in September and December respectively. The annual African American Festival takes place in June.

Lower Town originally began as a separate town that was once home to a number of mills and other industrial buildings. In 1832, founder Anson Brown built a structure in Lower Town that remains as the oldest commercial building in the city. Lower Town features New York City–based street names such as Wall Street and Broadway Street, as Mr. Brown hailed from New York City. In 1867, Lower Town was annexed into the city of Ann Arbor.

Also included in this section are a few photographs from "near" downtown. Places such as Ann Arbor High School, the Jones School building, and a few businesses are located just outside the traditional downtown but still have an interconnected history. These buildings, as much as anything located inside the Huron Street and William Street boundaries, have made Ann Arbor's downtown what it is today.

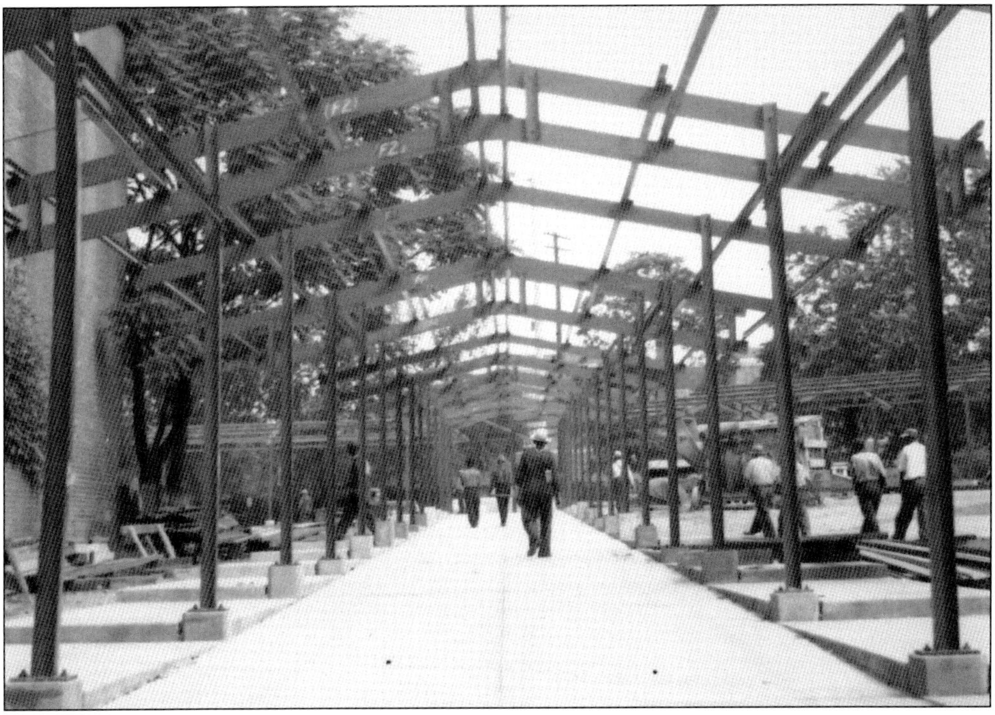

The new farmers' market is under construction in this 1941 image. Originally a curbside market at the old courthouse, the market has been in existence for over 90 years and is held every Saturday throughout the year. For part of the year (May through December), a Wednesday morning market is also in operation. On Wednesday evenings from June through October, an evening market features live music, along with local beer and wine.

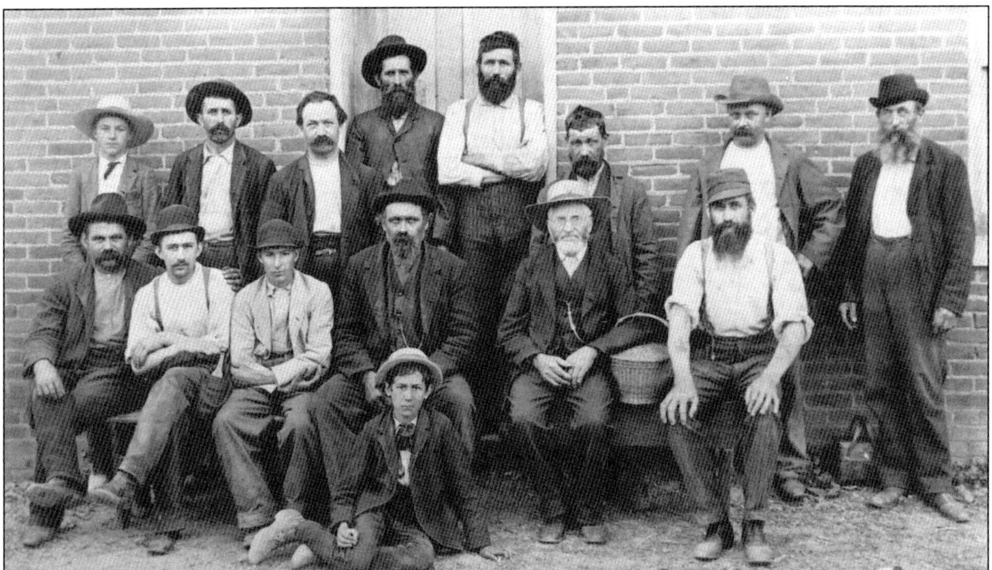

Employees of Luick Lumber are seen here in the 1890s. Located on Detroit Street, the company offered doors, door frames, blinds, and window frames for sale. Upon his retirement, Gottlob Luick gave this land to the city of Ann Arbor for use as a farmers' market.

A photograph taken on Detroit Street shows a parade float made completely of apples. The float was built by Luick Lumber employees and was decorated by Ann Arbor photographer Ernest Krueger. The float was reportedly built for a Cleveland/Thurman Democratic campaign rally and parade in 1888.

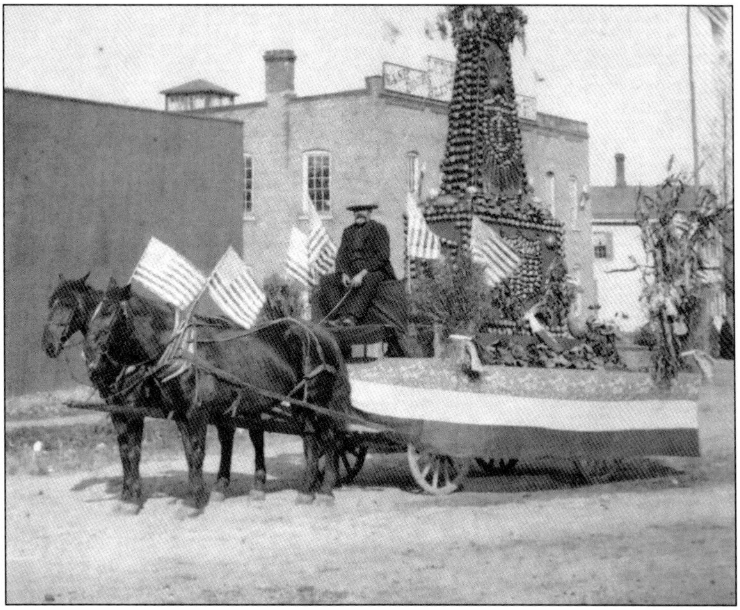

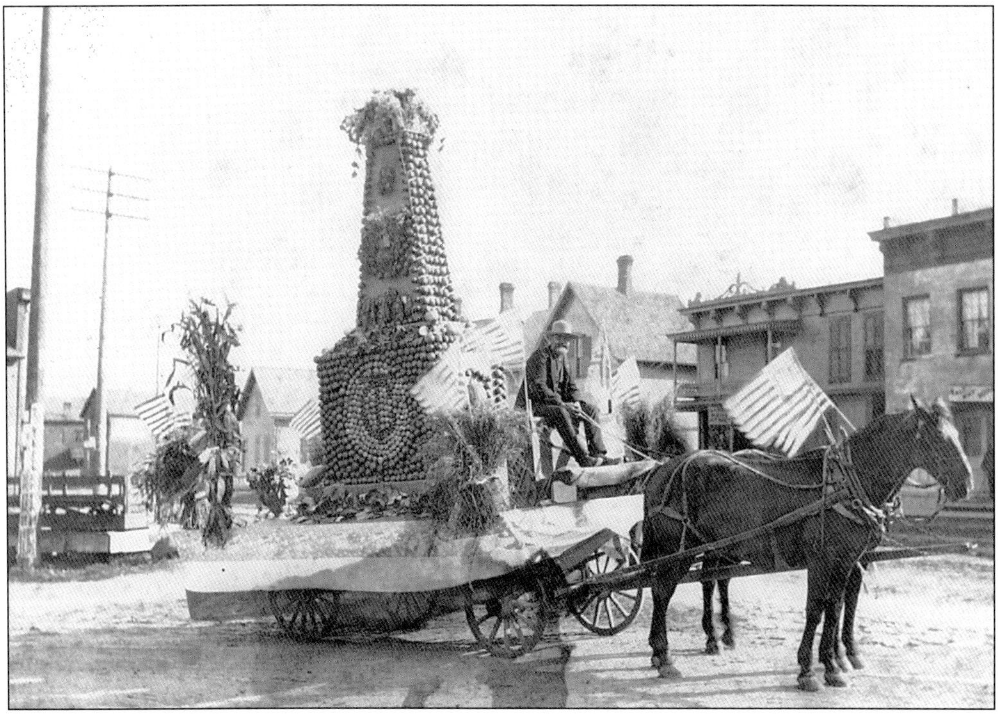

The Buchoz Block was built in 1851 on Detroit Street. In its heyday, the block housed tailors, cigar makers, cobblers, grocers, bakers, and dressmakers—everything a resident might require for his or her daily needs. There was even a saloon named the Half Way House; its name was a reflection of its location on the streetcar line, which was halfway between the depot and downtown.

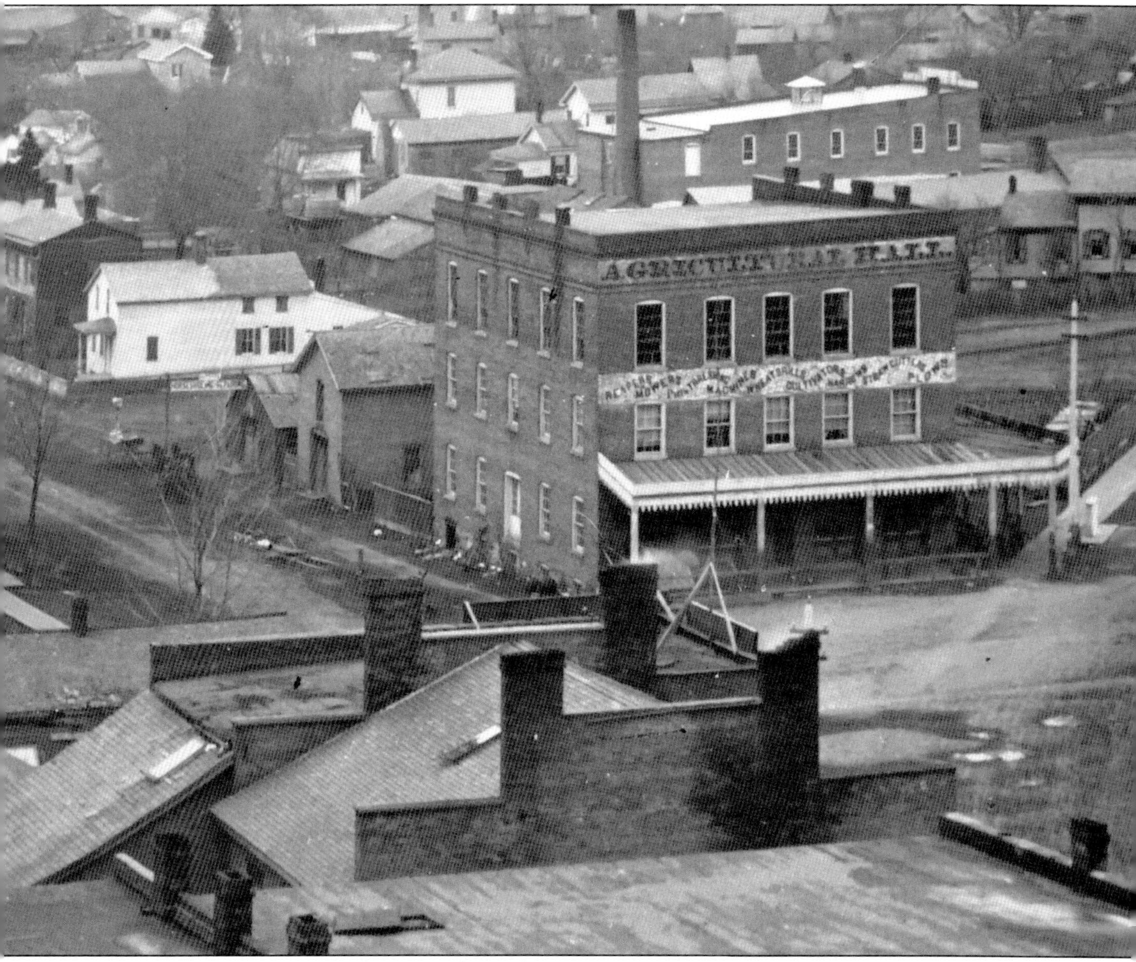

This is a pre-1882 view looking northeast from the courthouse toward Fourth Avenue and Detroit Street. Moses Rogers's agricultural implement factory/store, built in 1856, was located here during the Civil War. During the war years, the Soldiers' Aid Society for Civil War Relief met in the third-floor hall of Rogers's building. Rogers came to Ann Arbor from New York in 1831 after previously operating several similar factories. He was a key organizer of the aid society, which sponsored many social gatherings and contests to both raise money and morale.

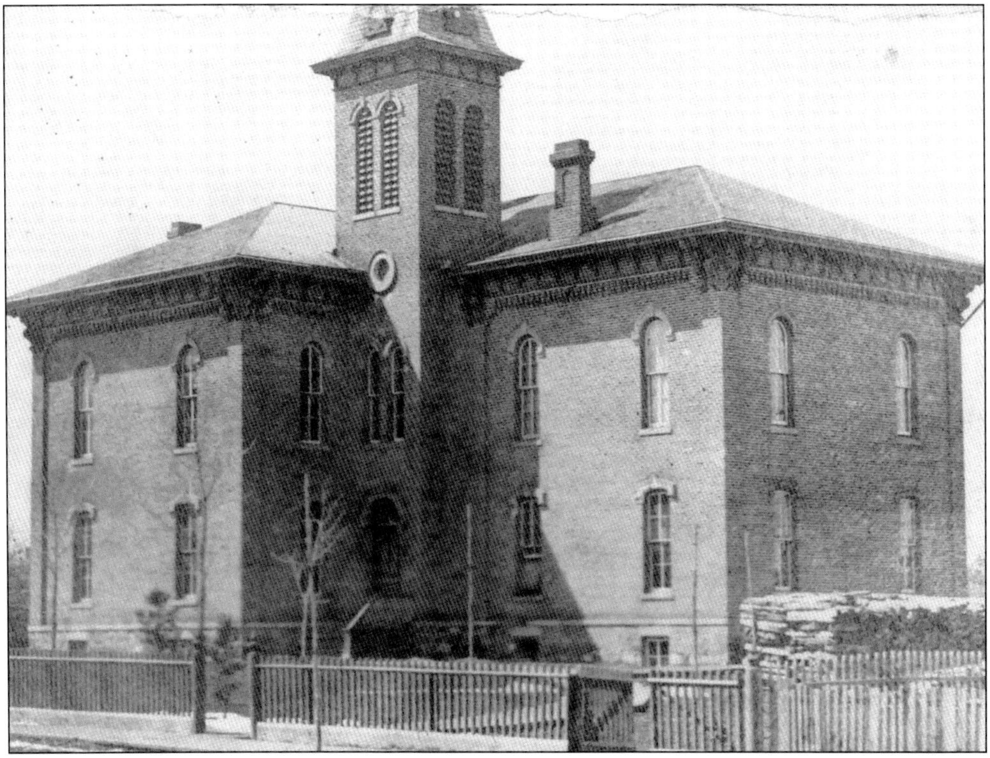

The Elisha Jones School was located at 401 North Division Street. Elisha Jones was the first superintendent of the Ann Arbor public school system, serving from 1867 to 1870. In addition, Mr. Jones taught Greek and Latin classes at the University of Michigan at various times from 1870 until 1888, when he passed away. The building is now home to Community High School.

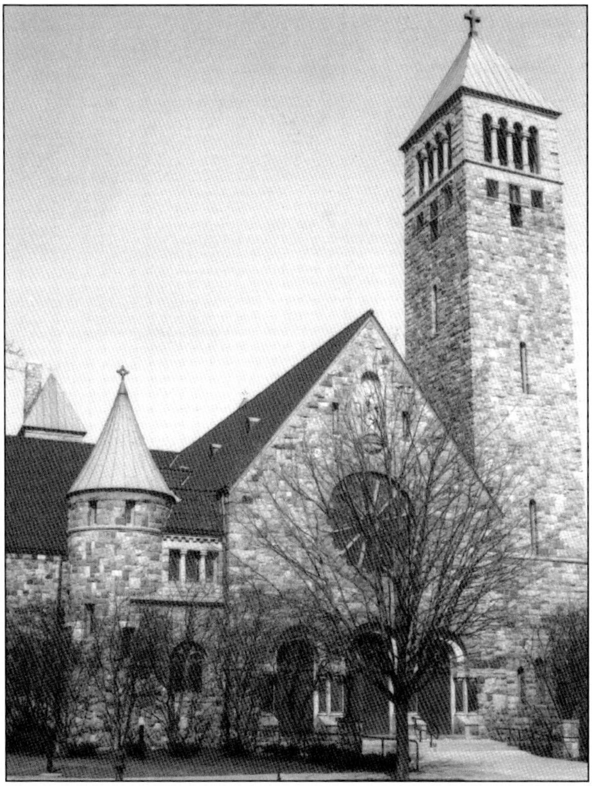

St. Thomas Church on Elizabeth Street in the Kerrytown neighborhood is shown here. Established in the 1840s, it was the first Catholic church in Ann Arbor. The St. Thomas the Apostle School was founded in 1868. Both the church and school still operate today. The school offers education from pre-kindergarten through the eighth grade, and the church boasts membership of over 1,700 families.

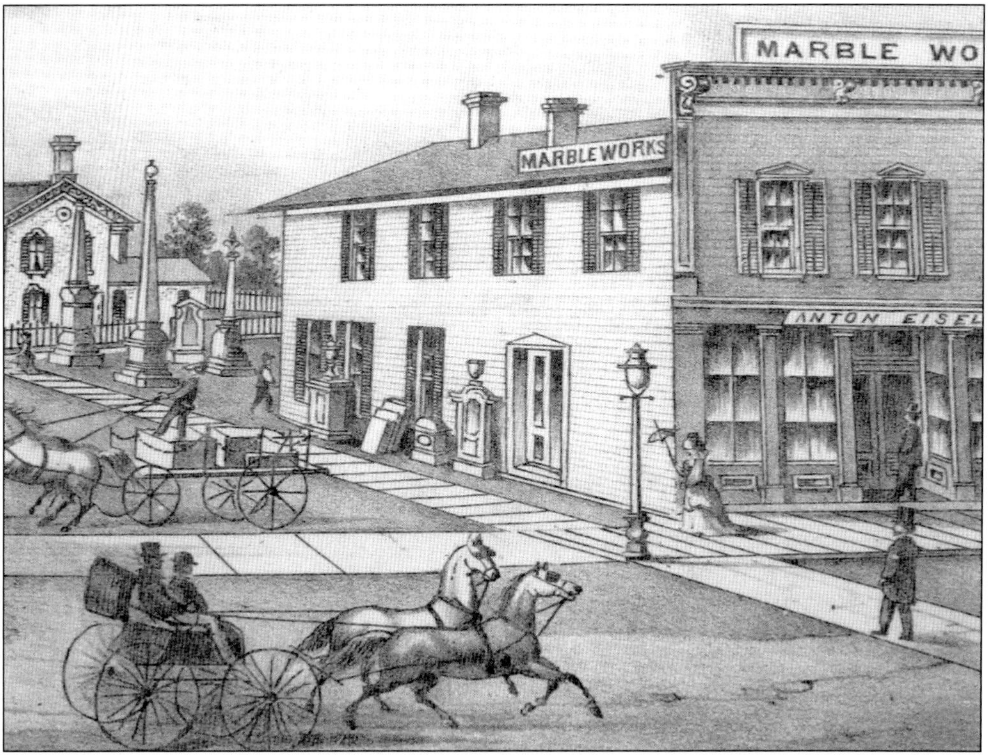

These images feature two prominent stonecutters, Anton Eisele and John Baumgardner. Eisele, a German immigrant, opened a marble works in 1868 at the southeast corner of North Fourth Avenue and Catherine Street. He built his home behind the business, located at 216 Catherine Street. Within 11 years, the business had expanded across the street and included several additions. The marble works itself is gone today, but the house remains. Eisele passed away in 1887, but John Baumgardner, who has been listed as either his stepson or his brother in various publications, carried on work in his shop, located on the northeast corner of Detroit and Catherine Streets. Baumgardner advertised marble and granite works, both imported and American made. Estimates, he advertised, were "cheerfully furnished." The image below shows Baumgardner's work crew as they unload stone slabs for sidewalks.

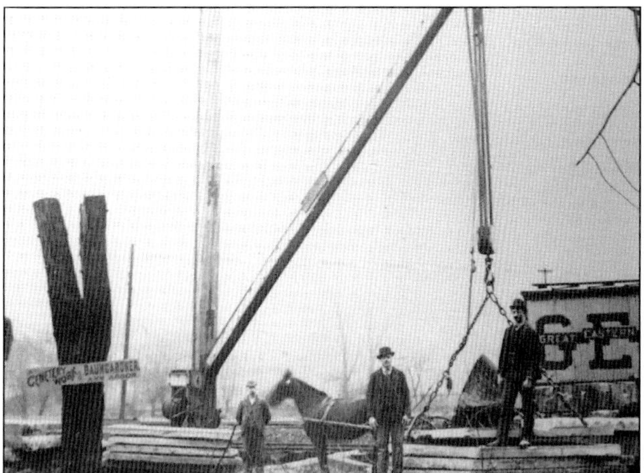

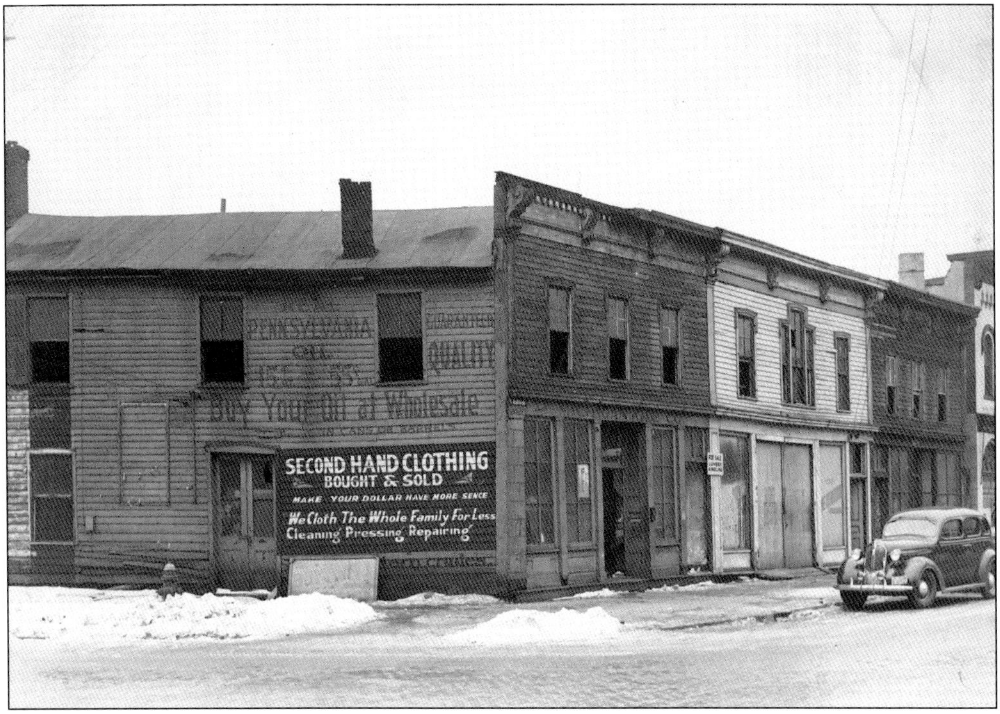

The corner of Catherine and Detroit Streets is pictured here. According to the "Polk Directory," the proprietor of this secondhand clothing store was Morris Schoenfield. The ad on the side of the building promises to "make your dollars have more sence [*sic*]." Argerio's Italian restaurant is now located on this corner.

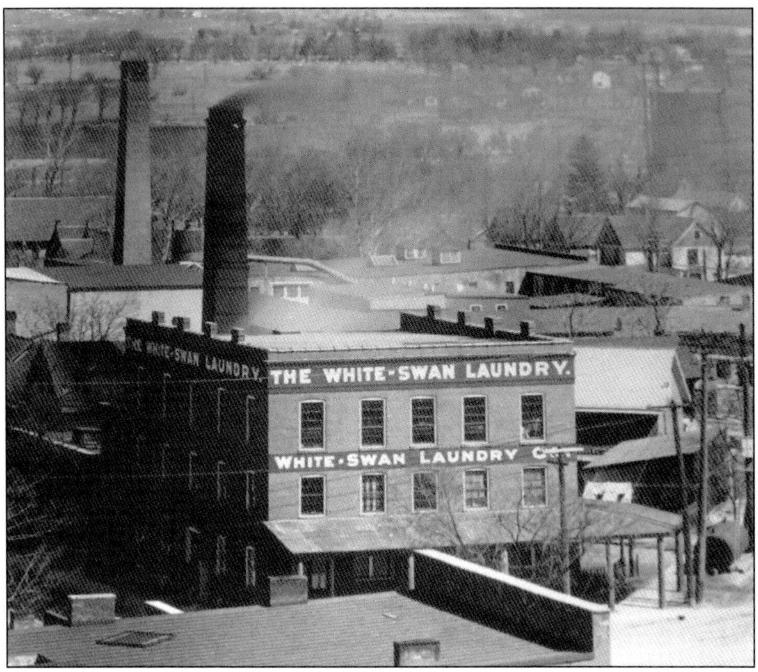

White Swan Laundry, located at 201 East Catherine Street, is seen here. At one time, the *Ann Arbor Observer* occupied this space, which now abuts to the farmers' market. This laundry should not be confused with White Star Laundry at 109 East Liberty Street. According to an *Ann Arbor News* article in February 1948, new owners took over White Swan Laundry.

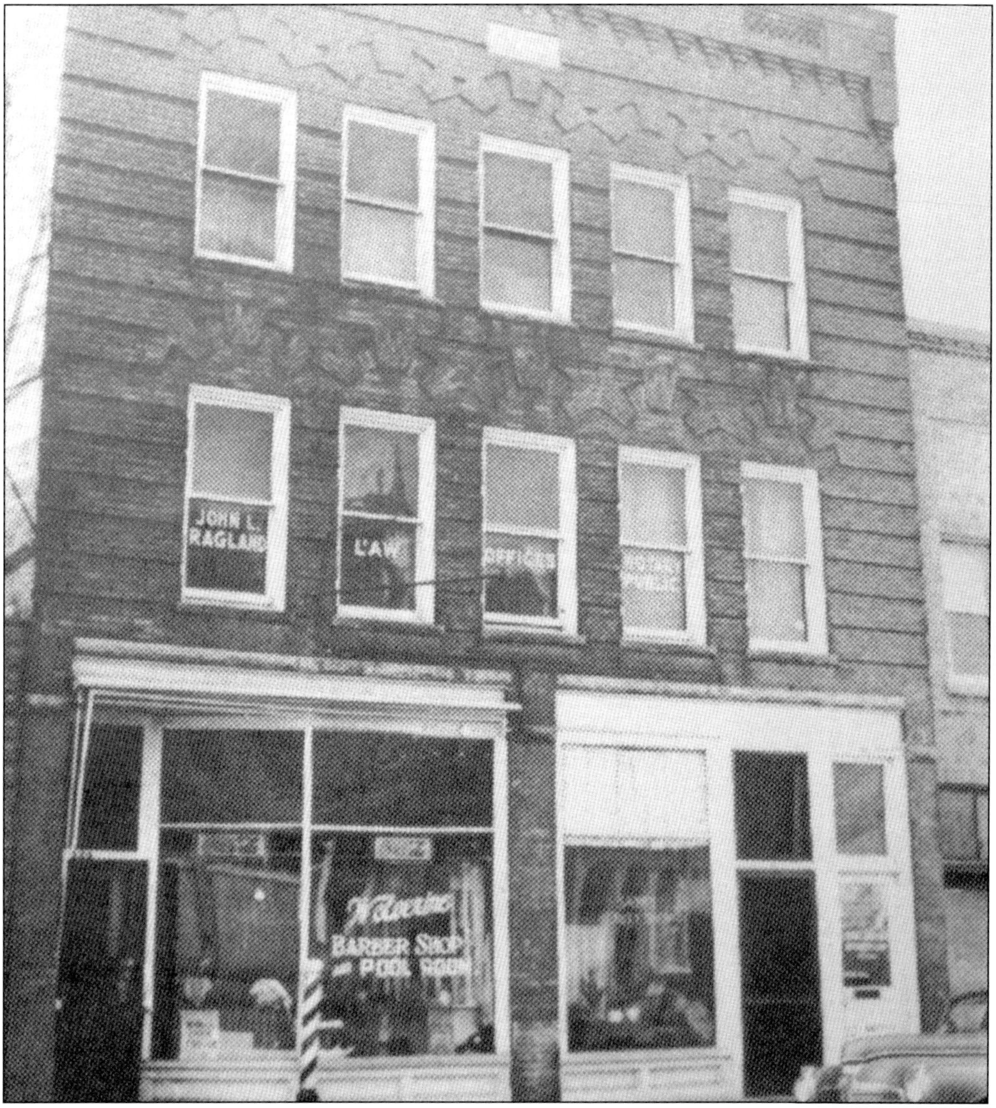

African Americans have been residents in Ann Arbor since the 1830s; by 1860, there were over 80 living in Ann Arbor and Lower Town. By the 1920s, the African American population was growing, so the Colored Welfare League (CWL) bought the Kayser Block on North Fourth Avenue. This block was made up of the buildings at 209 and 211 North Fourth, which were built by Charles Kayser in 1899. After the CWL bought the block, it set up a center to help new arrivals settle into town. Eventually, it became an African American community center for social gatherings. The block was later the first home of the Dunbar Center, which provided housing for black workers and also contained space for social events and meetings. This image shows the block when it housed the Dunbar Center. In 1926, under the auspices of executive secretary Savonia L. Carson, the center moved to East Catherine Street. Eleven years later, Douglas Williams came to Ann Arbor and charged himself with the task of revitalizing the center, which was moved to 420 North Fourth (currently home of Legal Services of South Central Michigan). With the revitalization of programs and events, the CWL's membership increased from 57 to 371. Currently, this building is occupied by the Fourth Avenue Birkenstock Store and a set of private offices.

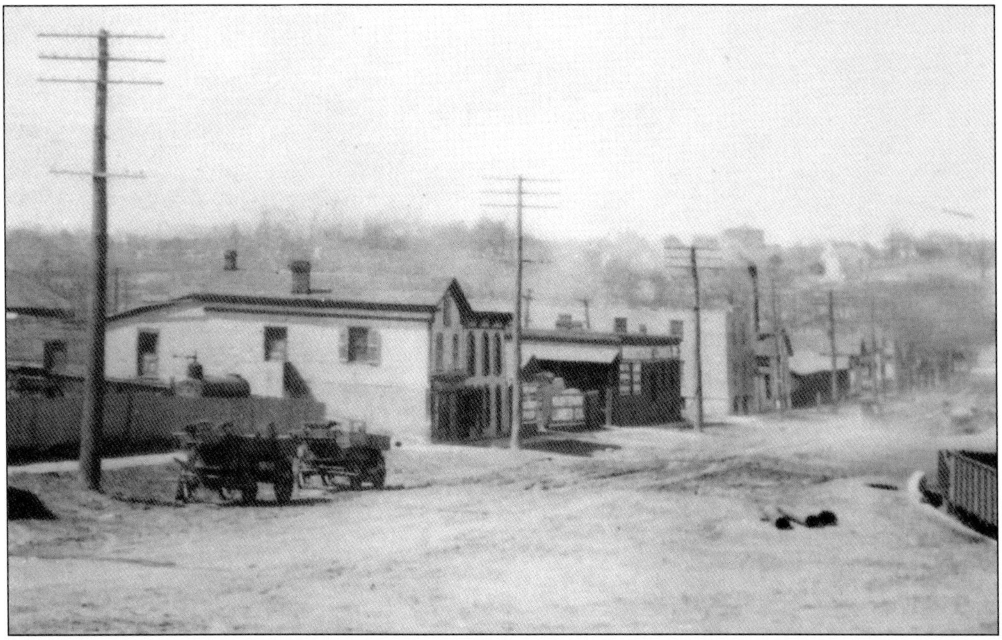

This is a view of Depot Street looking west. Currently, Wheeler Park is located on Depot between Fourth and Fifth Avenues. The park is named for Albert H. Wheeler, who was Ann Arbor's first African American mayor, a University of Michigan professor, and a civil rights activist.

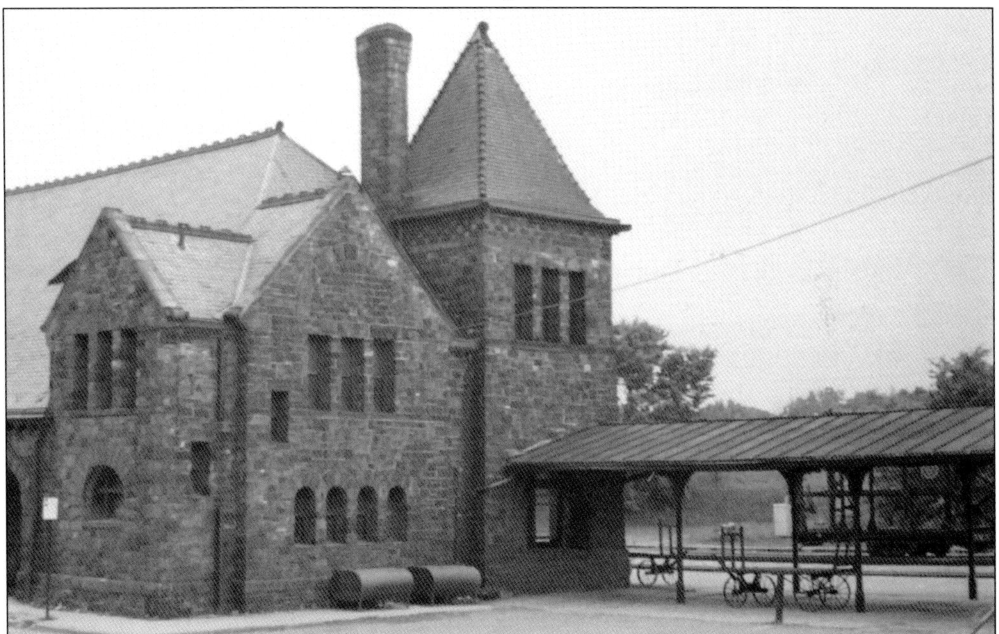

Construction of a railroad to connect the eastern and western sides of Michigan began in 1836 at the southeast corner of Jefferson Street and Woodward Avenue in Detroit. It ran out of money in four years and had only made it as far west as Dexter. In 1846, the Michigan Central Railroad was created to establish rail service between Detroit and St. Joseph. The Michigan Central Depot seen here was built in 1886.

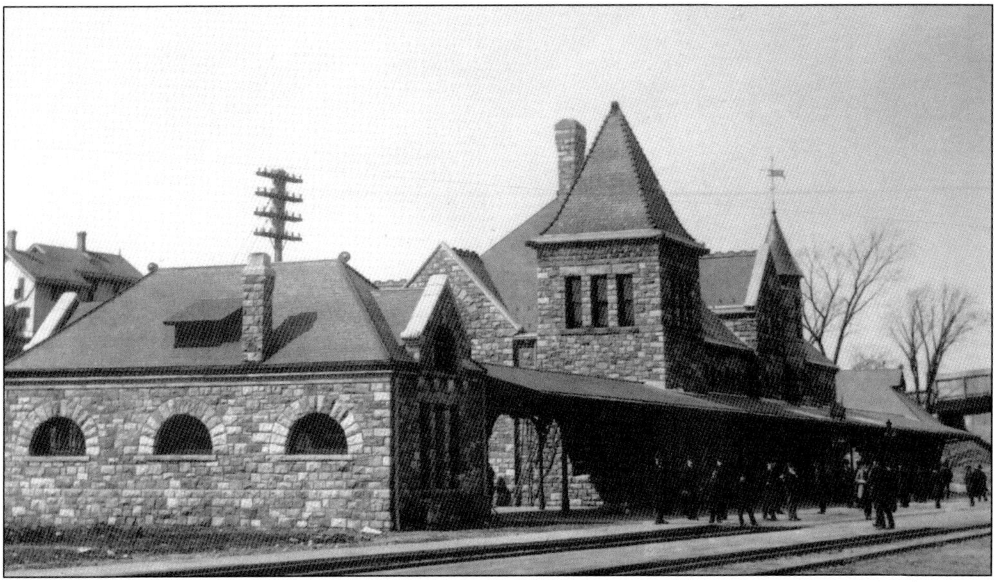

Architects Spier and Rohn from Detroit designed the Michigan Central Depot. The $33,000 building featured a centrally gabled tower with a circular opening, along with gabled corner towers. The structure consisted of two-foot-thick granite block walls made from stone that was quarried locally. The building was added to the National Register of Historic Places in 1975 and continues as the upscale Gandy Dancer restaurant to this day.

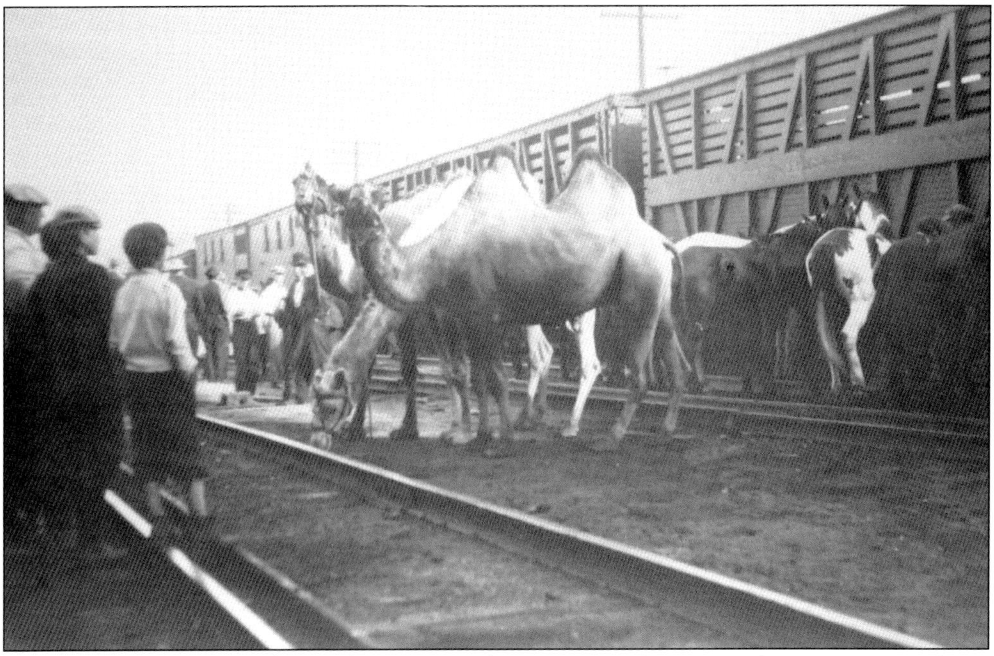

A circus train unloads at the Michigan Central Depot in 1913. In 1911, thirty-two circus shows traveled the country by rail, the high point for such events. Within 10 years, the Ringling Bros. and Barnum & Bailey circuses had over 100 cars in their fleets.

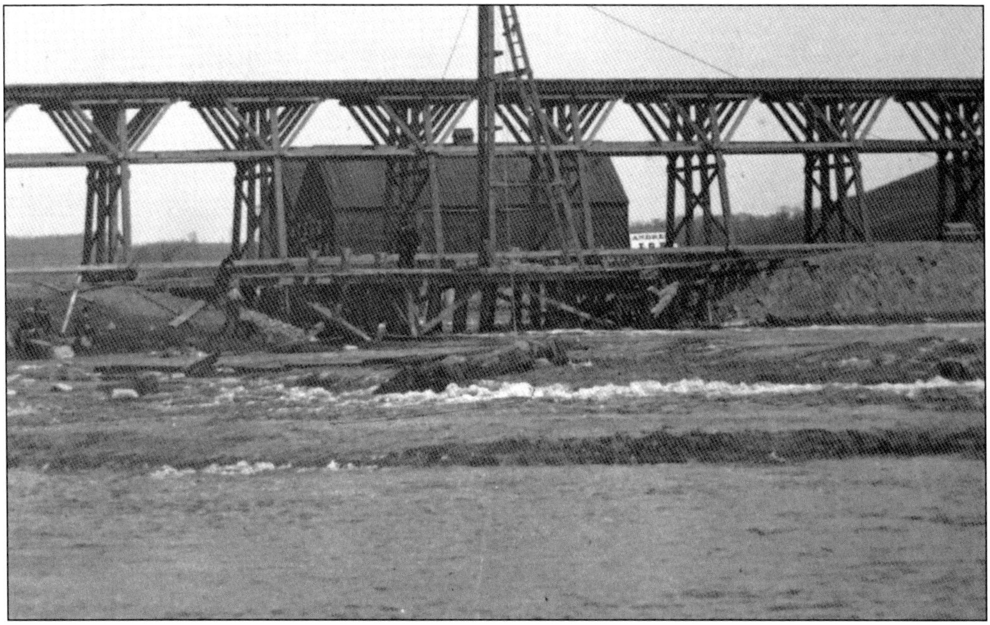

Here is a view of the Ann Arbor Railroad's trestle across Argo Pond. Later, a steel trestle replaced the wooden one. In its day, the Ann Arbor Railroad traveled from Toledo to Frankfort on Lake Michigan, and then the cars crossed the lake on car ferries. In the background, icehouses can be seen.

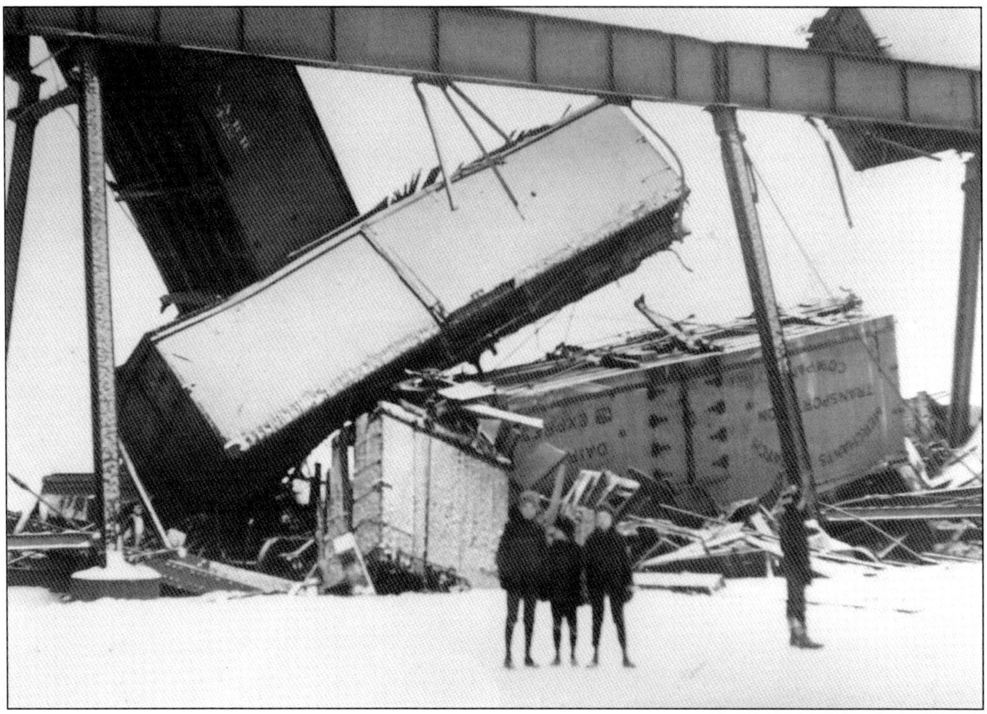

On January 28, 1904, a heavy Ann Arbor Railroad freight train collapsed the trestle over Argo Pond. Cargo from the freight cars fell onto the pond, and young people reportedly looted them. It was a bad month for Ann Arbor; just three weeks prior, the Argo Mill burned.

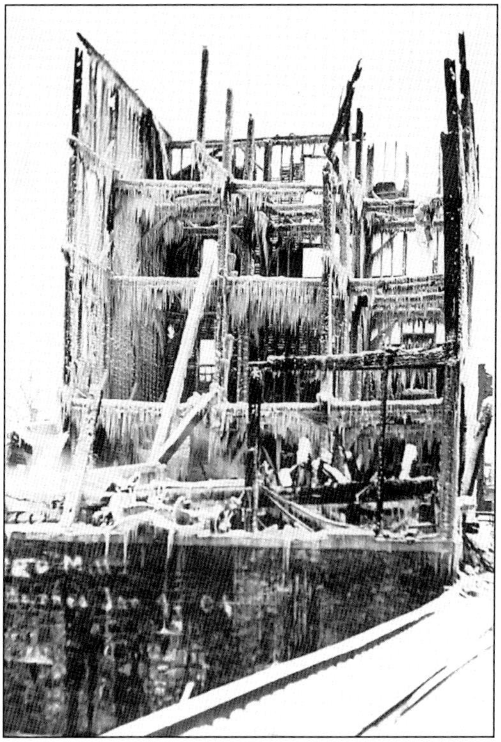

The ruins of the 1904 Argo Mills fire are seen here. According to the *Argus*, the fire started in the room that held the roller machine, which was used for grinding. An employee checked the room at 3:00 p.m. and found nothing amiss; however, five minutes later, the building was "all ablaze." Despite a prompt response by the fire department, the mill could not be saved.

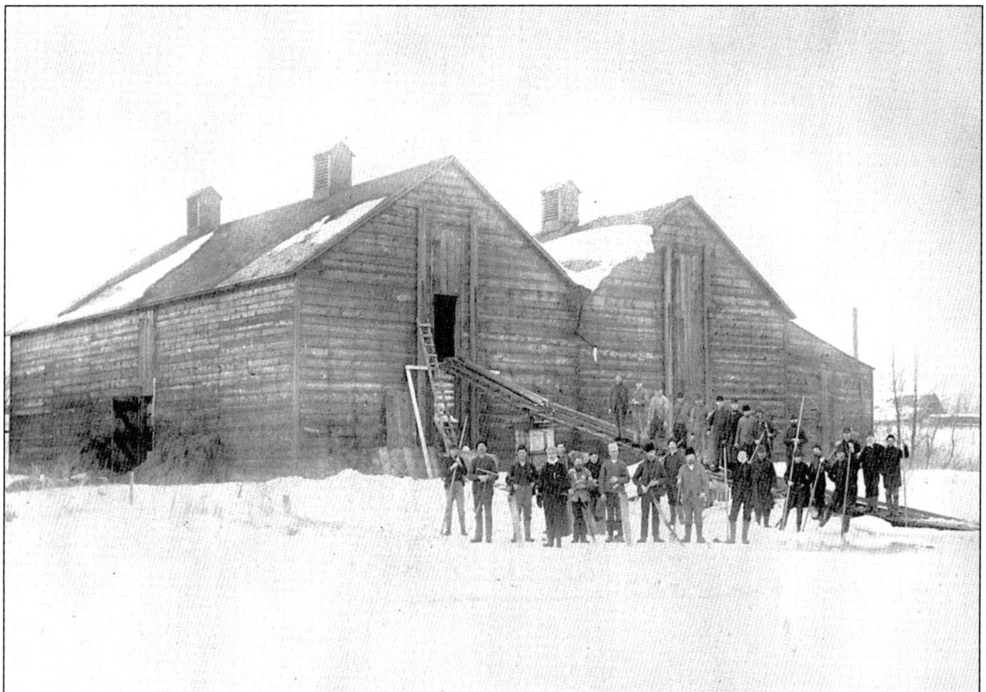

In this photograph, an Ann Arbor icehouse sits upon Argo Pond. Ice-harvesting businesses began on the river not long after the city was founded. Refrigeration eventually eliminated the need for icehouses, but the change was gradual.

This is a 1929 aerial view of the Washtenaw Gas Company (formerly the Ann Arbor Gas Company) on Broadway Street. The company bought the land between the first depot and the river and built its plant and storage tanks there.

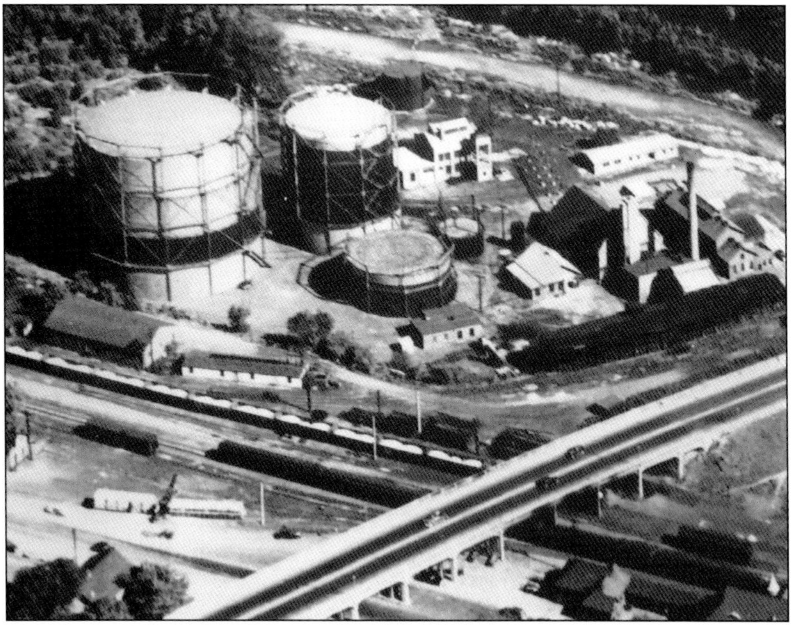

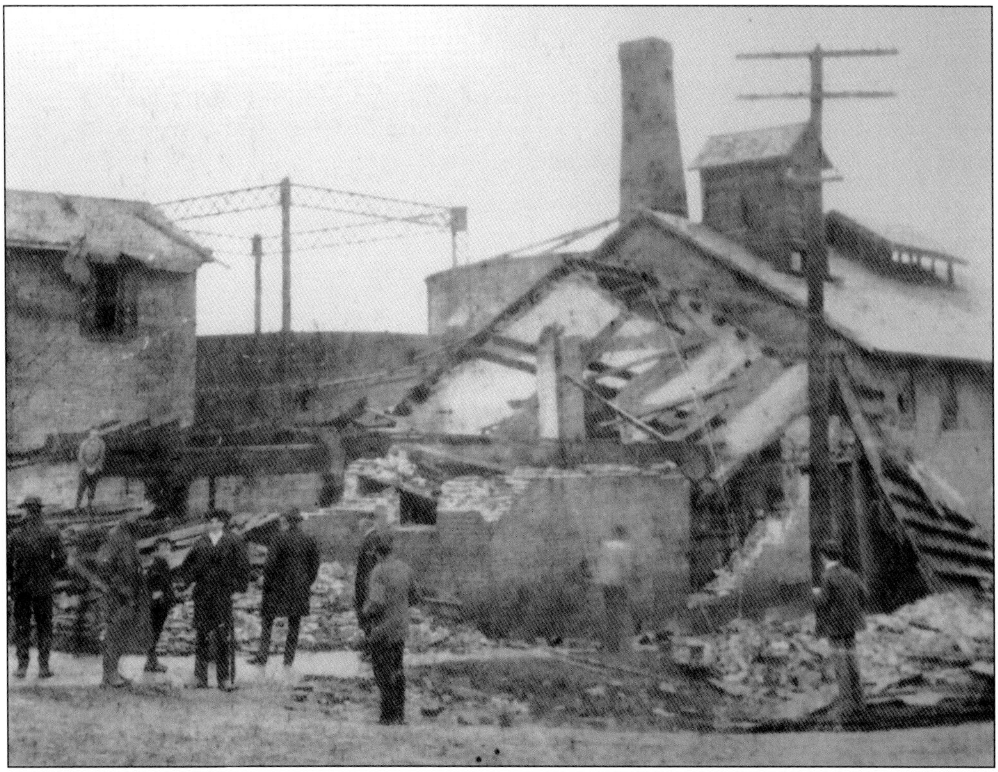

After an explosion in 1895 destroyed the Ann Arbor Gas Company's first plant, a larger plant was built on the other side of the railroad tracks. Ann Arbor's "1859 Revised Charter and Ordinances" contained Ordinance No. 33, which stated the desirability of being lighted by gas and thus granted the Ann Arbor Gas Light Company the exclusive "right and privilege of erecting Gas Works" and gave permission for laying the necessary piping.

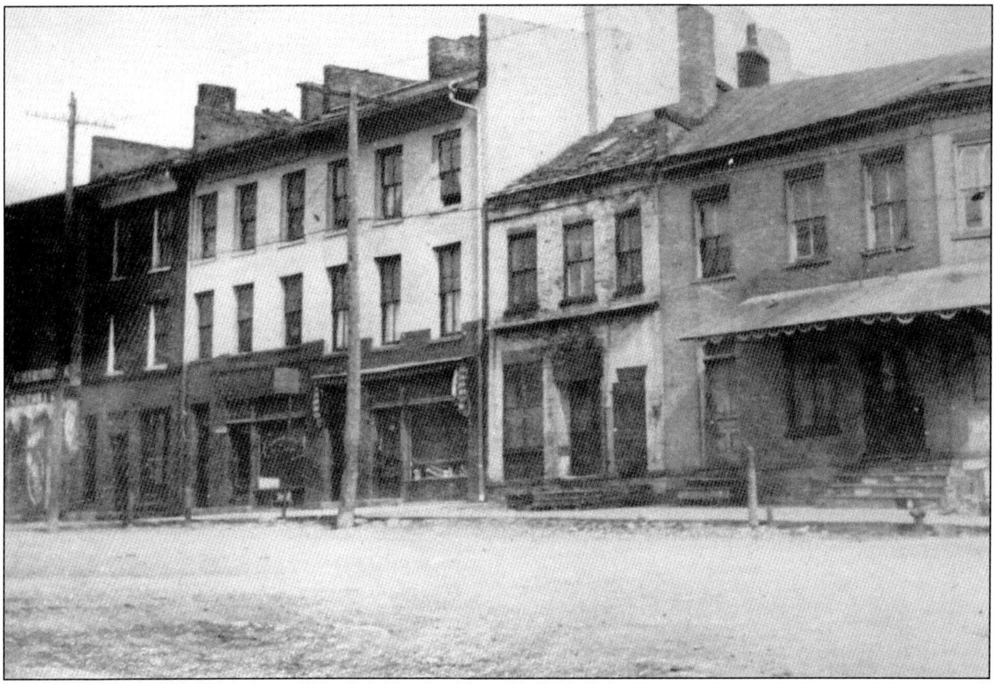

Once a separate town, here is the area known as Lower Town. This image shows the first brick structure in this section of Ann Arbor, erected in 1831 by Asa Smith. The three-story building next door was known as the Huron Block and was constructed by Josiah Beckley in 1833. The abolitionist newspaper the *Signal of Liberty* was published upstairs by Beckley's brother Guy. The entire block was torn down in 1959.

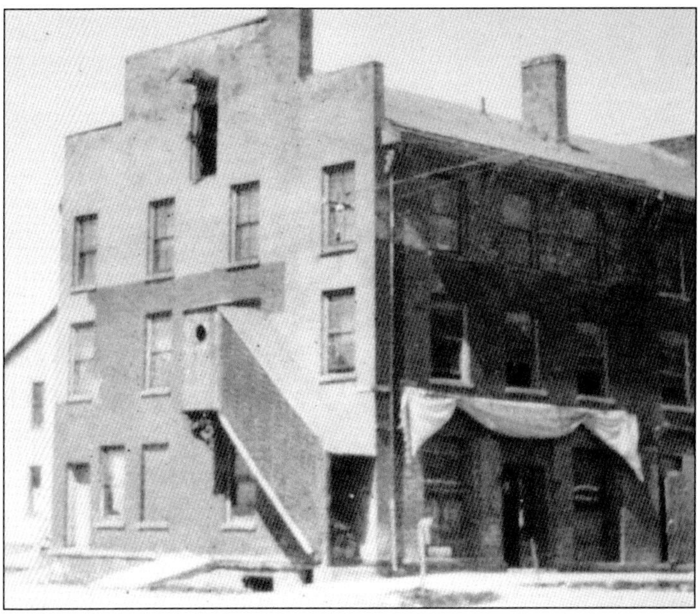

These Lower Town buildings were located on the west side of Broadway Street and include the Anson Brown Building. Handwritten notes indicate that the businesses shown belonged to grocers and a blacksmith, with a vacant store on the end. Brown's building remains standing and currently houses the St. Vincent de Paul shop. It has the distinction of being the oldest commercial building in the city that is still standing.

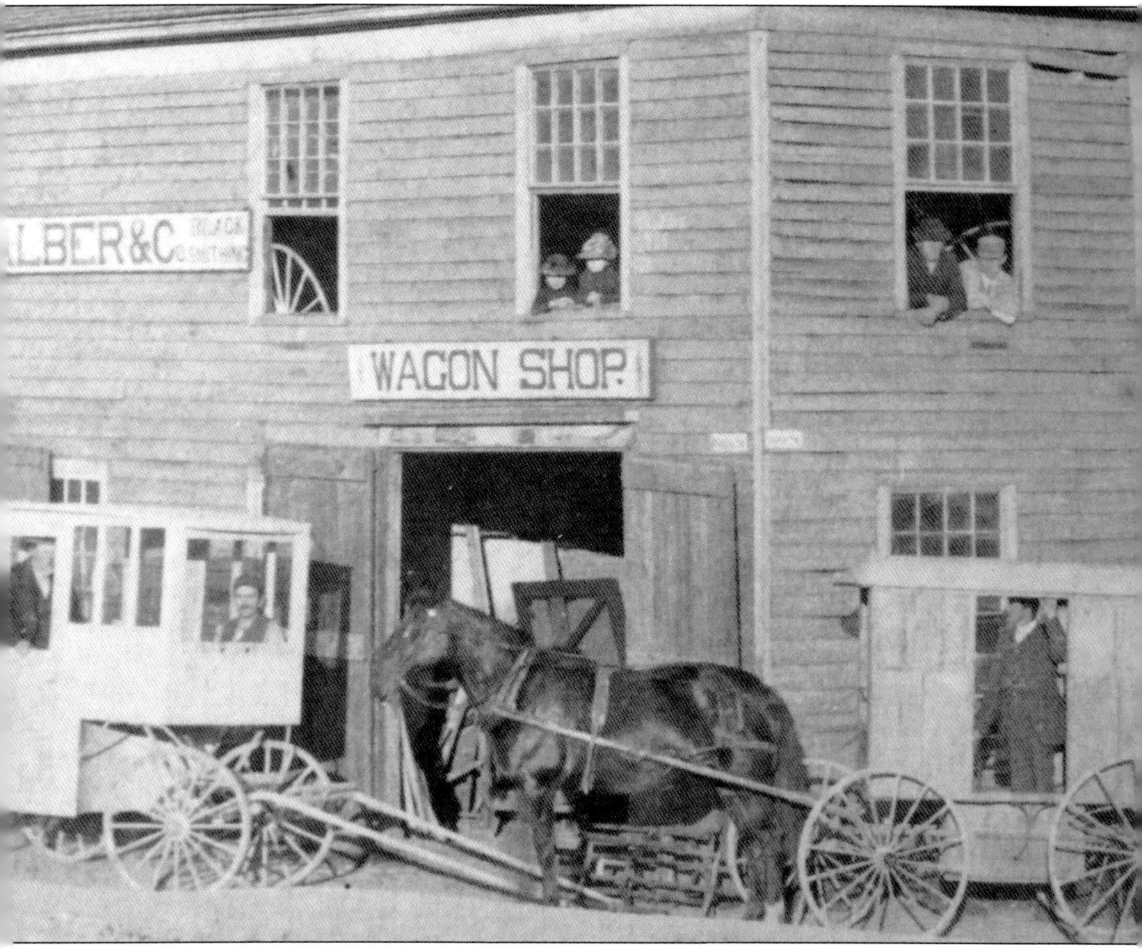

Alber & Co., one of the earliest blacksmith and wagon shops in the city, is pictured here. Factories, mills, slaughterhouses, and tanneries operated nearby, along with three spring-fed breweries. The Northern Brewery on Jones Street (formerly Mills Street) advertised "bottled beer in cases of 2 dozen or 1 dozen bottles, quart or pint, delivered to any part of the city." The brewery closed in 1908, and in 1922 the building became a foundry, which lasted until 1972. It was renovated for offices in 1976 and is now called the "Tech Brewery," as it houses a number of technology-centered businesses.

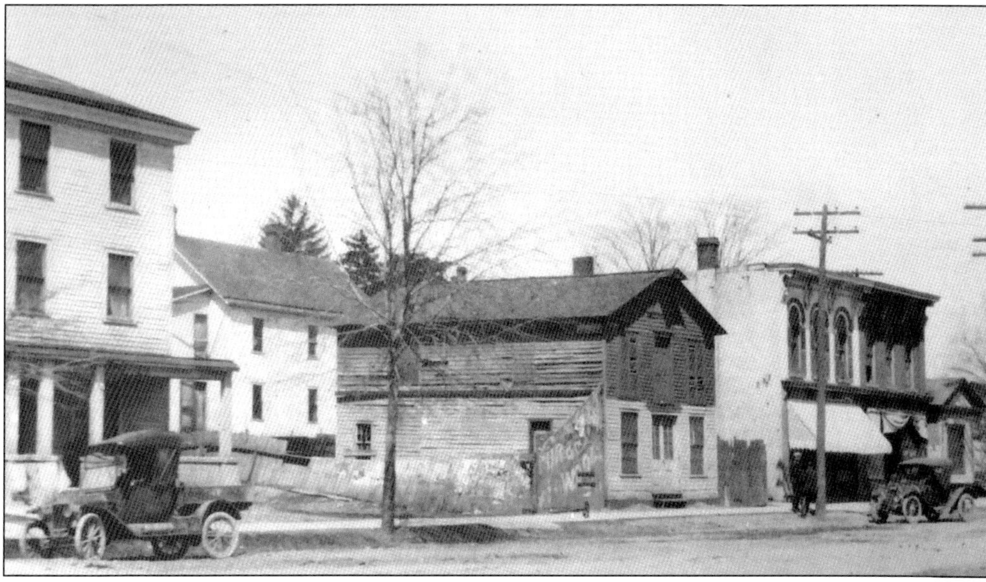

This is a view of Broadway Street. Notes on the photograph state that these are the "five most important buildings which would have to be removed for the relocation of Pontiac Street and the making of a small park." In the 1900s, a number of buildings in the area were torn down to make space for parks. A 1902 petition to the parks committee called for land north of the railroad tracks to be made into a public common or park.

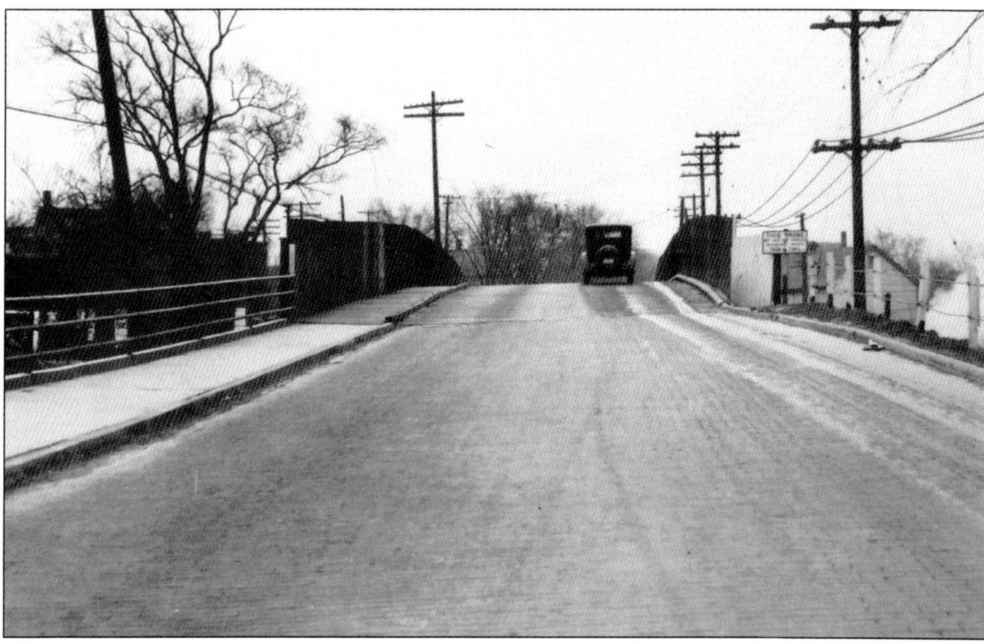

Here is the northern approach to the Broadway Bridge. The bridge connects the central part of the city with the northern part and has a rich history. Originally constructed from wood in 1828, the bridge spans the same stretch of the Huron River where city founders John Allen and Elisha Rumsey are said to have crossed as they made their way into the area from Detroit. The bridge was reconstructed with concrete in 1926 and rebuilt again in 2004.

The Ann Arbor Milling Company, located near Argo Pond, dominates this scene. The Agricultural Works on the other side of Broadway Street used power from the mills. In the 1890s, it was the largest employer in the city, making hay tedders, rakes, horse-drawn mowers, and other farm machinery.

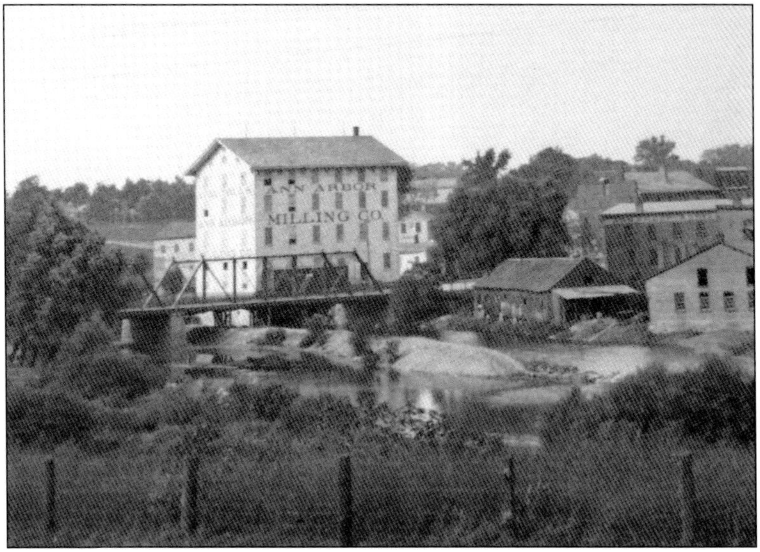

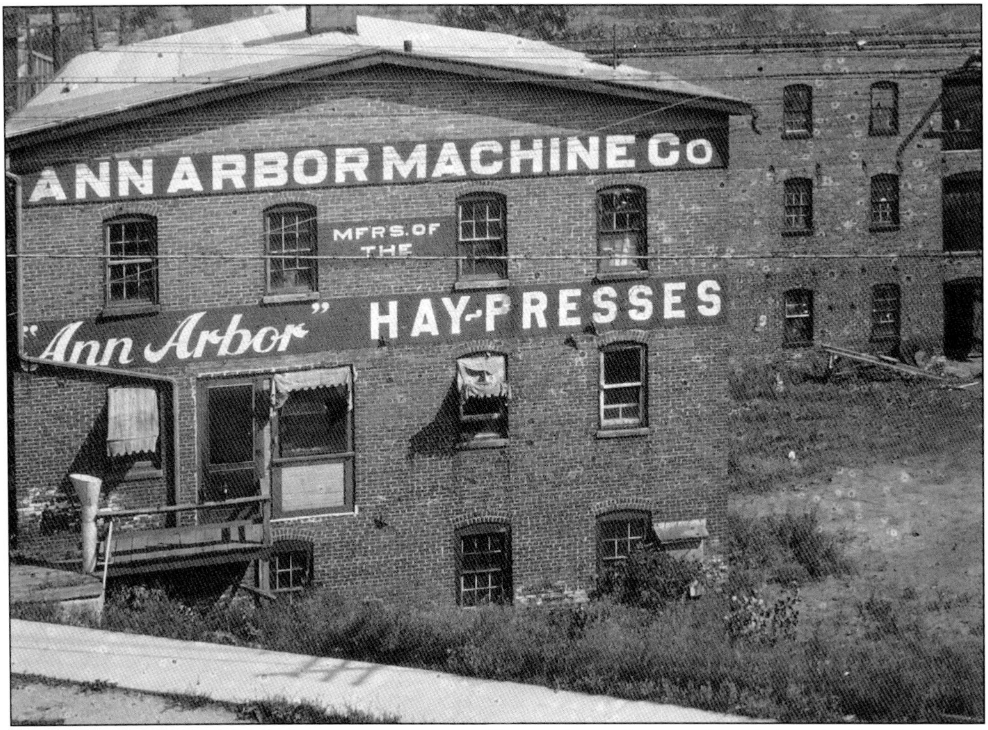

The Ann Arbor Machine Company is pictured here. According to *Ann Arbor the First Hundred Years*, John Christensen, a longtime company employee, patented a hay press. In 1906, the Ann Arbor Hay Press Company was started with the intention of building this press. The Ann Arbor Machine Company objected to the name of the new firm, claiming it would take business away, as people would think the two companies were the same. Ultimately, a judge disagreed and the machine company lost its suit.

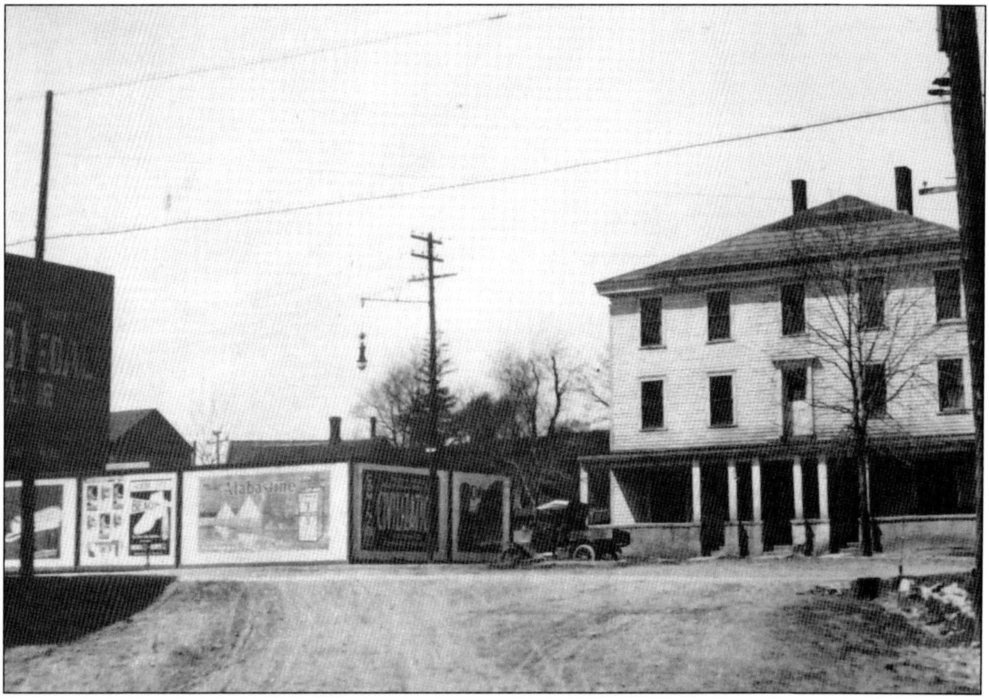

This is a view looking up Wall Street at its junction with Broadway Street. This intersection now dead-ends next to a currently vacant building with the popular Northside Grill located to its left and a party store to its right.

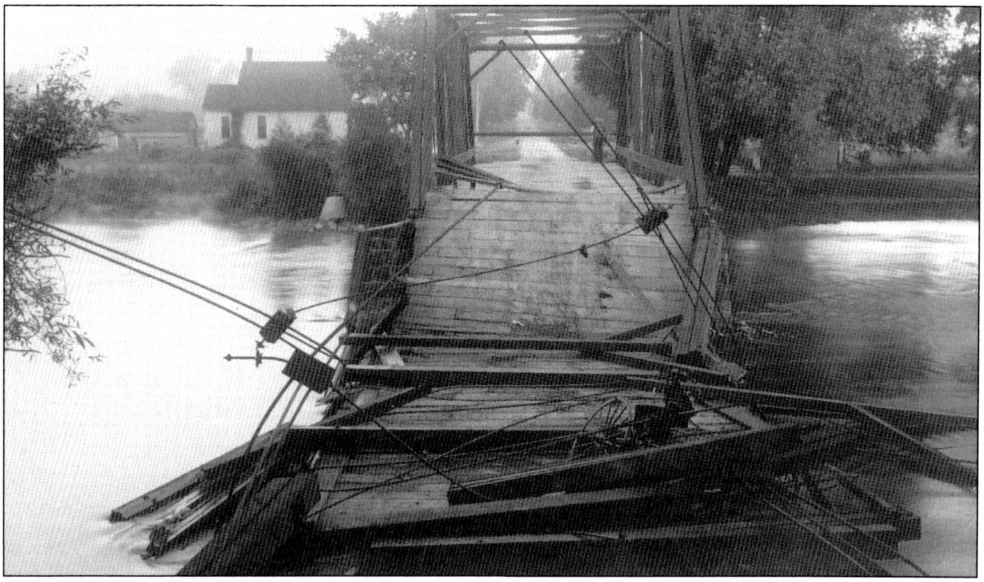

The Wall Street Bridge collapsed on August 6, 1909. A woman, who was giving several children a ride around Ann Arbor in a horse-drawn buggy, was crossing the bridge when it collapsed. She was reportedly injured badly but survived, and several children in the buggy were injured as well; the horse did not survive. Later, the Hermann Tapp Construction Company of Fort Wayne, Indiana, built a new concrete bridge at this location. The current bridge on Maiden Lane eventually replaced the one on Wall Street.

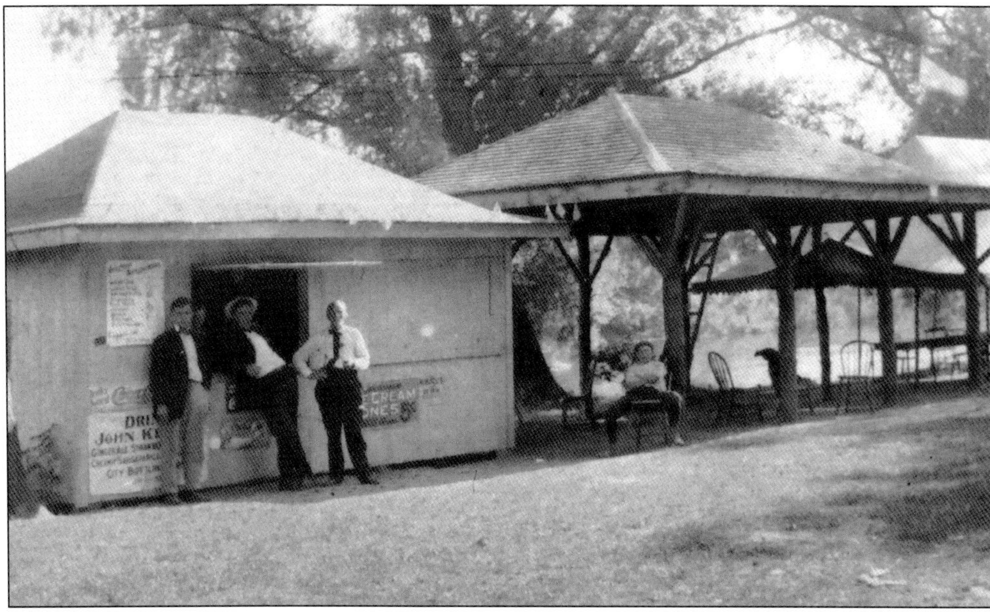

Located on Island Drive and surrounded by the Huron River, Island Park boasted a concession stand that sold drinks and ice cream (only 5¢ for a cone). While the park still exists, the stand has been lost to the ages.

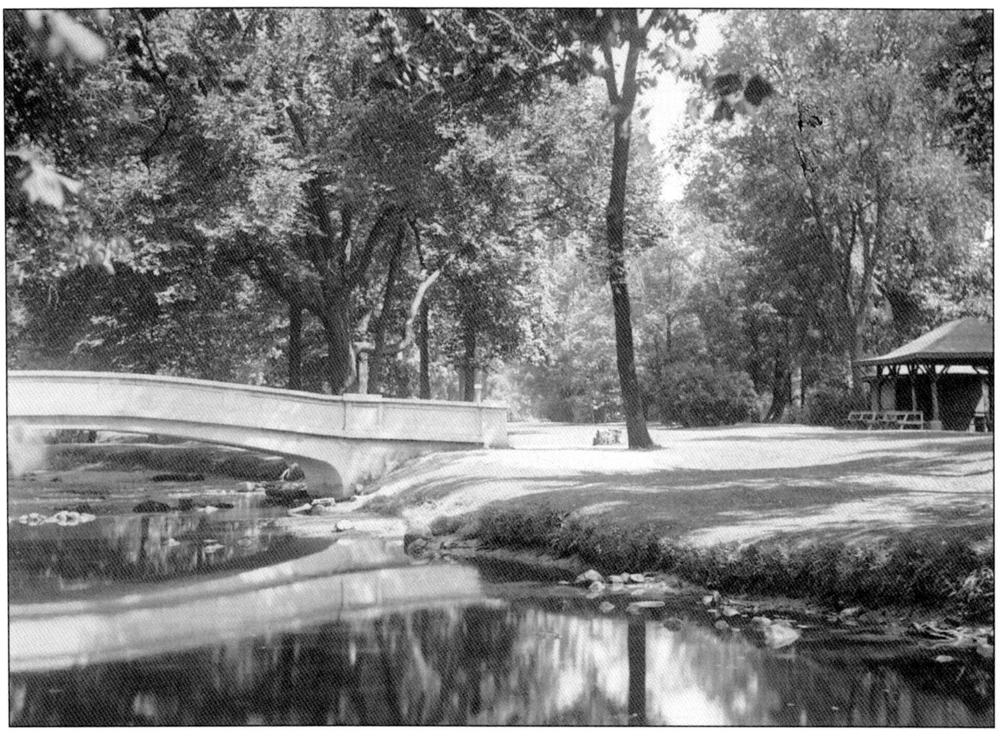

This view of Island Park shows a lovely bridge. Parks have long played a role in Ann Arbor life. According to the *Ann Arbor Sesquicentennial Journal*, the first board of park commissioners was appointed in 1905, marking the first "official" recognition of the park system. Island Park continues to be a popular spot for picnics, weddings, and other special occasions.

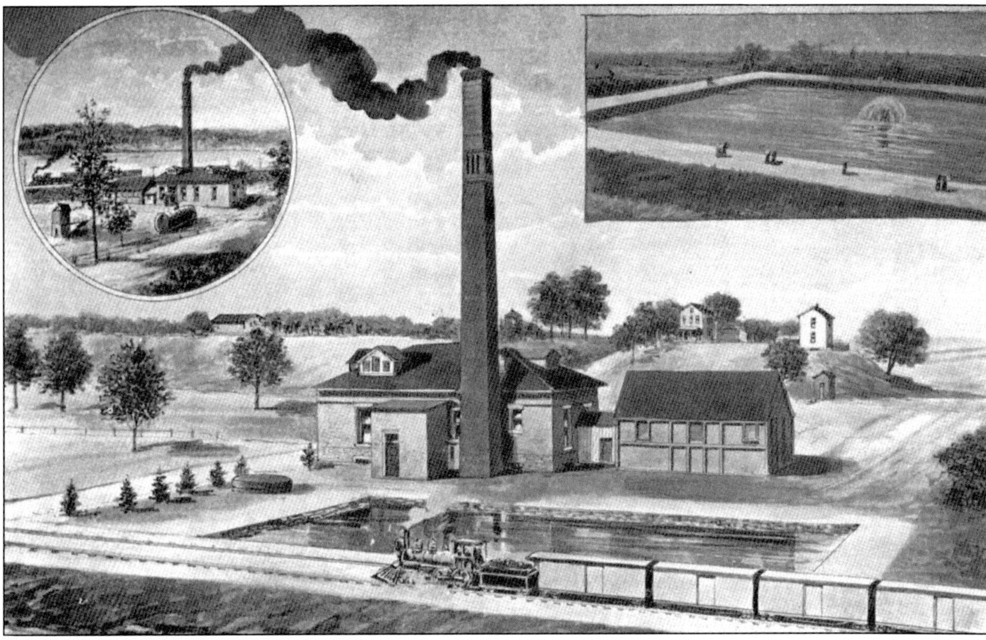

Fire was one of the biggest concerns of early life in Ann Arbor. For safety, wells were dug, and cisterns were placed at intersections. Demand for a more reliable supply of water was answered when the Ann Arbor Water Company installed 100 fire hydrants. Water was pumped from the river into a reservoir on Sunset Road and then flowed into town through pipes. The city purchased the water company in 1914.

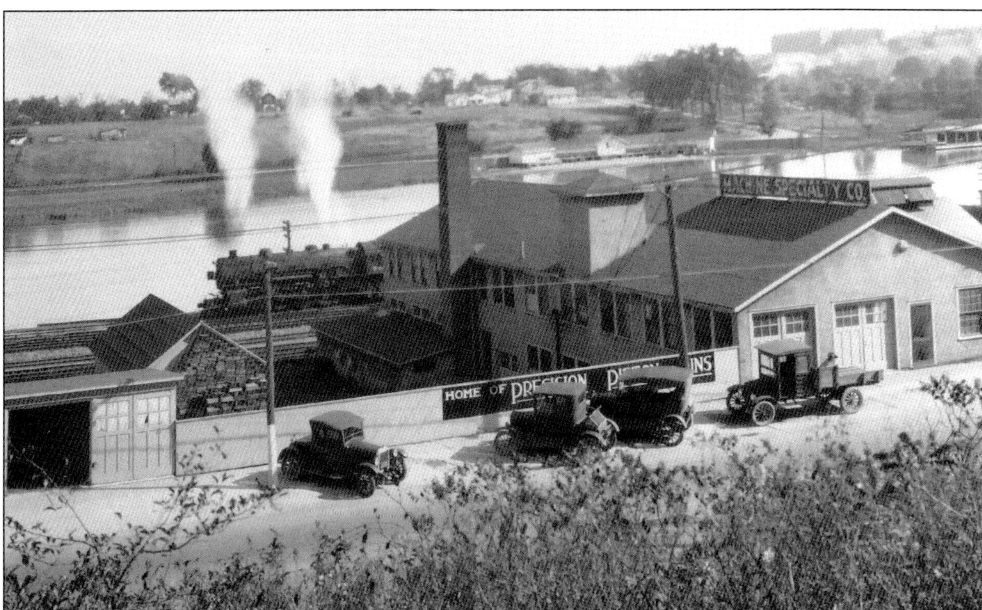

The Machine Specialty Company factory was located on North Main Street near Argo Pond. Among its products was the Zeta radio, which was manufactured briefly during the 1920s. Under the names Consolidated Radio and Precision Products, the company also produced Arborphone radios and auto parts.

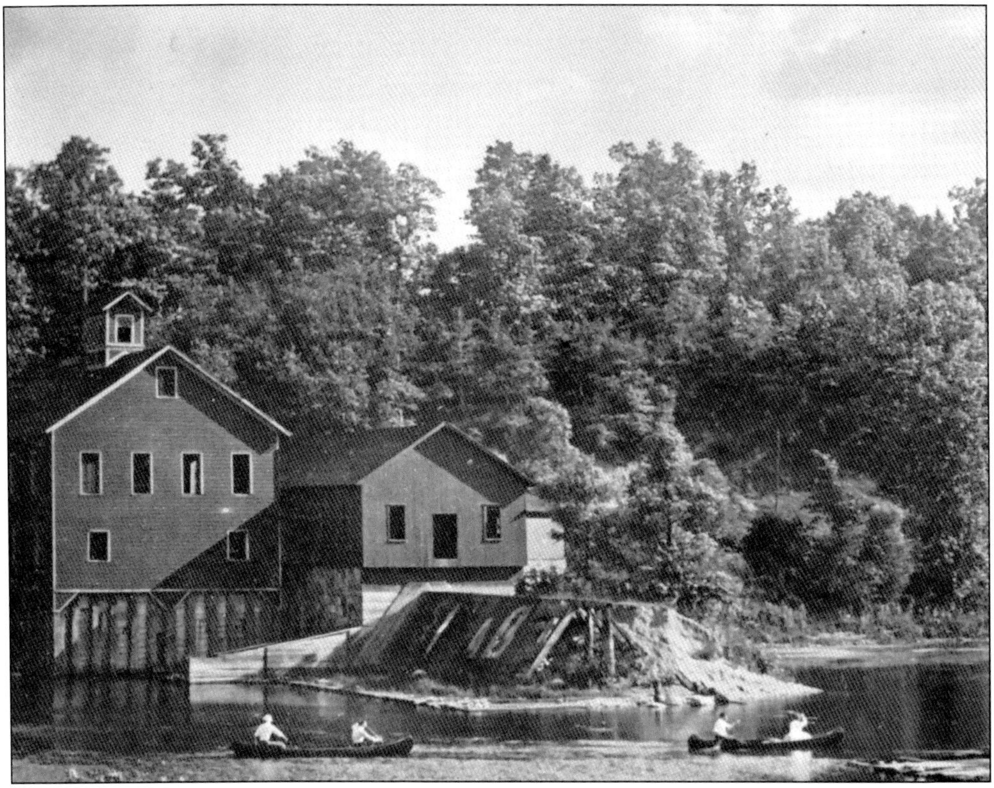

The Cornwell Paper Mill and Dam were built in 1885. The Michigan Milling Company (MMC) operated the Argo Milling Company downstream from the Cornwell Dam at Argo Pond. Argo Mills predated the construction of the Cornwell Dam, so in the late 1880s the MMC sued for water-rights infringement. An 1895 court order forced the removal of the Cornwell Dam, and the mill was subsequently abandoned.

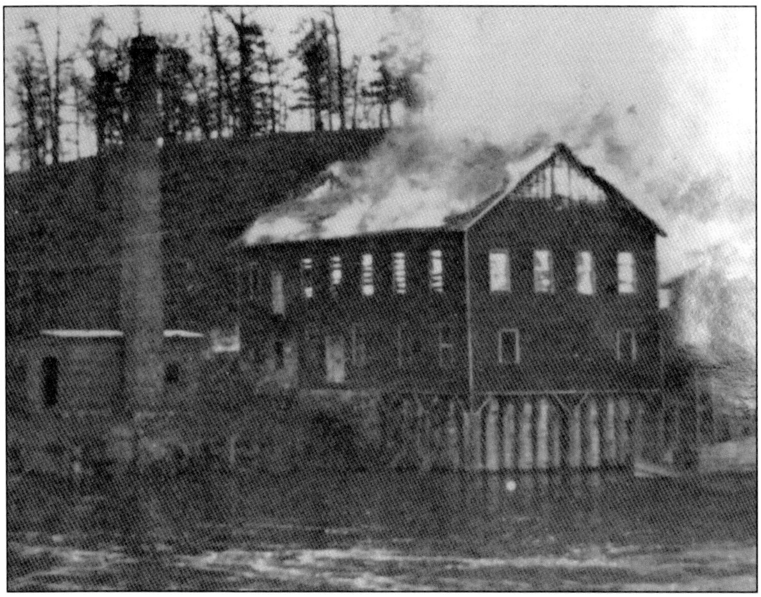

The vacant Argo Mills burned on May 8, 1913. Hobos often squatted in the abandoned mill and were blamed for the fire—or perhaps, as some thought, nearby residents were weary of the abandoned mill and started the blaze. Ruins of the mill are still visible when water levels are low.

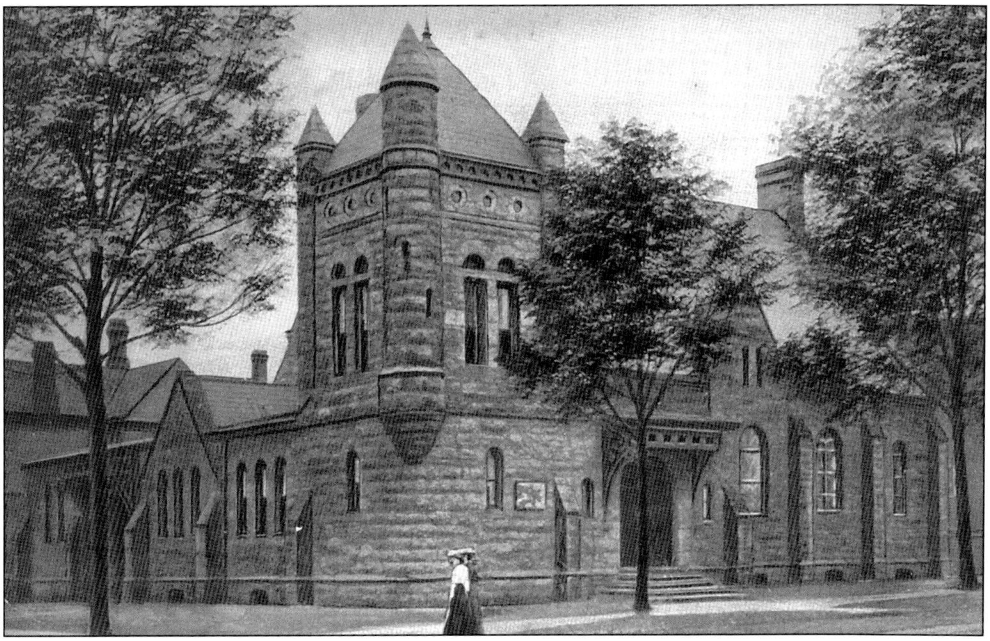

First Unitarian Universalist Church is featured in this photograph. The building, erected in 1882, stands at the corner of State Street and Huron Street. Today, the building is occupied by the architectural firm Hobbs+Black. The Unitarian church has moved to nearby Scio Township.

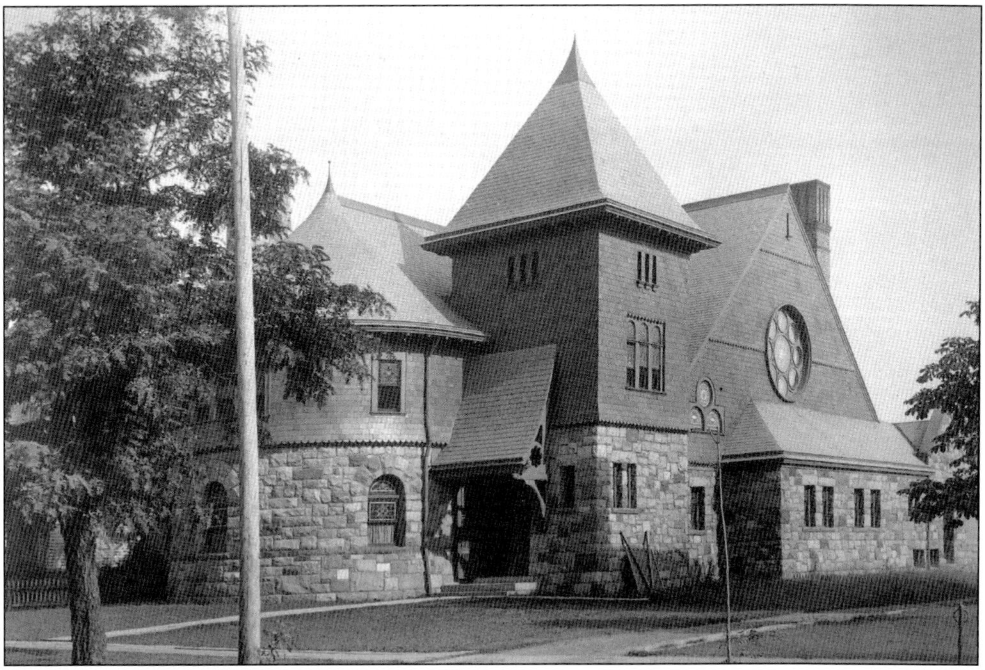

This 1920s photograph shows the Church of Christ. It was dismantled, rebuilt at Tappan and Hill Streets, and renamed Memorial Christian Church. The new building was constructed as a mirror image of the original church. In 2012, a fraternity purchased the building. The congregation has relocated again and has changed its name to Journey of Faith Christian Church.

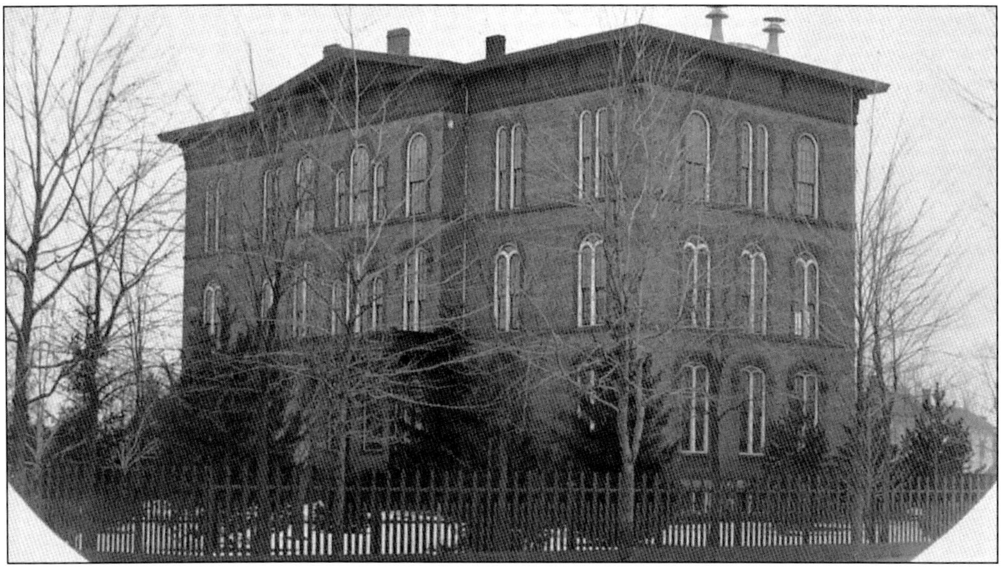

Union School, which was later renamed Ann Arbor High School, is seen here. Ann Arbor High School moved to a new site at Stadium Boulevard and Main Street in 1956, directly southwest from the University of Michigan's football stadium. In 1967, the school's name was changed to Pioneer High School.

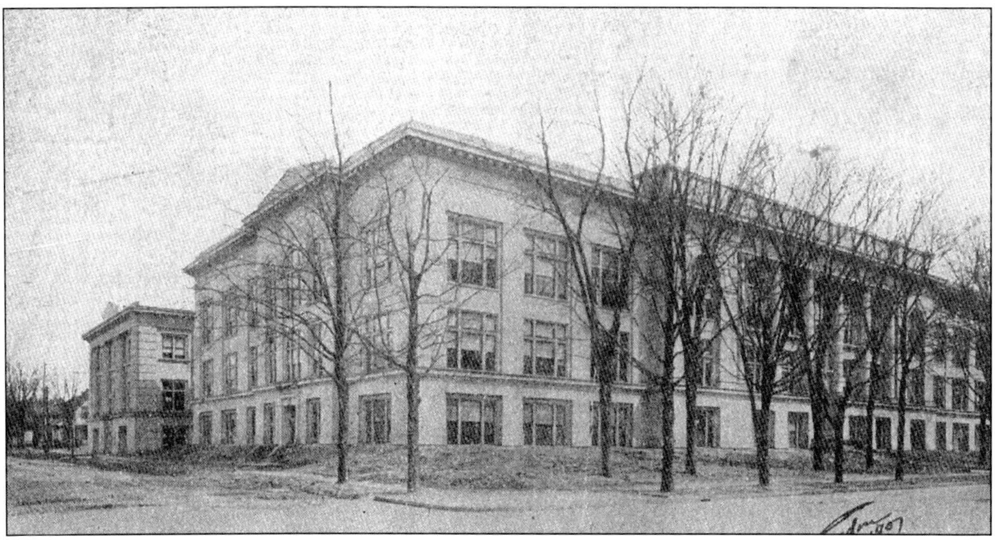

Ann Arbor High School, seen in this 1907 image, later became the University of Michigan's Frieze Building (housing the communications and theatre and drama departments) and is now the site of an expansion of the university's North Quadrangle. Today, Ann Arbor enjoys some of the most outstanding public schools in the state, but this was not always so. The original public schools were neither well organized nor properly funded. When Union School opened in 1856, things began to improve.

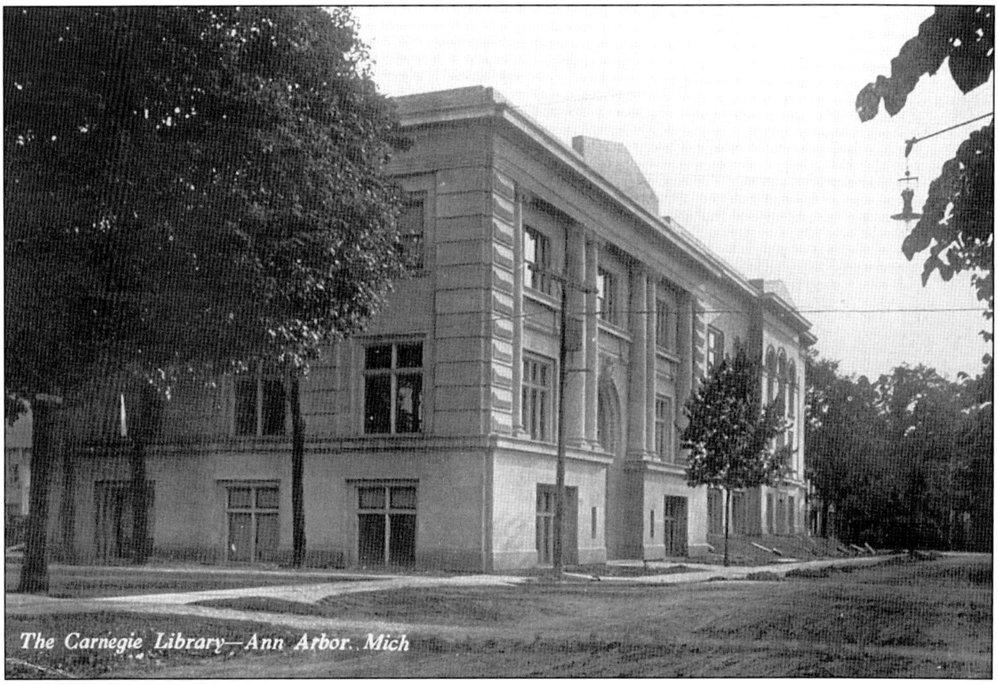

The Carnegie Library was attached to the second Ann Arbor High School. When the school burned down, students and faculty saved most of the school's library books. Voters later approved a bond for a new school, and the library and school were built together.

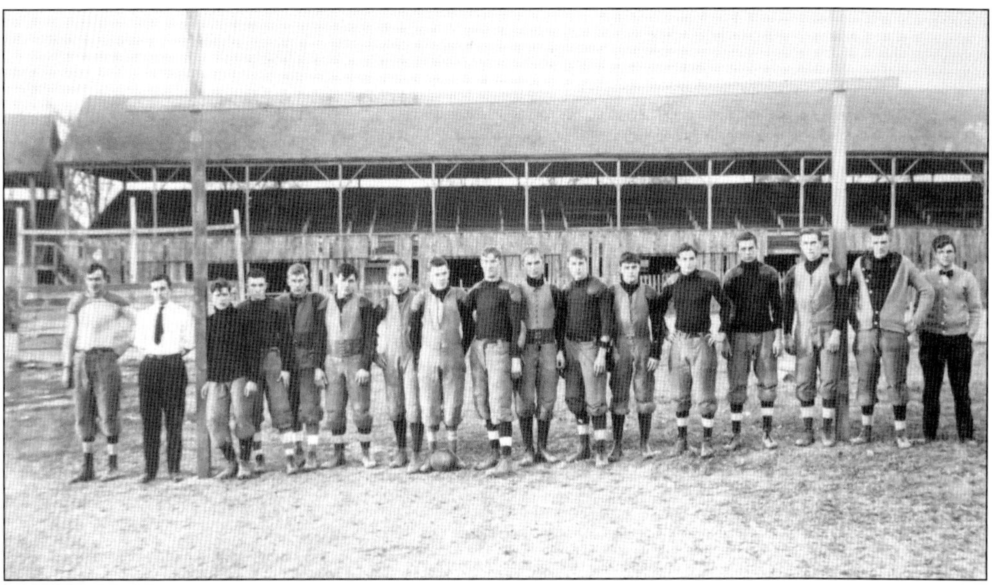

Ann Arbor has enjoyed football and victorious teams for well over a century. This photograph of the 1908 Ann Arbor High School football team looks very different from today's players—no helmets or big padding on these players. Fullback John Maulbetsch led the team to back-to-back state championships in 1908 and 1909.

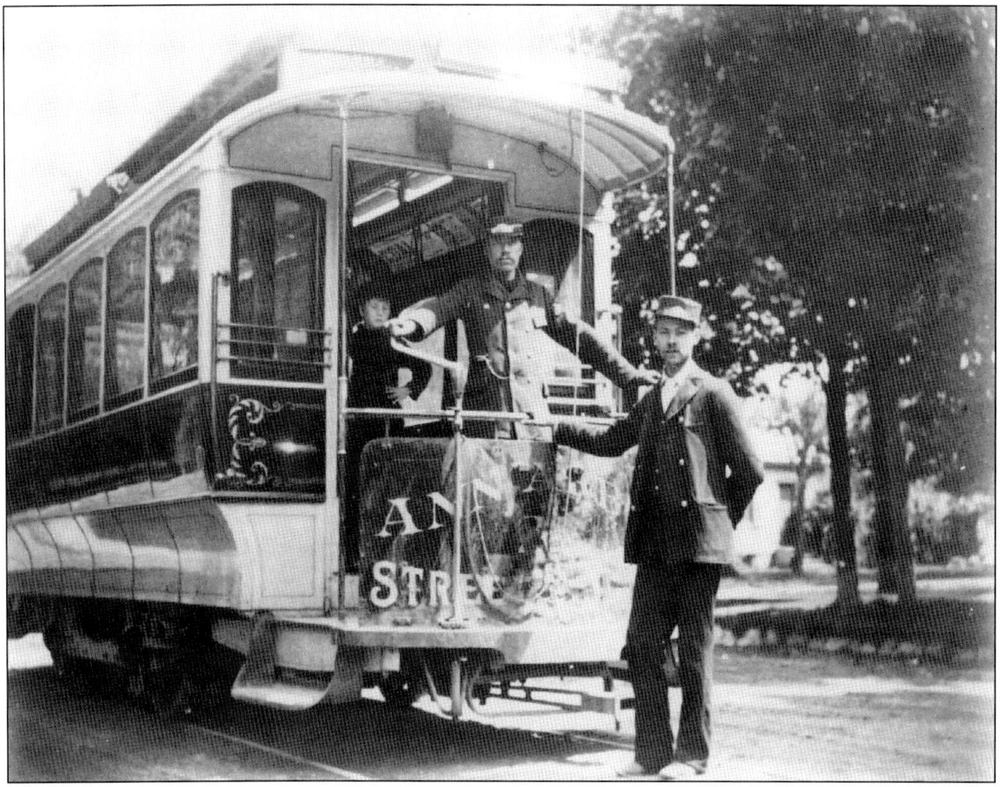

Posing with the local streetcar on Packard Street are its motorman Jim Love and conductor Marion Darling. Grace Shackman's "Then & Now" column in the *Observer* called them "two of the most famous streetcar employees." At times, the motorman would call out, "Ready, Darling?" with the conductor replying, "Yes, Love."

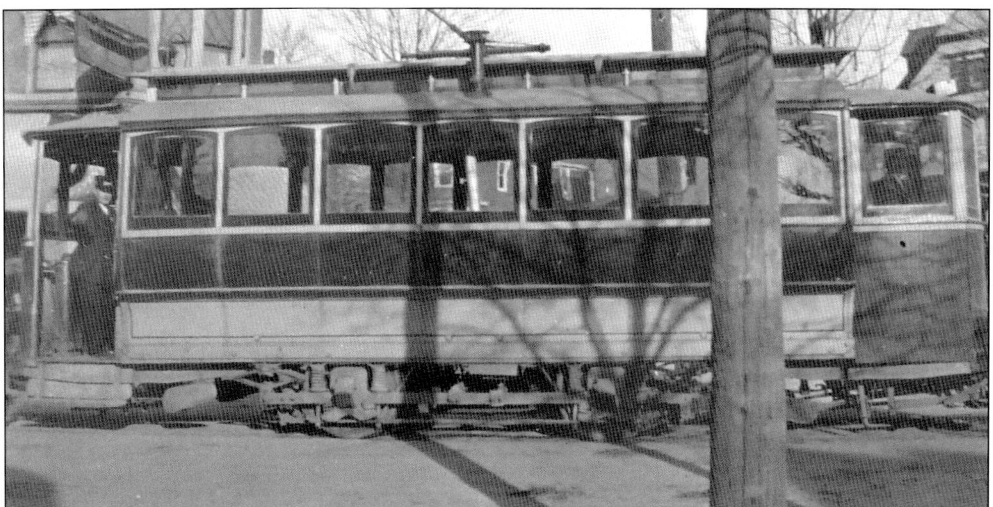

A streetcar has stopped in front of the Fischer and Finnell Cigar Store in this c. 1910 image. The store was located at the corner of Packard and State Streets, which has been a home to other businesses since. A waiting room for the interurban was located inside.

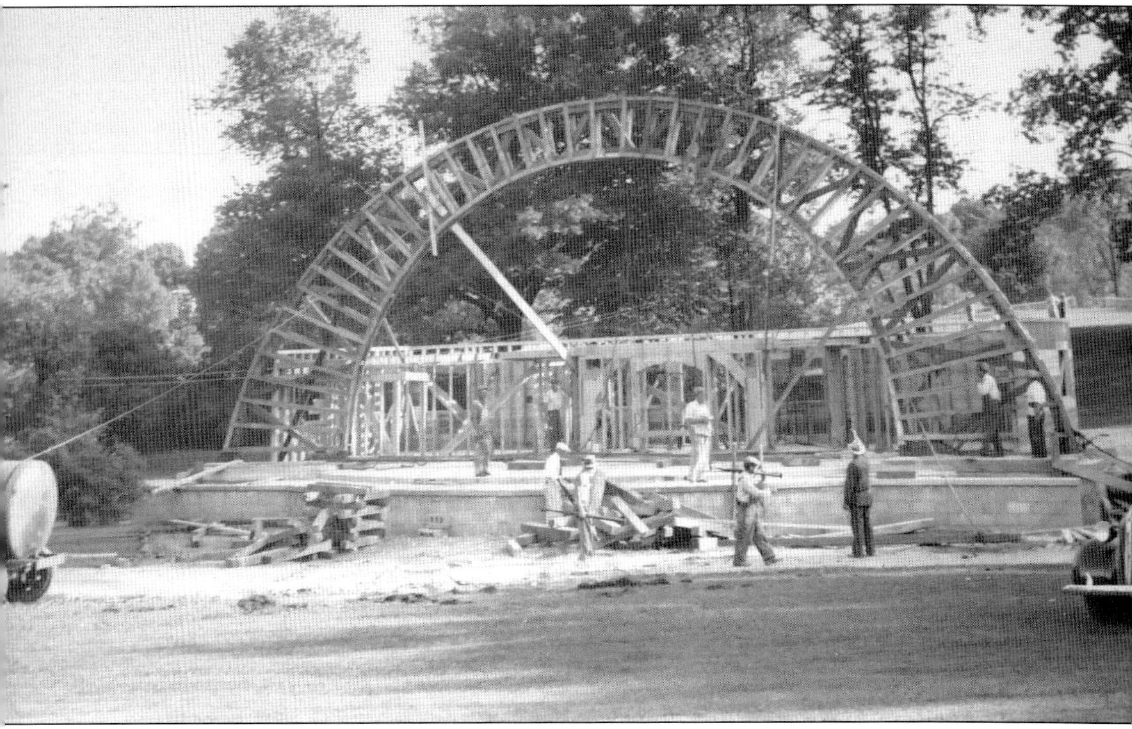

The construction of the West Park Band Shell began in 1938 as part of a Works Progress Administration project. Its initial budget was a little over $8,400. The dedication concert took place the following year, which featured music from University of Michigan students. A 50th anniversary and rededication ceremony was held in 1988. Outdoor plays, such as those put on by the Penny Seats theatre group, are often performed here. On five or six perfect summer evenings, the Ann Arbor Civic Band performs in the shell, celebrating all that is good about Ann Arbor in the summertime.

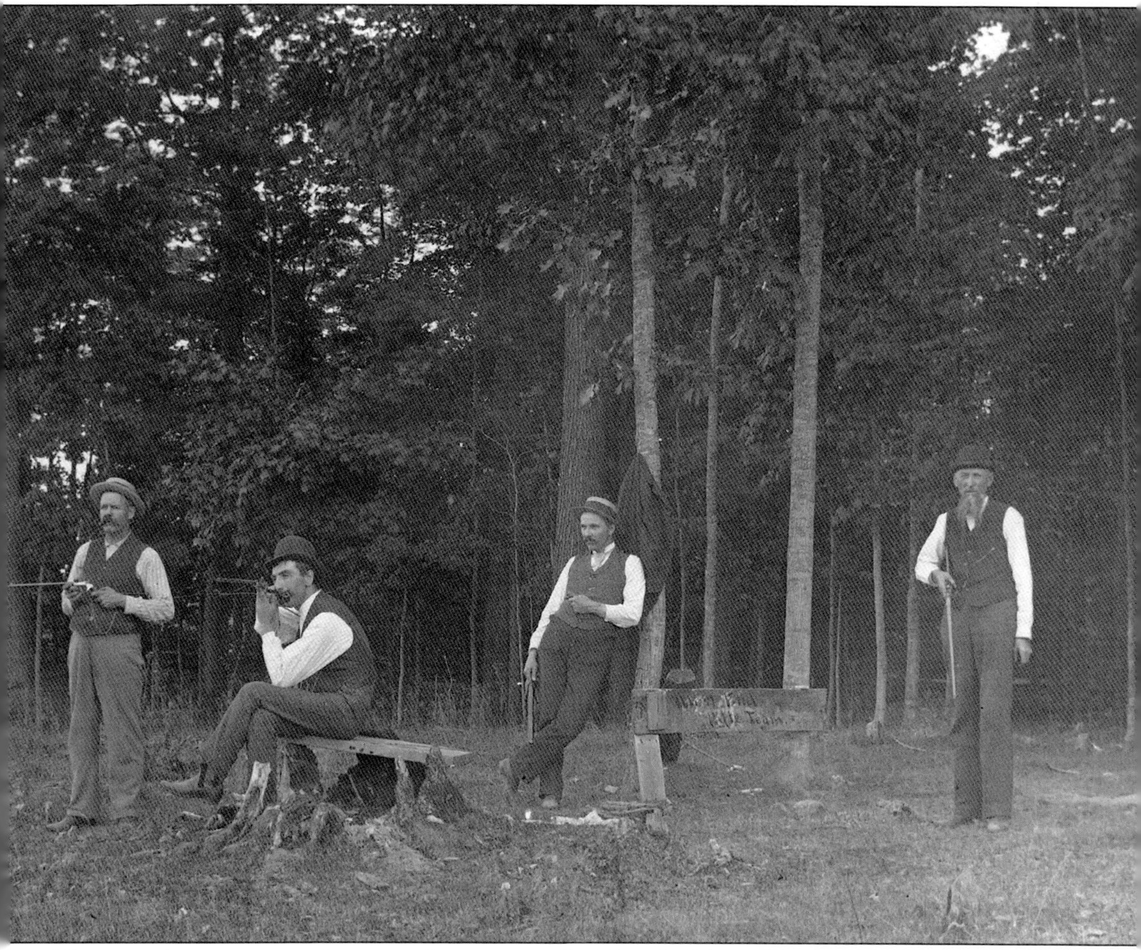

These gentlemen are socializing in what is now called Fritz Park but what was then the gun range for the Schuetzenbund (Shooting Club) park. As noted elsewhere in this book, there were many German immigrants living on the west side of town where this photograph was taken. There was also a gymnastics club that was located south of Madison Street between Fourth and Fifth Streets. German volunteer firemen owned the Relief Fire Company Park. According to an 1895 mentioning in the *Argus*, the Schuetzen Bund (as they were also known) would rent its practice range to light infantry. For the first year, rent was $75 but only $35 for the second year and $25 for each year thereafter.

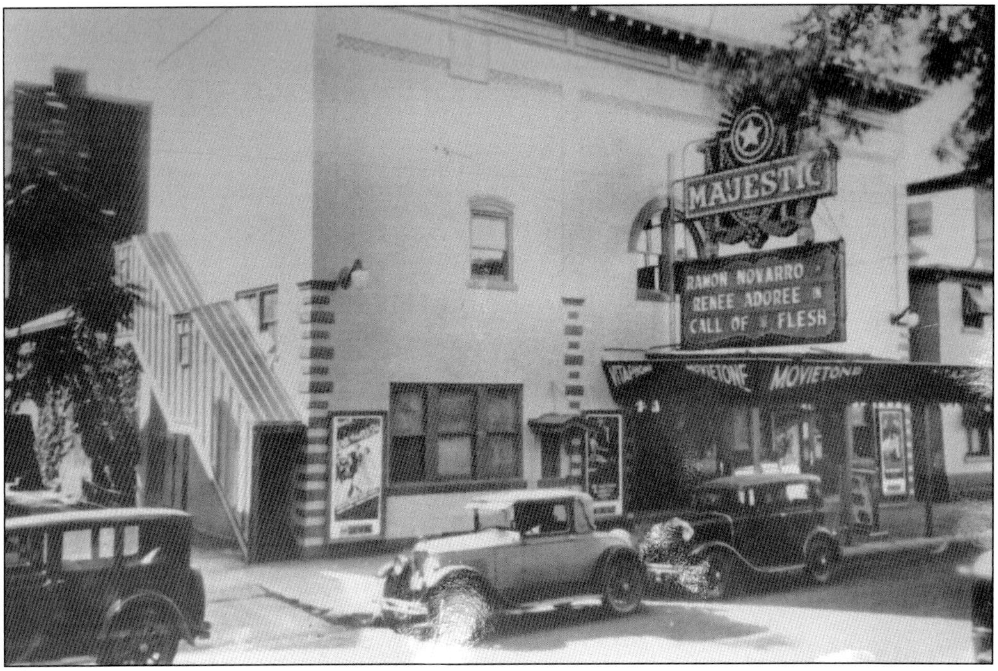

The Majestic Theater is shown here. It opened in 1909 with over 1,900 seats. Like many other theaters of its era, it began with live vaudeville performances and transitioned into films sometime in the 1910s. The theater closed in 1942 and was replaced by a parking structure. People now park their cars where hundreds of people once sat to enjoy the likes of Buster Keaton and the Marx Brothers.

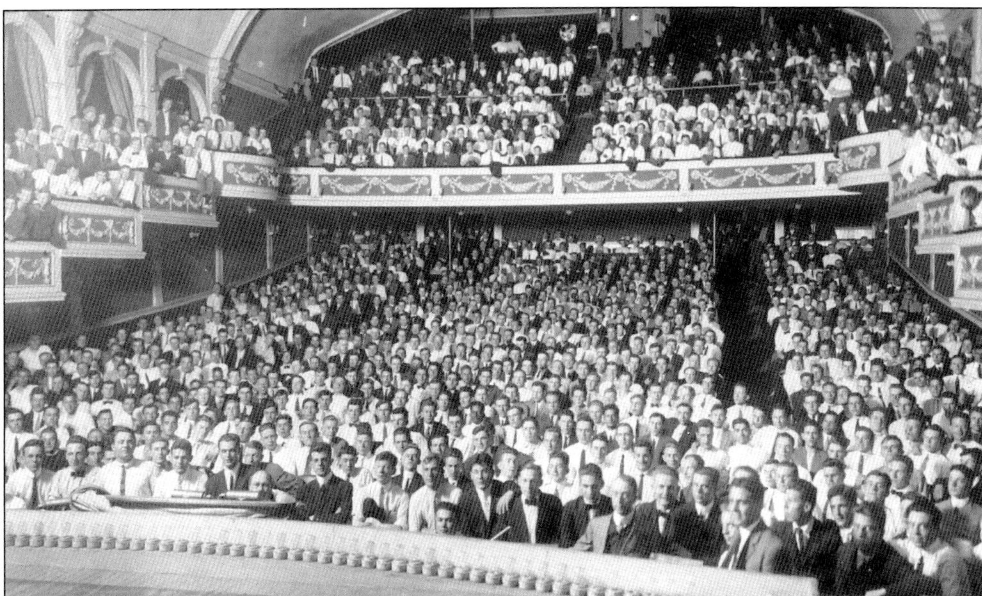

Here is a look inside of the Majestic Theater. Charles Sauer, a lumberyard owner, converted a skating rink into this theater. In addition to the stage, it featured dressing rooms, box seats, a confectionery, and a balcony. *The Girl of the Golden West* opened the theater. Although the "Maj" showed movies, vaudeville acts were also a big attraction.

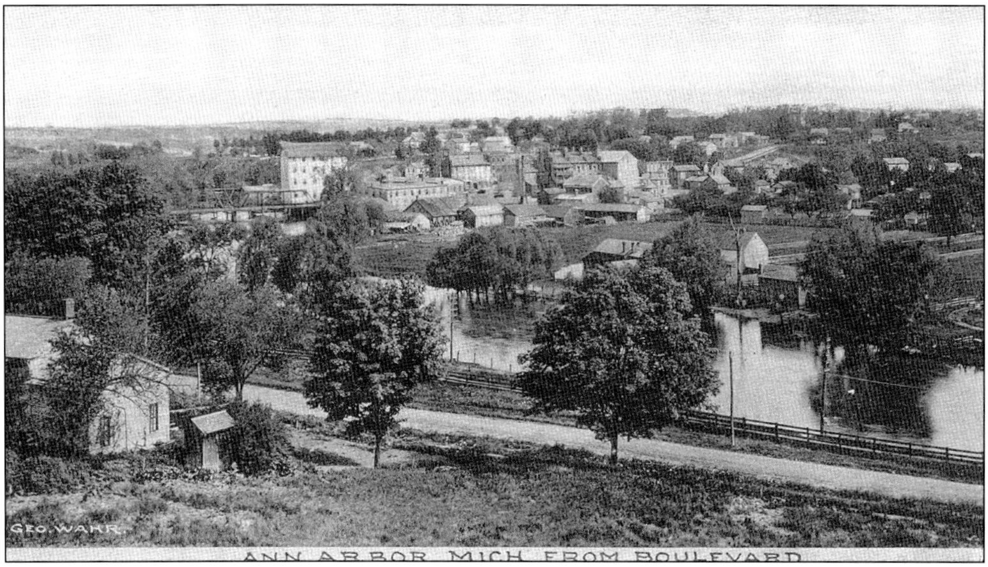

The street formerly known as the "Boulevard" is now Cedar Bend Drive. Judge Noah Cheever, author of *Pleasant Walks and Drives About Ann Arbor*, described it as "extending from the north river road to Broadway . . . only about three-quarters of a mile in length"; however, he added it "makes up in beauty for what it lacks in extent."

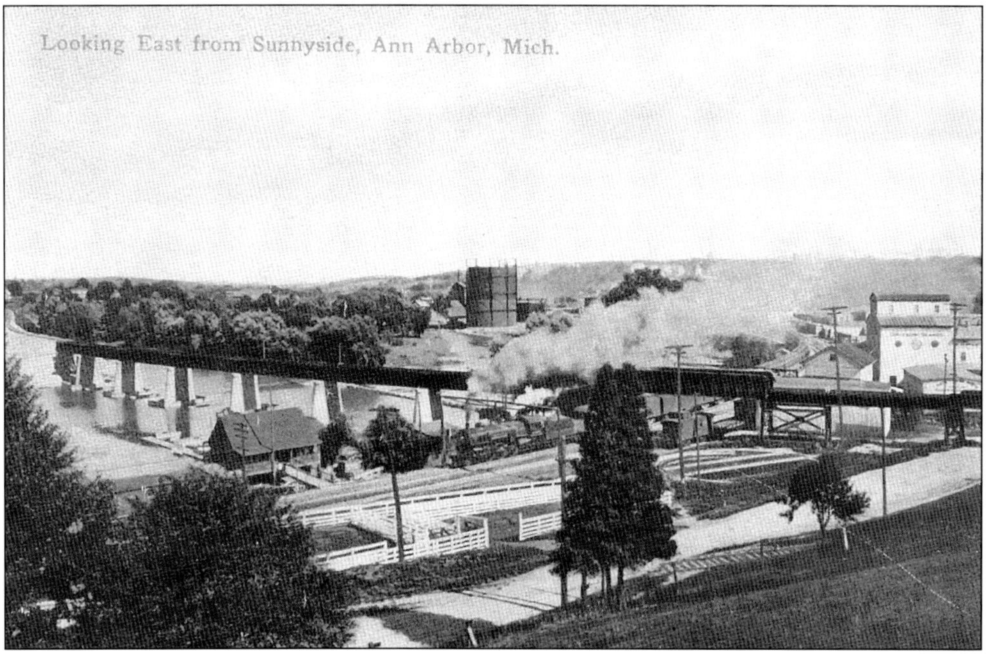

Here is a postcard labeled "Sunnyside." This image was actually taken from Sunset Road, which was mistakenly called Sunnyside. This neighborhood has grown up into a beautiful place, hosting the annual Water Hill Music Festival. Begun in 2011 by Fourth Avenue Birkenstock owners Paul and Claire Tinkerhess, the festival features neighbors performing on their front porches for passersby who wander from house to house. There is lots of dancing in the streets and much fun—just like the good times that were had in old Ann Arbor!